Entrepreneur MAGAZINE'S

LEGAL GUIDE

Michael Spadaccini

Forming
an LLC
in Any State

EP
Entrepreneur.
Press

Editorial director: Jere L. Calmes
Cover design: Desktop Miracles, Inc.
Composition and production: MillerWorks

This publication is designed to provide accurate and authoritative information in regard to the subject matter covered. It is sold with the understanding that the publisher is not engaged in rendering legal, accounting, or other professional services. If legal advice or other expert assistance is required, the services of a competent professional person should be sought.

Scales ©Rzymu

Library of Congress Cataloging-in-Publication Data
    Spadaccini, Michael, 1964-
        Forming an LLC : in any state / by Michael Spadaccini.
        p. cm.
        ISBN-13: 978-1-59918-105-9 (alk. paper)
        ISBN-10: 1-59918-105-3 (alk. paper)
        1. Private companies—United States—States. I. Title.
    KF1380.Z95S68 2007
    346.73'0668—dc22   2007011672

Printed in Canada

12 11 10 09 08 07   10 9 8 7 6 5 4 3 2 1

Contents

Acknowledgments

I'd like to thank Jere Calmes, editorial director of Entrepreneur Press, for giving me the opportunity to write this book. I am also grateful to:

- Attorney, friend, and fellow golfer Dan Sweeney, who contributed to this volume by providing invaluable legal research.
- My law professors at Quinnipiac University School of Law, who taught me the foundations of corporate and business law which I now offer to you.
- My family and friends, who offered their support throughout the drafting of this volume.

- All the clients who have sustained my law practice throughout the past ten years and whose support helped me grow to become an expert in my field, with special thanks to Don LeBuhn and his family's business, Evolution Furniture of Berkeley, California (my first clients) for whom I organized my first corporation back in 1993.
- Finally, and most importantly, my wife Mai, for enduring an admittedly imperfect man.

Introduction

This book is intended for everyone: business-person, manager, lawyer, and accountant. Its goal is to give the business professional all the tools necessary to plan, organize, form, operate, and maintain a basic LLC.

The book begins by providing a basic understanding of the law surrounding business organizations. It examines the fundamental differences and advantages of sole proprietorships, partnerships, limited liability companies, and corporations, and compares and contrasts the various business forms. It then takes you step by step through the organization of an LLC in any of the 50 states and the District of Columbia. Among the topics covered are how to do the following:

- Select the proper state for organization of your business.
- Select a name for your business without running afoul of the law or the rights of others.
- Conduct a search for prior use of business names and trademarks.
- Draft the foundational documents to organize your LLC: the articles of organization. Appendix A and the CD-ROM include many helpful and relevant documents that would cost thousands of dollars if drafted by an attorney.
- Choose and elect directors, officers, or managers for your company.
- Select and appoint a registered agent.
- File your organizational papers.
- Maintain proper formalities and records for your entity.
- Conduct your organization so that you can protect your personal assets and earnings from liability.

In addition, this book will assist you with the ongoing responsibilities of running an LLC. Record-keeping and internal governance are importance topics in business law. You will learn about organizing annual and special meetings of executives and owners, taking business actions by written consent in lieu of a formal vote, drafting minutes, reporting and paying annual franchise and corporate income taxes, and meeting the periodic reporting requirements that most states impose on LLCs.

One of this book's most valuable features is the model documents it provides. These documents, included in Appendix A and on the CD-ROM, can be easily modified to suit your specific needs. The CD-ROM features the documents in rich text format (RTF), a universal document standard that is readable by nearly every word processing software package. The model documents also appear on the web at www.learnaboutlaw.com, along with additional documents. These documents are meant to be general and can be suited to your needs with a little modification.

Appendix B includes LLC reference information for all 50 states and the District of Columbia. The reference section includes contact information for the secretary of state's office, fee schedules and requirements for filing LLC papers, links to model organizational forms for LLCs, information on periodic reporting and tax requirements, taxation summaries, and much more.

Understand, of course, that this volume cannot possibly serve as a substitute for the legal advice of a qualified attorney or accountant tailored to your specific needs. The information in this book is not intended as specific legal advice; it is intended as a broad educational overview. By using this book, you will step into the role of an attorney. If your goal is to form a small and simple LLC, then this book can serve your needs perfectly. But understand its limitations, and note that this volume occasionally warns about certain topics that present potential pitfalls and complex issues that warrant a visit to your local attorney's office. Heed these warnings, because small legal errors have a way of becoming enormous legal problems over time. Business law has some simple topics and some complex ones, so if your needs are obviously complex, don't try to do everything yourself. Sometimes the best advice an attorney can give is "get a qualified attorney."

That said, let's get started.

An Overview of Business Organizations

The most common forms of business enterprises in use in the United States are the sole proprietorship, the general partnership, the limited liability company (LLC), and the corporation. Each form has advantages and disadvantages in complexity, ease of setup, cost, liability protection, periodic reporting requirements, operating complexity, and taxation. Also, some business forms have subclasses, such as the C corporation, the S corporation, and the professional corporation. Choosing the right business form requires a delicate balancing of competing considerations. Each of these business forms is briefly discussed in this chapter.

The Sole Proprietorship

The sole proprietorship is a popular business form due to its simplicity, ease of setup, and nominal cost. A sole proprietor need only register his or her name and secure local licenses and the sole proprietorship is ready for business. The sole proprietorship is not a legal entity; it simply refers to a natural person who owns the business and is personally responsible for its debts. A sole proprietorship can operate under the name of its owner or it can do business under a fictitious name, such as Nancy's Nail Salon. The fictitious name is simply a trade name—it does not create a legal entity separate from the sole proprietor owner. Fictitious names are covered at length in later chapters.

> **Definition:**
>
> A sole proprietorship is a business owned and managed by one person. The sole proprietorship is not a legal entity; it simply refers to a natural person who owns the business and is personally responsible for its debts.

The owner of a sole proprietorship typically signs contracts in his or her own name, because the sole proprietorship has no separate identity under the law. The sole proprietor owner will typically have customers write checks in the owner's name, even if the business uses a fictitious name. Sole proprietorships can bring lawsuits and can be sued using the name of the owner. Many businesses begin as sole proprietorships and graduate to more complex business forms as the business develops.

Business Names

Although a sole proprietorship is indivisible from its owner, that is not to say that the sole proprietorship cannot operate under a trade name separate from its owner. Many sole proprietorships adopt and operate under what is called a *fictitious business name*. A fictitious business name is simply a trade name (the fictitious business name) that an owner of a business (the legal name) uses in the marketplace. A business that is using a fictitious business name is said to be "doing business as" the fictitious name—the terms are interchangeable. "Doing business as" is commonly abbreviated to DBA, which some businesses often include in corre-

> **Definition:**
>
> A fictitious business name is the operating name of a company that differs from its legal name.

spondence or in advertisements. A simple example of a DBA would be if Ritchie Rizzo, a sole proprietor, operated a business called Ritchie's Plumbing. Thus, Ritchie Rizzo is the legal name and Ritchie's Plumbing is the fictitious business name. Remember, the fictitious business name is just a name and does not create a separate entity.

Often, states require a person operating a sole proprietorship (or any other business form) under a fictitious business name to register that business name with either the state or the county. Requiring business owners to register fictitious names protects consumers and vendors. A consumer or creditor who has a legal dispute with a business can use the registry of fictitious names to determine what person or entity is ultimately responsible.

> **The following are examples of sole proprietorships:**
>
> 1. Jake is a plumber who owns his own tools and truck and has no partners.
> 2. Nancy has a nail salon. She rents the storefront where she operates in her own name and calls the business Nancy's Nail Salon.
> 3. Michael Johnson buys and sells sports memorabilia online.

Sole proprietor owners can, and often do, commingle personal and business property and funds, something that partnerships, LLCs, and corporations cannot do. Sole proprietorships often have their bank accounts in the name of the owner. Sole proprietors need not observe formalities such as voting and meetings associated with the more complex business forms.

Many businesses begin as sole proprietorships and later graduate to one of the more complex business forms.

Forming a Sole Proprietorship

As noted above, you may already be operating a sole proprietorship. One of the great features of a sole proprietorship is the simplicity of formation. Little more than buying and selling goods or services is needed. In fact, no formal filing or event is required to form a sole proprietorship; it is a status that arises automatically from one's business activity.

See Chapter 2, Information for All Businesses, for information on local taxes and local licenses.

Taxes for the Sole Proprietor

Because a sole proprietorship is indistinguishable from its owner, sole proprietorship taxation is quite simple. The income earned by a sole proprietorship is income earned by its owner. A sole proprietor reports the sole proprietorship income and/or losses and expenses by filling out and filing a Schedule C along with the standard Form 1040.

A sole proprietor need not pay unemployment tax on himself or herself, although he or she must pay unemployment tax on any employees of the business. Of course, the sole proprietor will not enjoy unemployment benefits should the business suffer.

Suing and Being Sued

Sole proprietors are personally liable for all of the debts of their businesses. Let's examine this more closely, because the potential liability can be alarming. Assume that a sole proprietor borrows money to operate, but the business loses its major customer, goes out of business, and is unable to repay the loan. The sole proprietor is liable for the amount of the loan, which can potentially consume all her personal assets. Imagine an even worse scenario:

a sole proprietor (or one of his employees) is involved in a business-related accident in which someone is injured or killed. The resulting negligence case can be brought against the sole proprietor owner and against his personal assets, such as his bank account, his retirement accounts, and even his home.

Consider the preceding paragraph carefully before selecting a sole proprietorship as your business form. Accidents happen. Businesses go out of business all the time. Any sole proprietorship that suffers such an unfortunate circumstance is likely to quickly become a nightmare for its owner.

If a sole proprietor is wronged by another party, he or she can bring a lawsuit in his or her own name. Conversely, if a corporation or LLC is wronged by another party, the entity must bring its claim under the name of the company.

Advantages of the Sole Proprietorship

- Owners can establish a sole proprietorship instantly, easily, and inexpensively.
- Sole proprietorships carry little, if any, ongoing formalities.
- A sole proprietor need not pay unemployment tax on himself or herself (although he or she must pay unemployment tax on employees).
- Owners may freely mix business and personal assets.

Disadvantages of the Sole Proprietorship

- Owners are subject to unlimited personal liability for the debts, losses, and liabilities of the business.
- Owners cannot raise capital by selling an interest in the business.
- Sole proprietorships rarely survive the death or incapacity of their owners and so do not retain value.

The Partnership

A partnership is a business form created automatically when two or more persons engage in a business enterprise for profit. Consider the following language from the Uniform Partnership Act: "the association of two or more persons to carry on as co-owners a business for profit forms a partnership, whether or not the persons intend to form a partnership." A partnership—in its various forms—offers its multiple owners flexibility and relative simplicity in organization and operation. In the case of limited partnerships and limited liability partnerships, a partnership can even offer a degree of liability protection.

Partnerships can be formed with a handshake—and often they are. Responsible partners, however, will seek to have their partnership arrangement memorialized in a partnership agree-

> **Definition:**
>
> A partnership is a business organization formed when two or more persons or entities come together to operate a business for profit. Partnerships do not enjoy limited liability, except in the case of limited partnerships.

The following are examples of partnerships:

1. Jake and Nancy open a convenience store together and have an attorney draft a formal partnership agreement between them.

2. Jake and Nancy agree orally to join together to run a convenience store and split the profits 50/50. (However, note the warning against forming oral partnerships!)

ment, preferably with the assistance of an attorney. Because partnerships can be formed so easily, partnerships are often formed accidentally through oral agreements. A partnership is formed whenever two or more persons engage jointly in business activity to pursue profit.

Don't operate a partnership without a written partnership agreement! Because of their informality and their ease of formation, partnerships are the most likely business form to result in disputes and lawsuits between owners—and oral partnership arrangements are usually the reason.

The cost to have an attorney draft a partnership agreement can vary between $500 and $2,000, depending on the complexity of the partnership arrangement and the experience and location of the attorney.

How Partnerships Are Managed

Partnerships have very simple management structures. In the case of general partnerships, partnerships are managed by the partners themselves, with decisions ultimately resting with a majority of the percentage owners of the partnership. Partnership-style management is often called *owner management*. Corporations, on the other hand, are typically managed by appointed or elected officers, which is called *representative management*. (Representative management is discussed throughout the sections on LLCs and corporations.) Keep in mind that a majority of the percentage interest in a partnership can be very different from a majority of the partners. This is because one partner may own 60 percent of a partnership, with four other partners owning only 10 percent each. Partnerships (and corporations and LLCs) universally vest ultimate voting power

Liability Protection Alert:

General partnerships are poor vehicles for business persons wishing to protect their personal assets. A debt incurred by a general partnership can be collected from any general partner.

with a majority of the percentage ownership interest.

Of course, partners and shareholders
don't call votes every time they need to
make some small business decision such as
signing a contract or ordering office sup-
plies. Small tasks are managed informally,
as they should be. When voting becomes
important, however, is when a dispute
arises among the partners. If the dispute
cannot be resolved informally, the partners

> **The following is not an
> example of a partnership:**
>
> Jake and Nancy agree that Nancy will work in
> Jake's existing plumbing business, he will pay
> her a salary, and he will pay her a bonus based
> on the amount of profit the business earns.
> Nancy is merely an employee with a profit-
> sharing bonus, not a partner.

call a meeting and take a vote on the matter. Those partners representing the
minority in such a vote must go along with the decision of the partners representing the majority.

Partnerships do not require formal meetings of their partners like corporations do. Of course, some partnerships elect to have periodic meetings any-
way. Overall, the management and administrative operation of partnership is
relatively simple, which can be an important advantage. Like sole proprietorships, partnerships often grow and graduate to LLC or corporate status.

How Partnerships Are Governed

Partnerships are governed by the law of the state in which they are organized
and by the rules set out by the partners themselves. Typically, partners set
forth their governing rules in a partnership agreement.

Often the governance rules determined by the partners differ from the governance rules set by state law. In most cases, the rules of the partners override
state law. For example, state law typically dictates that a partnership's profits
are to be divided among partners in proportion to their ownership interests.
However, the partners are free to divide profits by a formula separate from
their ownership interests and the decision of the partners will override state
law. Thus, the governance rules in state law are default provisions that apply
in the absence of any rules set by the partners in a partnership agreement.

Definition:

Agency is status as the legal representative (the agent) of an entity or another person (a principal).

This fact underscores the need for a partnership agreement. Otherwise, the partnership will by default be governed by state law. The laws set forth by state law may not be appropriate for every partnership. For the most part, however, the default state rules are fair and well-balanced.

An Important Concept: The Law of Agency

Agency refers to one's status as the legal representative (the *agent*) of an entity or another person. The party on whose behalf an agent acts is called a *principal*. A person is said to be the agent of a partnership or other entity if he or she has the legal authority to act on behalf the company.

An agent can bind a partnership to contracts and other obligations through his or her actions on behalf of the partnership. Of course, when an agent acts on behalf of a partnership or another company, the company is bound by those acts and decisions. A third party dealing with an agent of a company can rely upon the agency relationship and enforce the obligations undertaken by the agent—even if the agent made a foolish or selfish decision on the company's behalf. If the agent acts within the scope of his or her authority, the partnership becomes bound by his or her actions, no matter how foolish.

Definition:

The law of agency is the law concerned with the contractual or quasi-contractual relationship between a principal or principals and an agent who is authorized to represent the legal interests of the principal(s) and to perform legal acts that bind the principal(s).

The *law of agency* applies to corporations and LLCs as well as to partnerships. However, a discussion of the law of agency is particularly pertinent to a discussion of partnerships because in a general partnership, all of the partners usually have the status of agent with respect to the general partnership. The law of agency applies differently to corporations. Shareholders in a corporation are not necessarily officers and directors of that corporation and agent status will not automatically apply to them. So, partners in a partnership must be careful to delineate authority and keep abreast of decisions by their co-partners.

Partnerships can grant specific authority to specific partners, if such a grant appears in the partnership agreement. Without an agreement to the contrary, however, any partner can bind the partnership without the consent of the other partners, as described above.

Varieties of Partnerships

There are several varieties of partnerships. They range from the simple general partnership to the limited liability partnership.

The General Partnership

By default, a standard partnership is referred to as a general partnership. General partnerships are the simplest of all partnerships. An oral partnership will almost always be a general partnership. In a general partnership, all partners share in the management of the entity and share in the entity's profits. Matters with respect to the ordinary business operations of the partnership are decided by a majority of the partners. Of course, some partners can own a greater share of the entity than other partners, in which case their vote counts according to their percentage ownership—much like voting of shares in a corporation. All partners are responsible for the liabilities of the general partnership.

> **Definition:**
>
> A general partnership is a standard partnership, the simplest form. All partners share in the management and in the profits and decide on matters of ordinary business operations by a majority of the partners or according to the percentage ownership of each partner. All partners are responsible for the liabilities.

The Limited Partnership

The limited partnership is more complex than the general partnership. It is a partnership owned by two classes of partners: general partners manage the enterprise and are personally liable for its debts; limited partners contribute capital and share in the profits but normally do not participate in the management of the enterprise. Another notable distinction between the two classes of partners is that limited partners incur no liability for partnership debts beyond their capital contributions. Limited partners enjoy liability

> **Definition:**
>
> A limited partnership is a business organization owned by two classes of partners: general partners who manage the enterprise, and limited partners, who contribute capital and share in the profits but normally do not participate in the management of the enterprise. The limited partners enjoy limited personal liability while general partners have unlimited personal liability.

protection much like the shareholders of a corporation. The limited partnership is commonly used in the restaurant business, with the founders serving as general partners and the investors as limited partners.

A limited partnership usually requires a state filing to establish the business entity. Some states, most notably California, allow the oral creation of a limited partnership. Of course, establishing a limited partnership with nothing more than an oral agreement is unwise. Oral limited partnership agreements will very likely lead to disputes and may not offer liability protection to limited partners.

Limited partnerships have fallen out of favor recently because of the rise of the limited liability company. Both forms share partnership-style taxation and partnership-style management, but the LLC offers greater liability protection because it extends liability protection to all of its managers. Thus, today the LLC is often selected instead of the limited partnership.

Because of the complexity of limited partnerships, the formation of limited partnerships is not covered in this volume. The formation of a limited partnership is best left to a qualified attorney.

The Limited Liability Partnership

Yet another form of partnership is the limited liability partnership. A limited liability partnership is one composed of licensed professionals, such as attorneys, accountants, or architects. The partners in an LLP may enjoy personal liability protection for the acts of other partners, but each partner remains liable for his or her own actions. State laws generally require an LLP to maintain generous insurance policies or cash reserves to pay claims brought against the LLP.

Because of the complexity of limited liability partnerships, as well as the small audience for whom LLPs are appropriate, the formation of LLPs is not covered in this volume. That is best left to a qualified attorney.

Advantages of the Partnership

- Owners can start partnerships relatively easily and inexpensively.
- Partnerships do not require annual meetings and require few ongoing formalities.
- Partnerships offer favorable taxation for most smaller businesses.
- Partnerships often do not have to pay minimum taxes that are required of LLCs and corporations.

Disadvantages of the Partnership

- All owners are subject to unlimited personal liability for the debts, losses, and liabilities of the business (except in the cases of limited partnerships and limited liability partnerships).
- Individual partners bear responsibility for the actions of other partners.
- Poorly organized partnerships and oral partnerships can lead to disputes among owners.

> **Definition:**
>
> A limited liability partnership is a partnership composed of licensed professionals, each of whom may enjoy personal liability protection for the acts of other partners while remaining liable for his or her own actions.

The Limited Liability Company (LLC)

The limited liability company (LLC) is America's newest form of business organization. There is little historical precedent for LLCs. They are essentially creations of the state legislatures, although some commentators trace the origin of the LLC to a 19th-century form of business organization called the *partnership association* or *limited partnership association*. The great bulk of laws authorizing LLCs in the United States were passed in the 1980s and 1990s. Wyoming passed the first law authorizing the LLC in 1977. Florida followed in 1982. The watershed event in the rise of the LLC was a 1988 Internal Revenue Service ruling that recognized partnership tax treatment for LLCs. Within six years, 46 states authorized LLCs

> **Definition:**
>
> A limited liability company is a new and flexible business organization that offers the advantages of liability protection with the simplicity of a partnership.

as a business form. By 1996, Vermont, the last state to recognize LLCs, had an LLC statute in place.

The LLC is often described as a hybrid business form. It combines the liability protection of a corporation with the tax treatment and ease of administration of a partnership. As the name suggests, it offers liability protection to its owners from company debts and liabilities.

Simplicity and Flexibility

While LLCs are essentially new creations of state legislatures, corporations are truly ancient—and today's corporate law still carries some unwanted baggage. The modern American corporation has antecedents that date to Roman times and that we inherited through English law. The basic principles of American corporate law have not changed significantly in centuries. Probably the single greatest disadvantage of the corporate form is the burdensome range of formalities that corporate managers must observe. A modern corporation's heavy administrative burden is a remnant of the more traditional and formal legal system under which corporate law was cultivated.

The LLC changed all that. The LLC offers the liability protection benefits of the corporation without the corporation's burdensome formalities. It is this simplicity that has made the LLC an instantly popular business form with businesspersons operating smaller companies.

Another attractive feature of LLCs that we will discuss throughout this book is their flexibility. The management of an LLC can elect to be taxed either as a partnership or as a corporation. An LLC can be managed like a partnership (a member-managed LLC) or like a corporation (manager-managed LLC). LLCs can create a board of directors and can have a president and officer just like a corporation. Management of an LLC can choose to have periodic meetings of its membership or choose to ignore such formalities altogether.

Potential Disadvantages of the Limited Liability Company

The LLC does carry some disadvantages that make it an undesirable business form for some purposes. It is a new business form and courts have not yet developed a body of legal precedent governing LLCs. Thus, LLC owners and professionals may face operating questions and issues for which they have little or no legal guidance. However, this concern lessens as the states develop a reliable body of law concerning LLCs and it is no issue at all for very small companies.

Furthermore, for companies that wish to pursue venture capital, accumulate a large number of shareholders, and/or eventually pursue an initial public offering, the LLC is not an appropriate alternative to a corporation. Venture capitalists and angel investors tend to shy away from investing in LLCs. The overwhelming number of large publicly held companies are corporations, not LLCs.

What should the owners of an LLC do if their company grows in size such that an LLC is no longer the appropriate business form? The answer is simple: it is possible to convert an LLC into a corporation. Thus, some small companies begin life as LLCs, outgrow the LLC form, and then the owners transfer the assets of the LLC to a newly formed corporation with the same owners as the LLC. Thereby, the LLC is converted to a corporation. Furthermore, as one might imagine, it is also possible to convert a corporation into an LLC—or nearly any business form into any other. It is also possible to reorganize a business in another state by transferring the assets of a business into a newly chartered entity. Converting business forms requires some sophisticated legal and tax analysis, however, and should not be attempted without the services of a qualified attorney and accountant.

The cost of setting up an LLC is roughly equivalent to the cost of setting up a corporation. The secretary of state's fees for filing articles of organization and for filing annual reports are often the same for both LLCs and corporations. Organizers that wish to seek help with organizing an LLC through an LLC formation service or through an attorney will find the fees to be roughly the same.

> **Insider Tip:**
>
> LLCs are the favorite choice for entities with one to three owners working in a small local business that they do not plan to grow significantly and who do not expect to raise significant amounts of capital. As the number of owners grows, the corporation becomes a more attractive choice as a business form.

Advantages of the LLC

- LLCs do not require annual meetings and require few ongoing formalities.
- Owners are protected from personal liability for company debts and obligations.
- LLCs enjoy partnership-style, pass-through taxation, which is favorable to many small businesses.

Disadvantages of the LLC

- LLCs do not have a reliable body of legal precedent to guide owners and managers, although LLC law is becoming more reliable as time passes.
- An LLC is not an appropriate vehicle for businesses seeking to become public eventually or to raise money in the capital markets.
- LLCs are more expensive to set up than partnerships.
- LLCs usually require annual fees and periodic filings with the state.
- Some states do not allow the organization of LLCs for certain professional vocations.

Corporations

The term corporation comes from the Latin *corpus*, which means body. A corporation is a body—it is a legal person in the eyes of the law. It can bring lawsuits, buy and sell property, contract, be taxed, and even commit crimes.

Its most notable feature: a corporation protects its owners from personal liability for corporate debts and obligations—within limits. See Chapters 6 and 7 for information on the limits of corporate liability protection.

> **Definition:**
>
> A corporation is a legal entity that has most of the rights and duties of natural persons but with perpetual life and limited liability.

A corporation has perpetual life. When shareholders pass on or leave a corporation, they can transfer their shares to others who can continue the corporation's business. A corporation is owned by its shareholders, managed by its board of directors, and, in most cases, operated by its officers. The shareholders elect the directors, who in turn appoint the corporate officers. In small corporations, the same person may serve multiple roles—shareholder, director, and officer.

Corporations are ideal vehicles for raising investment capital. A corporation seeking to raise capital need only sell shares of its stock. The purchasing shareholders pay cash or property for their stock and they then become part owners in the corporation. Of course, the sale of corporate stock is heavily regulated by the U.S. Securities and Exchange Commission and by state securities laws.

A corporation's shareholders, directors, officers, and managers must observe particular formalities in operating and administering the corporation. For example, decisions regarding a corporation's management must often be made by formal vote and must be recorded in the corporate minutes. Meetings of shareholders and directors must be properly noticed and must meet quorum requirements. Finally, corporations must meet annual reporting requirements in their state of incorporation and in states where they do significant business.

Advantages of the Corporation
- Owners are protected from personal liability for company debts and obligations.
- Corporations have a reliable body of legal precedent to guide owners and managers.
- A corporation is the best vehicle for eventual public companies.
- Corporations can more easily raise capital through the sale of securities.
- Corporations can easily transfer ownership through the transfer of securities.
- A corporation can have an unlimited life.
- Corporations can create tax benefits under certain circumstances, but note that C corporations may be subject to "double taxation" on profits.

Disadvantages of the Corporation
- Corporations require annual meetings and require owners and directors to observe certain formalities.
- Corporations are more expensive to set up than partnerships and sole proprietorships.
- Corporations require periodic filings with the state and annual fees.

Business Form Comparison

Table 1.1 highlights the main advantages and disadvantages of each business form. Use this table to focus in on your specific needs. It outlines the various features of corporations, LLCs, partnerships, and sole proprietorships.

TABLE 1-1. **Business Form Comparison**

	Corporation	Limited Liability Company	Partnership	Sole Proprietorship
Ease of setup	More Difficult	More Difficult	Less Difficult	Easy
Initial costs such as filing fees, state fees, and legal fees	High	High	Medium to High	Low
Owners are personally protected from liability for the organization's debts	Yes	Yes	No, except in limited partnerships	No
Entity must make annual or biennial state filings	Yes	Yes	Almost never	No
Entity must pay annual or biennial state fees	Yes	Yes	Almost never	No
Annual meetings	Required by law, except for close corporations	Not required, but recommended	Not required, but recommended	No
Formalities required in connection with voting and internal governance	Yes	Relaxed formalities	Relaxed formalities	No
Can exist indefinitely	Yes	Yes	Yes*	No
Can issue shares or interest in exchange for cash	Yes	Yes	Yes	No
Appropriate entity to raise venture capital	Yes	No	No	No
Appropriate entity to become publicly traded	Yes	No	No	No
Entity can elect to be taxed as a corporation	Yes	Yes	No	No
Entity can elect to be taxed as partnership	Yes	Yes	Yes	No
Can choose fiscal year other than that of its owners	Yes	No	No	No
Owner can mingle personal and business assets and funds	No	No	No	Yes
Registration required in foreign states in which company does business	Yes	Yes	No, except for limited partnerships	No
State laws governing entity are uniform throughout nation	Laws vary widely	Laws vary moderately	Laws vary very little	Laws vary very little
Maximum Number of Members	Unlimited, except S Corp. maximum is 75 owners	Unlimited	Unlimited by law**	One

*Partnerships can, conceivably, have unlimited life if new partners are admitted into the partnership as old partners exit the partnership.

**While general partnerships are not limited in size by law, prudence dictates that they not have too many partners, because each partner is liable for the acts of the other partners acting on the partnership's behalf. Any general partnership of more than ten persons is likely to become difficult to manage.

CHAPTER 2

Information for All Businesses

The following information applies equally to sole proprietorships, partnerships, LLCs, and corporations.

Local Taxes, Local Licenses

You can reasonably expect that your state and local jurisdiction will carry licensing and filing responsibilities for your business—regardless of the business form you choose. Local licensing rules will vary from jurisdiction to jurisdiction; expect more stringent requirements in cities.

Insider Tip:

If you get stuck in the bureaucracy trying to figure out your local regulations, call the office of an elected representative such as a county supervisor or the mayor (you probably won't reach them, you'll reach an assistant) and ask them to point you to the right person or department. Typically, elected representatives are more responsive than bureaucrats who are not elected.

Here are some requirements to watch for:

- City and/or county business license
- City and/or county local taxation
- State sales tax registration and filings for owners who sell goods to which sales tax is applicable
- Need to pay unemployment tax on employees
- Registration for certain industries—a requirement that varies wildly from state to state
- Registration for fictitious business names

Of course, the wide variation of local regulations places this topic far beyond the scope of this book. The best ways to learn about your local regulations are to call or visit your city hall or county administration. Some municipalities even have helpful guides to get you started.

Partnership/LLC Taxation

Partnership and LLC taxation deserve mention. A notable feature of LLCs is that they are typically taxed in the same manner as partnerships. Technically speaking, partnerships are not taxed. Their income passes freely through the partnership, but is taxed as the partnership or LLC pays the income out in the form of wages, dividends, and distributions of profits. This manner of taxation is familiarly known as *partnership taxation*. In most circumstances, smaller businesses will incur a lower overall tax liability if they follow partnership taxation. Another common term applied to partnership taxation is *pass-through taxation*—which refers to the way income passes through a partnership to its members. Although partnerships and LLCs pay no tax, they are required to disclose their earnings and distributions to the Internal Revenue Service and state tax authorities on annual information returns.

Definition:

Pass-through taxation is when entities are not taxed on their income, but the income and profits that the entities pay out to owners and employees are taxable. Partnerships and LLCs enjoy pass-through taxation.

Partnerships report their annual income or loss on U.S. Federal Form 1065. Also, each partner submits his or her individual Schedule K-1, Partner's Share of Income, which is part of Form 1065.

How LLCs report their income depends upon if they are single-member LLCs or multimember LLCs. If a single-member LLC has an individual as its owner, the LLC income and expenses are reported just like a sole proprietorship, on Schedule C and Form 1040. Multimember LLCs (those that do not elect to be taxed as a corporation) report their annual income, loss, and expenses just as a partnership does, on Form 1065.

Corporate Taxation

A corporation, in contrast, pays tax twice—once on its corporate profit and again when its employees or owners are taxed personally on income, distributions, and dividends. The dual effect of corporate taxation is aptly referred to as *double taxation*. Although LLCs typically follow partnership taxation, in some cases LLCs elect to be taxed as corporations. Corporations may elect partnership taxation if they elect to be taxed as subchapter S corporations. Thus, the flexibility afforded to organizers of both LLCs and corporations reveals the modern trend towards fluidity in the law of business organizations.

> **Definition:**
>
> Corporate taxation is the taxation of a corporation both on its profit and when its employees or owners are taxed personally on income, distributions, and dividends.

Double taxation sounds much worse than it is. Remember that salaries are a tax-deductible expense for a corporation. Thus, only profit is subject to double taxation. Some corporations deal with the double taxation problem by simply paying out all of the corporation's profits as salaries and bonuses.

The corporate federal income tax rate (like the individual tax rate) begins at 15 percent and graduates to a maximum of 35 percent, but certain surtaxes cause tax "bubbles" at lower incomes. Table 2.1 illustrates the federal corporate income tax rates at various income levels. Note that Congress routinely adjusts income tax rates, so this table is subject to change. See the instructions to Form 1120 for current tax rates. By comparison, individual tax rates graduate to a maximum of 39.6 percent.

TABLE 2–1. **U.S. Federal Corporate Income Tax Rates**

Income Level	Effective Tax Rate
0–$50,000	15%
$50,001–$75,000	25%
$75,001–$100,000	34%
$100,001–$335,000	39%
$335,001–$10,000,000	34%
$10,000,001–$15,000,000	35%
$15,000,001–$18,333,333	38%
Above $18,333,333	35%

Corporations may choose a fiscal year that differs from the fiscal year of its shareholders. This creates opportunities to achieve tax savings through deferring income. For example, a business that receives a large increase in revenues in December can make its fiscal year end on November 30, thereby deferring the December receipts until the following fiscal year. You should seek the advice of an accountant when making decisions regarding your fiscal year.

How corporations report their annual income, loss, and expenses at the federal level depends upon whether they are C corporations or S corporations. C corporations file Form 1120, U.S. Corporation Income Tax Return. S corporations file Form 1120S, U.S. Income Tax Return for an S Corporation. Form 1120S closely mirrors a partnership return (because S corporations are taxed like partnerships) and each S corporation member must file a Schedule K-1, Shareholder's Share of Income, which is part of Form 1120S.

Corporations are also taxed at the state level. The states have adopted a dizzying variety of approaches to corporate taxation. The most common is the corporate income tax. Corporate income tax rates are lower than federal rates and tend to range between 4 percent and 11 percent, depending on the state. Not all states levy an income tax. Also common are state corporate taxes based upon assets in use in the state and taxes based upon outstanding shares of stock.

A common theme in state corporate taxation is that a given state will tax only corporate activity that occurs within that state. This doctrine is called *apportionment*. For example, a state will tax corporate income only to the extent that such income flows from activities within the state.

A corporation or other business operating in more than one state must file a tax return with the IRS as well as with all states in which it operates. Of course, each state has its own legal definition of what degree of business operation will trigger taxation.

Business Entity Terminology

Because LLCs, corporations, and partnerships differ fundamentally from each other, the basic language varies. For example, LLCs do not have shareholders or partners; they have "members." They do not have shares like a corporation; they have "membership interests." Understand, of course, that calling an LLC member a "shareholder" is not technically incorrect. Nevertheless, the legislators, lawyers, administrators and judges who govern the body of law surrounding LLCs will universally use the proper terminology.

Table 2.2 shows how some basic terms differ with respect to partnerships, corporations, and LLCs.

TABLE 2-2. **Business Entity Terminology**

	PARTNERSHIP	**CORPORATION**	**LLC**
Owners	**Partners**	**Shareholders**	**Members**
Ownership share	Partnership interest or percentage interest	Shares or stock certificate	Membership interest, percentage interest, membership unit, or unit
Charter document filed with state	Statement of partnership (for general partnerships, but it is permissive and not mandatory), certificate of limited partnership (for limited partnerships)	Articles of incorporation, or certificate of incorporation	Articles of organization or certificate of organization
Operating/governing document	Partnership agreement	Bylaws	LLC operating agreement
Company organizer	Organizer, founding partner	Incorporator	Organizer
Managers	In limited partnership, general partners	Directors and officers	Managers or managing members

Forbidden Business Purposes

Some licensed professions may not be conducted as LLCs and corporations. The practice of law and the practice of medicine are the most universal and most illustrative examples of this prohibition. Because lawyers and doctors face professional malpractice liability for errors that they make in the conduct of their practices, it would be unfair to the public to allow such professionals to enjoy liability protection from such errors. The types of business purposes that will be allowed in a given state will vary widely from state to state. For example, California forbids any profession that requires a "license, certification, or registration" from using the LLC or corporate form. This prohibition excludes more than 100 individual professions, including such diverse businesses as lawyers, real estate brokers, and pest control operators.

In states that allow it (not all do), licensed professionals must use a special form of LLC, the professional limited liability company (PLLC), or a special form of corporation, the professional corporation (often called a PC).

CHAPTER 3

The Features of LLCs

An LLC is formed in a manner much like a corporation. Both LLCs and corporations are chartered entities. This means that, unlike some types of partnerships that can be created without state registration, LLCs can be created only by filing a charter document in the state of organization. An LLC's charter document is called its *articles of organization*—a name obviously borrowed from the corporation's equivalent, *articles of incorporation*.

Interestingly, articles of organization are very similar to articles of incorporation. For example, both state the entity's name, require the appointment of a resident agent (more on this later), and usually require a statement of purpose.

> **Definition:**
>
> Articles of organization are the document by which an LLC is formed. Articles of organization cover foundational matters such as the name of the LLC, its business purpose, and its agent for service of process.

How LLCs Are Governed

Because LLCs do not have directors like a corporation, they are managed differently than corporations. LLCs are either *member-managed* or *manager-managed*.

Member-managed LLCs are governed by the LLC's owners (members) equally, just like a standard partnership. Manager-managed LLCs are governed by one or more appointed managers, who typically need not be members of the LLC. This management by appointment is called *representative management*. Manager-managed LLCs are managed much like corporations—with an appointed body of persons other than the company's owners. The body that undertakes governing responsibilities can be in the form of a board of managers or a committee of managers.

Of course, an LLC that wishes to use a representative form of management will require operating rules. Typically, an LLC sets forth its operating rules in a document called an *operating agreement*. An operating agreement is a close equivalent of a corporation's *bylaws*. LLC operating agreements cover matters such as who governs the LLC, the appointment of managers, the manner in which members can be ousted from the LLC, and such. Operating agreements, like bylaws, are not filed with the state. In fact, typically an LLC is not required to have any operating agreement in place, although it is advised. In the absence of an operating agreement, the LLC will follow the default rules of governance set forth in the laws of the state of organization. LLCs that operate without operating agreements are extremely rare.

> **Definition:**
>
> An operating agreement is the document that governs the internal structure and operation of an LLC and governs the relationship between its members and its managers.

Professional Limited Liability Companies

Professional LLCs (sometimes called PLLCs) are simply LLCs in which the members are engaged in rendering professional services, such as the practice of medicine or law. Forming a professional LLC is slightly more difficult than forming a standard LLC. Much like professional corporation shareholders, professional LLC members may enjoy personal liability protection for the acts of other members, although each member remains liable for his or her own professional misconduct. State laws generally require professional LLCs to maintain generous insurance policies or cash reserves to pay claims brought against them.

Note that professional LLCs are not recognized in all states, most notably California. Professional LLCs are more sophisticated enterprises than standard LLCs, and their organization should be left to a qualified attorney.

Definition:

A professional LLC is an LLC organized to offer services that normally require a license, such as the practice of medicine or law.

CHAPTER 4

The Ten Steps to Organizing an LLC

Organizing an LLC yourself can seem daunting upon first glance, but it is actually a series of small, simple tasks. At the end of this chapter, you will find an Organization Worksheet that will help you organize these activities. Appendix A offers model organizational documents. Text versions of the documents are also included on the CD-ROM and are always available at www.learnaboutlaw.com. The State Reference Tables in Appendix B offer contact information and resources for all 50 states and the District of Columbia.

Defining the Essential Roles

The Role of the Organizer

An LLC's organizer is the person or entity that organizes an LLC and signs and files its articles of organization or certificate of organization with the secretary of state's office or its equivalent. An organizer is necessary because a brand-new LLC does not yet have appointed managers, members, or owners. The organizer is much like the incorporator of a corporation. The organizer may be an owner or manager of the LLC, but need not be.

The organizer is the LLC's first representative and gives birth to the LLC by signing and filing the articles of organization. By signing the LLC's articles of organization, the organizer attests to the truthfulness of the articles, but the organizer does not incur any real liability or assume any ongoing duty. When an attorney forms an LLC on behalf of a client, he or she serves as organizer. If you intend to use this book to guide you with the formation of your LLC, you will be serving as the organizer. After completing the organization of the LLC, the organizer then turns over the LLC to its owners.

The Role of Members

Members are the owners of an LLC. Once the organizer forms the LLC, persons then become owners of the LLC by purchasing membership interests in the LLC by making initial capital contributions. Typically, the founders of an LLC will join an LLC soon after the LLC is organized. When members join an LLC, they also typically execute an LLC operating agreement, discussed at length below. The LLC operating agreement is the equivalent of a corporation's bylaws—it outlines the operating rules of an LLC and governs the rights and responsibilities of its members.

The Role of Managers

LLCs are managed either by the members themselves or by managers appointed or voted into office by the members. In a member-managed LLC, all members participate in management, much as the partners in a general partnership. In such cases, the managers are the members. In manager-managed

LLCs, the members do not necessarily participate in the daily operations and decision making of an LLC. The managers of a manager-managed LLC are appointed by the members to operate and manage the LLC. They are the equivalent of directors and officers of a corporation.

An LLC's managers may be members of the LLC, but need not be. Again, the LLC's operating agreement will govern the relationship between members and managers, such as how managers are appointed (and, if necessary, removed). An LLC's managers enjoy broad powers. They typically have authority to take the following actions:

- Issue units of stock
- Vote on acquisitions and mergers
- Approve loans to the LLC
- Approve plans for employee incentive compensation
- Approve large purchases of real estate and capital equipment
- Manage the LLC on a day-to-day basis
- Hire and fire employees
- Negotiate and signing contracts
- Deal with customers and vendors
- Maintain the limited liability company's records.

The Management Structure of LLCs

The management structures of LLCs are limited only by the imagination of their organizers. They can be operated like sole proprietorships or partnerships. LLCs, because of their inherent flexibility, can even be designed to imitate the management structure of a corporation. For example, an LLC can have an elected board of directors and officers such as a chief executive officer (CEO) and a president. All that is required to design an LLC management structure is an LLC operating agreement that outlines the structure. This subject is reexamined in Step 9 and Appendix A contains two examples of LLC operating agreements.

Many small LLCs will have very few members and managers, sometimes as few as one member. It is not uncommon for an LLC to have one person who is the sole owner and sole manager.

The Role of the Secretary of State

A secretary of state is the state official charged with responsibility for receiving and archiving legal documents, including corporation and LLC papers. Of course, you will not deal with the secretary of state (typically an elected official) directly; you will deal with employees of the office of the secretary of state. Understand, however, that your state may have an equivalent department with a different name, such as Hawaii's Department of Commerce and Consumer Affairs or Arizona's Corporation Commission. Regardless of the name, each state's business filing office operates much the same.

Your LLC's most foundational document is its articles of organization, which you file with the secretary of state to begin the life of your LLC. But the secretary of state's role does not end there. The secretary of state's office is also the department that receives periodic information reports from LLCs and corporations and maintains records on business entities. If an LLC fails to pay its taxes or fails to file its periodic reports, the secretary of state may withdraw an LLC's good standing status. LLCs do not file their operating agreements or other records with the secretary of state.

The records of LLCs and corporations are public records and are available for inspection by anyone. In my role as an attorney, I often make requests of the secretary of state's office when trying to locate the business address of a corporation or to determine if a particular corporation still enjoys good standing status. More often than not, I seek such records when attempting to collect a debt on behalf of my clients. The secretary of state is entrusted with maintaining accurate business records and with responding to such requests for information.

If an LLC becomes seriously delinquent in its tax and reporting responsibilities, the secretary of state may eventually order an administrative dissolution of that LLC. An administrative dissolution is one way an LLC may conclude its life. Each state has different rules for what constitutes a delinquency serious enough to warrant an administrative dissolution. Both the withdrawal of good standing status and dissolution lead to a failure of a LLC's liability protection. (See Chapter 5 for further information on maintaining good standing with the secretary of state.)

Step 1: Where Should You Organize?

Your LLC's life begins when you file articles of organization with the secretary of state or an equivalent department of state government. (The federal government does not charter LLCs or corporations.) Several factors should guide your decision on which state is the best for your LLC. Those factors include the following:

- The state or states in which your business operates (the most important consideration for most companies)
- Initial LLC filing fees
- Annual filing fees and annual reporting requirements
- State-specific advantages such as privacy rights

The LLC That Does Business in Only One State

As a general rule, if your business is small and operates in and sells products or services in only one state or even just mostly in one state, you should organize your LLC in the state where you conduct business. Most readers of this book will follow this course. Corporations differ from LLCs in an important respect: because corporation law differs widely in the 50 states (especially with respect to corporate taxation, director's rights, and privacy rights), it is quite common to incorporate out-of-state.

LLC law, however, is more uniform throughout the states (especially with regard to taxation), which lessens the advantages of shopping around when picking a state in which to organize an LLC. In short, you should probably organize in your home state if your company operates solely in that state.

The LLC That Does Business in Several States

But what if your LLC operates or does business in several states? You may be required to register in all of the states where you do business—regardless of the state you choose for your organization. States generally require out-of-state LLCs (called *foreign LLCs*) to register and pay fees in the state in which they are operating as a guest. (See Chapter 5, Operating Your LLC, for more information on foreign LLC status and reporting requirements and considerations.) For example, a Delaware LLC that transacts business in California must register in

> **Definition:**
>
> A foreign LLC is an LLC that operates in one state but whose articles of organization are filed in another state or another nation. In the state where its articles of organization are filed, it is considered a domestic LLC.

California as a foreign LLC, pay a filing fee in California, and also pay the annual minimum California franchise tax. Registration of an out-of-state LLC in a state where the LLC is conducting business operations is often called *qualification.* So the benefits of organizing out-of-state are limited by such foreign registration rules, because you will probably be required to register in your home state in any case.

This raises an important question: what constitutes "operations" or "business activity" in a particular state? Well, all states will define it somewhat differently—but universally states define business activity broadly. For example, California defines "doing business" as "actively engaging in any transaction for the purpose of financial or pecuniary gain or profit." It does not take a lawyer to get the crux of the meaning of that phrase. Quite simply, California interprets a single transaction taking place in California as doing business.

Why do states define business activity so broadly, thereby requiring local registration of out-of-state LLCs? There are two reasons. First, registered LLCs pay lucrative filing fees and franchise fees. The second reason is less sinister: each state has an interest in protecting its consumers from unscrupulous out-of-state companies, LLC or otherwise. A state can better protect its consumers from misconduct by out-of-state businesses if the state has registration and contact information on file for the company. Furthermore, a registered company automatically submits to jurisdiction (and so can be more easily sued) in jurisdictions where it is registered.

So, is every LLC in the United States properly qualified in every state in which it does business? No. Right or wrong, many thousands of LLCs regularly ignore the foreign registration requirements imposed by states. Foreign LLC registration in California, for example, runs about $1,000 per year.

The Nevada Advantage—Myth or Reality?

In my practice, I am often asked about organization in specific states. Nevada is a popular choice in recent years, and there are certainly some advantages to organization there. But why has Nevada become America's hottest corporate haven? Advertisements touting Nevada's advantages appear everywhere, from airline magazines to e-mail spam. The answer is that throughout the last few decades the Nevada Legislature underwent a conscious, deliberate, and effective program to make its state business-friendly and corporate-friendly.

Traditionally, the most popular state for incorporation was Delaware, and its dominance began early in our nation's history. Delaware is business-friendly, offers low corporate income taxation (although its franchise taxes max out at a wallet-busting $165,000!), and offers managers and owners a great degree of liability protection for their business decisions and actions. For this reason, the state of Delaware has traditionally enjoyed an abundant stream of registration fees, and a sizeable industry developed to serve the corporations (and to a lesser extent LLCs) that filed there. Eventually, other states grew wise and mirrored Delaware's business-friendly approach. Nevada is easily the most notable example; the state began an aggressive program in the early 90s to attract companies to incorporate and organize there.

Nevada is not a perfect business haven. Nevada recently increased its incorporation and organization fees, making it one of the most expensive states in the nation in which to incorporate. Also, Nevada requires organizers to name an initial owner or manager in the articles of organization. This appointment then becomes part of the entity's public record, ultimately searchable by anyone over the internet or through the Secretary of State's office. Despite this, Nevada is otherwise generally a "privacy state," one that offers its owners (but not its managers) a great degree of anonymity. We'll discuss Nevada's privacy rules at length below.

Advantages of Nevada Incorporation or LLC Formation

Nevada incorporation carries many benefits, among which are the following, and all of which are described in detail below:

- Nevada does not tax corporate profits or LLC profits.
- Nevada does not tax corporate shares or LLC ownership. Some states (not many, mind you) tax individual shares in a company.
- Nevada has no franchise tax.

- Nevada has no personal income tax.
- Nevada does not have an Information Sharing Agreement with the US Internal Revenue Service. (There is no information to share, because there is no income tax department).
- Shareholders in a Nevada corporation and owners in a Nevada LLC are not a matter of public record—shareholders can remain completely anonymous.
- Officers and directors of a Nevada corporation can be protected from personal liability for lawful acts of the corporation.
- Nevada corporations may purchase, hold, sell or transfer shares of its own stock.
- Nevada corporations and LLCs may issue stock for capital, services, personal property, or real estate, including leases and options. The directors may determine the value of any of these transactions, and their decision is final.
- The Nevada Secretary of State's office provides excellent customer service and excellent web support.

Nevada's Generous Taxation Rules for Businesses

Nevada enjoys a windfall of tax revenues from its most notable industry: gaming. As a result, Nevada's residents and business enjoy some of the lowest state taxes anywhere. Nevada does not impose a tax on corporate or LLC profits; many other states do, such as New York and California. California even imposes a 1.5% income tax on S Corporations, which do not pay income tax at the federal level.

Similarly, Nevada imposes no tax on corporate stock or LLC ownership shares. This isn't saying much; almost no states impose taxes based on stock or ownership. Nevertheless, by way of comparison, New York imposes an annual filing fee on LLCs of between $325 and $10,000, depending on the number of LLC members.

Nevada imposes no franchise tax, although it does collect a modest fee along with each LLC's List of Officers Report. A franchise tax is a tax levied in consideration for the privilege of either incorporating or qualifying to do business in a state. A franchise tax may be based upon income, assets, outstanding shares, or a combination. Put another way, a franchise tax is a tax one pays for "just being there." Many states impose franchise taxes on businesses.

While Nevada's Secretary of State touts the absence of a personal income tax as a benefit to businesses, this is more of a reason to reside in Nevada, and not really a reason to incorporate there. Personal income tax is paid in an individual's state of residency and not in the state where his entities are chartered. For example, a California resident that operates a Nevada corporation will be subject to California's personal income tax on corporation income paid to her despite her choice of Nevada for the state of charter for her corporation.

Nevada's Privacy Protection Rules

Nevada offers a tremendous degree of privacy to owners of business chartered there. Note that this degree of privacy is not extended to directors and officers of Nevada entities. Nevada has no US Internal Revenue Service Information Sharing Agreement—and Nevada is not afraid to boast about it. The IRS has in place an Information Sharing Agreement ("ISA") with about 33 states. The purpose of the ISA is to combat abusive tax avoidance. Even if Nevada participated in the agreement, it would have no information to share. Because Nevada has no corporate income tax and no personal income tax, it has no corresponding tax forms and no corresponding tax department. Under agreements with individual states, the IRS will share information (and vice versa) on abusive tax avoidance transactions and those taxpayers who participate in them. As reported by the IRS, states that participate in the ISA include Alabama, Arizona, Arkansas, Connecticut, Georgia, Florida, Hawaii, Idaho, Illinois, Indiana, Iowa, Kansas, Kentucky, Minnesota, Mississippi, Missouri, Montana, New Hampshire, New Mexico, North Carolina, North Dakota, Ohio, Oklahoma, Oregon, Pennsylvania, Rhode Island, South Carolina, South Dakota, Utah, Vermont, Washington, West Virginia and Wisconsin.

Along the same lines, owners of Nevada LLCs and shareholders of Nevada corporations need not identify themselves in any public records. This makes it very difficult for the government, police, or for third parties to determine who a Nevada entity's owners are.

Unfortunately, Nevada's privacy protections are widely misused. By way of example, and not by way of recommendation, many individuals and businesses have improperly and illegally used Nevada business entities to hide assets from creditors and even their own spouses. The other obvious misuse is tax avoidance.

Despite occasional abuse, Nevada's privacy protections do offer value to the legitimate and law-abiding businessperson. Probably the single greatest benefit of Nevada's privacy protections is that it serves to protect business owners from unscrupulous creditors, aggressive attorneys, and frivolous litigation. In my law practice, I have served as counsel to several companies that have been the victims of lawsuits that could only be fairly described as totally baseless. Often, the owners of businesses are dragged into the suit as defendants simply as an intimidation tool. Frivolous lawsuits are an unfortunate reality in today's business climate. Also, lawsuits are never win-win, they are always win-lose; the successful defense of a lawsuit following the time and expense of a trial is not a pure victory, it is a victory that comes at great cost.

The real victory is not to ever be sued. Experienced businesspersons and lawyers know this. Nevada's privacy protections can go a long way in achieving this goal by effectively hiding business owners from public view and thereby protecting them from litigation. Of course, Nevada's privacy protections are not absolute, they do have limits. A good plaintiff's lawyer with enough money and time (it would take a lot of both) could ultimately peek into a Nevada entity's ownership. Overall, though, Nevada's privacy protections are quite valuable.

The other obvious benefit to the businessperson of Nevada's privacy protections is shelter from the prying eyes of government. This benefit is obvious, even to a completely law-abiding company or company owner. Our government, police, and courts, while the finest anywhere, are capable of occasionally pursuing the innocent. Again, the successful defense of a criminal matter following the time and expense of a trial is not a pure victory, it is a victory that comes at great cost.

Privacy, for lack of a better term, is good. I am quite comfortable advising my business clients to maintain their privacy as much as possible in their business affairs regardless of the type of business they conduct. As a general rule, that which need not be disclosed should not be disclosed.

Nevada's privacy rules have an important exception, however. Nevada's privacy protection carefully protects owners and shareholders, but such privacy protection does not extend to company officers, directors, and in the case of LLCs, members. Nevada is one of a few states that requires an incorporator or organizer to appoint by name at least one initial director in a corporation's articles or in the case of an LLC, at least one member in the articles of organization. In both cases, the articles are a public record, and anyone can request copies by paying a small fee.

Even worse, however, is Nevada's requirement that every corporation and LLC file an "Annual List of Officers and Directors" each year. The oft-dreaded Annual List requires companies to disclose the full names of their officers and directors, and the information is then posted on the Nevada Secretary of State's web site

> **Insider Tip:**
>
> Nevada's two-sided approach to privacy (complete anonymity for shareholders, but complete disclosure of managers, directors, and officers) has produced an interesting cottage industry: the nominee director. A nominee director is an appointed manager/officer that serves as the appointed public representative of a corporation or LLC. The nominee director/manager is often charged with a solemn duty: to serve as the guardian of an entity's owners' privacy—the entity's owners "hide" behind the publicly disclosed nominee director. A common use of a nominee director is for asset protection; a Nevada entity owner that wishes to hide assets can assign the assets to the Nevada entity and can then appoint a nominee director and the owner can thereby direct the nominee director to serve the owner's interest. The use of nominee directors, however, has little value to an ordinary small business, but is an effective device for asset protection.

and is searchable through any web browser by anyone. This easily searchable public database makes it remarkably easy for any member of the public to determine a Nevada entity's management team. Keep in mind, however, that Nevada does offer a great degree of privacy to owners—as long as those owners do not participate as managers; such owners can easily remain anonymous. By comparison, Delaware (as well as many other states) require no disclosure of the identities of officers and directors.

Protection of Officers, Directors, and Managers From Personal Liability for Lawful Acts of the Corporation or LLC

Directors and officers of Nevada corporations enjoy generous protection (sometimes called "indemnity") from personal liability to the corporation or to a corporation's shareholders in connection with their service to the corporation. Nevada's rule on director and officer liability states:

> A director or officer is not individually liable to the corporation or its stockholders or creditors for any damages as a result of any act or failure to act in his capacity as a director or officer unless it is proven that:
>
> 1) His act or failure to act constituted a breach of his fiduciary duties as a director or officer; and
>
> 2) His breach of those duties involved intentional misconduct, fraud or a knowing violation of law.

The preceding passage is a pro-management version of the "business judgment rule." The business judgment rule that is in effect in most states dictates that courts will not review directors' business decisions or hold directors liable for errors or mistakes in judgment, so long as the directors were

- disinterested and independent;
- acting in good faith; and
- reasonably diligent in informing themselves of the facts.

Obviously, Nevada goes much farther, allowing liability to attach to directors and officers only when the director or officer breaches her fiduciary duty or commits fraud or a knowing violation of law.

So, how would this rule apply in the real world? Well, imagine a Nevada corporation with five shareholders and one director/officer. Assume the officer caused the corporation's funds to be withdrawn from the corporation's savings account. Using these funds, he caused the corporation to purchase a risky stock investment on a tip from a friend without making even a simple inquiry into the worthiness of the investment. Assume further that the stock investment went sour and caused the corporation to lose $50,000. This is a common model discussed in law school classes. The likely outcome depends on whose law applies.

In Nevada, the protective officer liability rule would shield the officer from liability. Sure, he made a bad investment of the corporation's funds, but he broke no law and committed no fraud. The corporation and its shareholders would therefore suffer the loss without recourse against the officer.

In a state that follows the general business judgment rule (keep in mind that every state will have a slightly different rule) the officer might face liability from the corporation or the shareholders. Because the officer was not diligent in informing himself, his decision would likely be found to be liable for his error.

Of course, when directors and officers enjoy enhanced rights, some other party will suffer diminished rights. Such is the case here. The protective business judgment rule in Nevada restricts the rights of the corporation and shareholders to pursue claims against the officer. Now, if you are contemplating a corporation where you are the sole shareholder and the sole officer, this rule is irrelevant—you would obviously never sue yourself for making a mistake. But, if you are an officer, director, or both you may want the protection against lawsuits and claims made by shareholders.

But what about liability protection for LLC managers? The preceding passages discussed the liability protection of corporate directors in Nevada. LLC managers do not enjoy the same protection that corporate directors and officers enjoy. Essentially, LLCs have the option of protecting managers to the same extent as corporate officers, but this decision can be overridden by a vote of the majority of the owners of the LLC.

If iron-clad indemnity protection is important to you, the corporate form will offer greater protection.

Purchasing, Owning, and Selling Shares of Corporation Stock

A Nevada corporation may purchase, own, hold, sell, transfer, pledge, or assign shares of its own stock. This may not seem important, but actually this is an important and convenient right that I find quite useful. Not all states allow corporations to own their own shares. Shares of a corporation held by the corporation itself are known as "treasury shares." The process of transferring shares into the name of the corporation is familiarly known as "returning shares to treasury." Keep in mind that the corporation cannot issue new shares to itself, treasury shares are only acquired through transfer back to the corporation from a third party that formerly owned the shares.

In practice, treasury shares might work as follows: Assume a corporation issues shares to a shareholder in exchange for services. If the shareholder fails to perform the services, or performs the services poorly, the corporation might have a claim against the shareholder. A convenient method of resolving that dispute is to have the shareholder transfer the shares into the corporation's treasury in exchange for a release of the corporation's claim. This is a very common way by which a corporation acquires treasury shares.

Once the corporation receives the shares, it can hold the shares or sell the shares to another party. Keep in mind, however, that treasury shares do not carry voting rights, and are not entitled to dividends and distributions.

Issue of Stock and the Valuation of Shares

Nevada corporations (and LLCs) may issue stock for nearly any sort of consideration: capital investment, services, personal property, or real estate, including leases and options. Not all states grant such power to a corporation. This is an important and convenient right that Nevada corporations enjoy. This freedom allows Nevada corporations to issue shares for the services of employees and consultants.

Perhaps more importantly, the corporation's directors may determine the value of any of these transactions, and their decision is final. This rule is advantageous to organizers of companies—it gives them the power to adjust stock ownership as they see fit. For example, if three persons come together and want to form a corporation, but only two of the three owners have capital to invest, the third owner can join the corporation or LLC as a one-third owner and her contribution to the entity can be an employment contract. The directors enjoy the power to value the employment contract as they wish, and that decision can never be questioned.

Customer Service and Web Support

Nevada has wisely organized the Secretary of State's office into an efficient and effective customer service organization. The office is not perfect, but generally speaking, it is an effective organization. First, the Secretary of State's web site is informative and easy to navigate. The searchable database allows one to quickly check on the status of one's own corporation or LLC. Is one's entity overdue in its annual report? Is one's entity in good standing with the Secretary of State's office? What are my filing fees for my annual report? A simple check on the web will answer these questions.

The Secretary of State's web site also offers a plethora of easy-to-use forms in portable document format (PDF) that can be easily viewed and filled out with a standard web browser. Note that in the last few years, Nevada has moved to a system where Nevada corporate and LLC filings are only accepted if filed on Nevada's pre-printed forms. Formerly, Nevada allowed both pre-printed forms and traditional typed documents.

Nevada also allows persons to make filings by facsimile—not every state allows this. I find this to be an invaluable convenience, and it can usually save one day and $20 of overnight charges.

Nevada processes filings quickly. A typical filing will be processed in three to seven days, but there is a variance depending on their workload. For a fee of $125, users can request 24-hour processing. So, a filing that is faxed on a Monday with the expedite fee will be processed on Tuesday and can be delivered by overnight delivery on Wednesday.

Disadvantages of Nevada Incorporation and LLC Formation

Nevada incorporation and LLC formation does carry a few drawbacks that are for the most part largely outweighed by the benefits, among which are the following, and all of which are described in detail below:

- In Nevada, you must select and name your initial directors in your articles of incorporation.
- Nevada requires an annual filing in which you must disclose the i d e n t ities of your management.

- Nevada recently increased its incorporation fees, making it one of the most expensive states in the nation in which to incorporate.
- Nevada corporations carry a slight stigma because Nevada corporations are often used by unscrupulous business persons to accomplish illegitimate goals, such as hiding assets. Many corporation service companies openly tout Nevada as the best state to incorporate in order to achieve certain illicit goals.

Disclosure of Directors and Officers

As discussed above, Nevada requires the comprehensive disclosure of the identities of officers and directors. This disclosure is required in three places. First, initial corporate directors or LLC members must be disclosed in a corporation's articles of incorporation or an LLC's articles of organization. Second, both LLCs and corporations must disclose their management teams soon after organization in a form called the Initial List of Officers (corporations) or the Initial List of Managers or Members (LLCs). Third, both LLCs and corporations must annually disclose their management teams in a form called the Annual List of Officers (corporations) or the Annual List of Managers or Members (LLCs). The information from the initial list and annual list are then posted on the Secretary of State's web site.

Here is a warning: if you operate a member-managed LLC, you must disclose the owners of the LLC, because the owners are the managers. Because of this, member-managed LLCs must endure complete transparency in Nevada.

As noted above, Nevada's approach to privacy has two faces: shareholders enjoy privacy, but officers do not. If you prefer not to have your management be so visible to the public, Delaware offers much greater privacy for management.

The Nevada Stigma

Unfortunately, Nevada corporations carry a faint stigma. Many corporation service companies openly tout Nevada as the best state to incorporate in order to achieve certain illicit goals. Furthermore, Nevada's reputation for vice in other areas may add to its "corporate stigma." True, Nevada corporations are often used by unscrupulous business persons to accomplish illegitimate goals, such as hiding assets.

On the other hand, the stigma is slight, and I have found that it has never hampered the goals of my clients and their business. Furthermore, in the day-to-day operation of your business, most persons you deal with will not necessarily know your state of incorporation. Your business correspondence will carry the name of your corporation, but you need not disclose your state of organization.

High Formation Expenses—and Balance

The initial incorporation expenses in Nevada (about $280 for a bare-bones incorporation) far exceed Colorado's $50 incorporation filing fee or Florida's $70 filing fee. Of course, Nevada charges far less than California's $900-plus organizational filing fee. Nevada has recently nudged its fees upwards, and based upon that, one can reasonably expect that it will continue to do so. Not only are the initial filing fees expensive, but the annual report filing fees are expensive ($125 minimum), as well as the fees for filing amendments to articles ($175 minimum), and articles of merger ($350).

On the other hand, Nevada's taxation is favorable. There are two lessons here. First, Nevada has likely had to raise its fees to keep the slim tax revenues up. Second, as a businessperson, you'll simply need to balance the incorporation and periodic expenses against the more forgiving tax environment.

Step 2: Select Your LLC's Name

At this stage in the organization process, you must choose a name for your LLC. Understand, of course, that you may use a trade name in the public marketplace other than your LLC's name. This is called doing business as (DBA) a fictitious name, as discussed earlier. For example, a company could operate a store under the trade name Evolution, but the LLC's name could be Evolution Trade Group, LLC, or any other name. The single greatest consideration when choosing a name is ensuring that no other person or entity is currently using the name. This consideration is guided by two factors. First, your use of a company name may infringe on the trademark or service mark rights of others. Infringing on the trademark rights of others may result in legal complications. Second, the secretary of state's office will not register a new LLC with the same name as an existing LLC. Keep in mind, however, that a secretary of state's office will have existing records only for company names in that state—the office will have no records for company names in the other 49 states. Thus, you may wish to search for existing trademarks and LLC names to ensure that your desired name is available.

Searching for Existing Trademarks

Begin by performing a trademark search. You can hire a professional service to do a trademark search for you. The cost can range between $300 and $1,200. The value of such professional search services has been eclipsed by free services on the internet. In my law practice, while I have used full-service search firms, I prefer to conduct trademark searches as follows.

You can search registered and pending trademarks at the U.S. Patent and Trademark Office's web site by pointing your browser to www.uspto.gov/main/trademarks.htm and click "Search" to use the Trademark Electronic Search System (TESS). Once there, use the New User Form Search. In the search window, enter the name that you wish to use in the box "Search Term." Make sure the "Field" term is set to "Combined Word Mark." To ensure that your search effectively locates all potential conflicts, do the following:

> **Definition:**
>
> A trademark is any symbol, word, or combination of either used to represent or identify a product or service. A trademark need not be registered to enjoy legal rights of protection. Trademark protection springs naturally from use of the mark in the public marketplace.

- Search for phonetic variants of your proposed name, because phonetically similar marks can cause a trademark conflict. For example, if your company name is Cybertech, search for Cybertek, Cybertex, Sybertex, etc.

- Search for both the plural and singular versions of your proposed name.

- If your name uses more than one word, search for each word individually.

- Follow the instructions in the use of wildcard search terms.

Searching for trademarks is an imperfect science, though, and no search can be expected to discover all users of a mark. Remember: trademark rights are created by the use of a trademark in the public marketplace and not by registration of the trademark. In fact, most trademarks are never registered, although they are used in the public marketplace. Thus, unregistered marks may be valid marks—and they are much more difficult to discover. The last step of your trademark conflict search should be an internet search with one of the popular search engines. Such a search will probably discover any users of your proposed name.

> **Insider Tip:**
>
> If protecting your personal assets from LLC liabilities is important to you, do not use your name within the name of the LLC, as in "Dave Doe Construction, LLC." If you do so, you create a strong evidentiary tie between yourself and the LLC. Separateness is a cornerstone in liability and asset protection.

Searching the Secretary of State's Records for Existing Company Names

Assuming that your name does not trigger a conflict with a registered or unregistered trademark, you should then search an online database of existing company names with the secretary of state in the state in which you intend to organize. Keep in mind that your LLC name must be distinguishable not only from other LLCs, but from corporations and partnerships as well. Nearly all secretary of state web sites offer free searching of existing company names. See Appendix B, State Reference Tables, for information on locating the secretary of state's web site in the state where you intend to organize. Alternatively, some secretary of state offices offer informal searches over the telephone. However, searching a database is always preferable.

Reserving Your LLC Name

When you have selected an appropriate name, you may wish to reserve the name of the LLC. This step is optional. In my law practice, I almost always skip reserving a company name. The form for reserving an LLC name is typically nearly as long as the form for filing the articles of organization! To me, name reservation just creates more work. If my search reveals that a name is not taken by any other company, I simply file the articles within a few days. If my filing is rejected, I work with my client to pick a new name and file again.

If name reservation is important to you, nearly all states offer a name reservation service. Typically, the service requires you to file a brief name reservation application with the secretary of state's office. See Appendix B, State Reference Tables, for information on name reservation in particular states, appropriate forms, and associated filing fees.

A Note on LLC Names

Your LLC's name should reflect LLC status. Most states require an LLC identifier. Perhaps more importantly, you should always hold yourself out to the public as an LLC to ensure maximum liability protection. Therefore, your LLC's name must include either Limited Liability Company, Limited Liability Co., or LLC. Some states allow Limited or Ltd., but this designation may imply a limited partnership.

Your LLC's name should *not* include any of the following terms, which are usually restricted by state and/or federal law, unless your LLC meets the legal requirements for such terms:

- Bank
- Trust or trustee
- Insurance
- Investment and loan
- Thrift
- Doctor
- Mortgage
- Cooperative
- Olympic or Olympiad

Step 3: Select the Registered Agent

A registered agent is a person or entity authorized and obligated to receive legal papers on behalf of an LLC. The registered agent is identified in the articles of organization, but can typically be changed upon the filing of a notice with the secretary of state.

The registered agent serves an important function. Because an LLC is not a physical person, service of legal papers on an LLC without such a designated representative would be impossible. The registered agent is designated by language such as the following:

> The name and address in the State of California of this LLC's initial agent for service of process is John Jones, 123 Elm Street, San Francisco, California 94107.

Your state of organization may use a different term than *registered agent*. Typical equivalents include *agent for service of process, local agent*, and *resident agent*.

The agent can be you, a family member, a corporate officer, an attorney, or a company that specializes in corporation and business services. The registered agent's name is a public record; if you desire anonymity, hire a professional to perform this service. The agent must have a physical address in the state of organization. Thus, if your business does not operate in the state of organization, you will need to hire a registered agent in that state. You must consider this additional expense when organizing out of state. Such services typically range from $50 to $150 per year. If you wish to hire a local agent and don't know where to turn, visit www.biz-filings.com. Business Filings, Inc. offers resident agent services in all 50 states at reasonable prices.

Having an attorney or a professional firm to serve as agent has advantages. Because the primary role of an agent is to receive service of legal papers, an attorney or a professional firm is likely to maintain a consistent address and to understand the nature of any legal papers served upon them. The agent will also receive important state and federal mail, such as tax forms, annual LLC report forms, legal notices, and the like.

Note that most secretary of state's offices where you file your LLC papers will not check to see if you have properly

Definition:

A registered agent is the person or entity authorized to receive legal papers on behalf of a corporation.

Insider Tip:

Don't use a P.O. box as a resident agent address. First, some states don't allow it. Second, any correspondence sent to a registered agent is likely to be important; with a P.O. box, you may receive that correspondence less quickly.

secured the services of a registered agent. If you do not select a registered agent properly, the secretary of state will mail you documents at the registered agent's address and you will not receive them. Thus, you should hire your registered agent either before or while filing your articles of organization. Appendix A contains a sample letter suitable for hiring a registered agent.

Step 4: Should You Organize Your LLC Yourself or Hire an Attorney?

At this stage in your organization, you must decide whether you will file and organize your LLC on your own, hire a discount LLC service, or hire an attorney. Each approach has its advantages and disadvantages.

Self-Organization

Obviously, the greatest benefit of organizing your LLC yourself is initial savings. Self-organizing an LLC carries the lowest initial cost. Of course, as with any legal matter, cutting costs can often cost more later. For example, if your LLC is not properly organized, ambitious creditors may later reach your personal assets by piercing the corporate veil. (The doctrine applies equally to corporations and LLCs.) See Chapters 6 and 7 for more information on preserving your LLC's full liability protection.

> **Insider Tip:**
>
> If you are organizing your LLC yourself, registered agents can be valuable sources of information about the state in which you are filing. Because most registered agents work so closely with the secretary of state's office on behalf of many companies, they become experts in dealing with that office. Remember: resident agents want your yearly fees, so they won't mind answering a few questions. You might confirm with them the amount of the filing fees to include with your articles of organization or you might ask for a free sample of articles of organization that they recommend.

Discount LLC Organization Services

A slightly more expensive alternative is to hire a discount LLC organization service. The prices range from $200 to $300 per company and the companies offer a streamlined but competent service. Such companies are essentially filing services and include only the following activities:

- They file articles of organization with the appropriate state office.
- They prepare a boilerplate operating agreement.
- They record the minutes of the initial meeting of LLC members.

Such companies generally do not include post-filing steps, such as the following, that you must do on your own:

- Reviewing and revising the operating agreement, if necessary
- Reviewing and revising the minutes for an organizational meeting of members, if necessary
- Conducting the organizational meeting of members
- Issuing units or membership interests
- Avoiding complications with state and federal securities laws
- Filing initial LLC reports
- Filing periodic LLC reports

Nevertheless, discount LLC organization services do offer value. They can often navigate the bureaucratic complexities of various states and provide prompt service and tested documents. However, the boilerplate operating agreement and proposed minutes of the organizational meeting that discount organization services provide often contain fill-in-the-blank and optional provisions that can baffle an inexperienced organizer.

Business Filings, Inc. offers competent incorporation and LLC services at reasonable prices. It also offers online filing, online customer service, and a free online name availability check. (However, name reservation services are not free.) The company can be reached at (800) 981-7183 or at www.bizfilings.com. Business Filings, Inc. can organize your business in any state; the fees range from $75 for a basic service to $295 for a comprehensive service.

Hiring an Experienced Business Attorney

Finally, you may wish to hire a business attorney to organize your LLC for you. A qualified business attorney can do the following:

- Suggest alternatives and solutions that would not occur to even the most diligent layperson.

- Assist with more complex features of LLCs, such as operating agreements and manager-managed LLCs.
- Anticipate problems before they arise.
- Prepare an operating agreement and minutes of the organizational meeting of members according to your specific needs.
- Ensure that no federal or state securities laws are violated when interests in the entity are sold to raise capital for the business.

There are several ways to find a qualified business attorney. Recommendations from friends and associates usually yield excellent matches between attorney and businessperson. Local bar associations in major metropolitan areas usually operate referral services. They prescreen attorneys, so you can be assured of the experience of any attorneys referred.

What you can expect to pay varies. The hourly rate for business attorneys ranges from $100 to $350 per hour. The lower end of the scale will apply outside of major metropolitan areas and for less experienced attorneys. For services such as forming LLCs and corporations, business attorneys often charge a flat fee. You can expect to pay between $500 and $2,000 for complete organization services.

Step 5: Determine the LLC Ownership

Your LLC will issue ownership shares, called units, to its members as part of the organization process. A member's units in an LLC are referred to in the aggregate as her percentage interest. So, if an LLC issues 100 units to its members and one member receives 60 units, that member's ownership percentage is 60 percent. You should choose your ownership structure early in the organization process, before filing your articles of organization.

The owners of an LLC will have the right to vote their units in proportion to their ownership interest. Thus, majority voting power ultimately exercises control over LLCs. Even if the LLC members choose to delegate management and operating authority to appointed managers, the members ultimately enjoy the right to elect managers and, if necessary, remove managers. In short, LLC members never delegate all of their voting power and they have ultimate authority and control over the LLC.

How Many Members?

In the early years of the development of the American LLC, many states required LLCs to have two or more members—single-member LLCs were prohibited. This led to an interesting work-around: many company organizers would simply grant a one percent ownership share to a family member or spouse and keep 99 percent ownership, thus avoiding the single-member prohibition. Today, all states allow single-member LLCs.

There are no legal prohibitions on the maximum number of LLC owners, but you should try to keep the number of members small.

Each member admitted to the LLC should execute an *investment representation letter*. We have included a sample in Appendix A. The investment representation letter offers some measure of protection to the entity because the member being admitted to the LLC makes certain representations regarding his or her qualifications and fitness to serve as a member of the LLC. Also, in the investment representation letter, the member makes certain representations regarding his or her investment objectives, which are necessary representations in order to comply with state and federal securities laws.

Owners' Contributions Determine Their Percentage Ownership

Business owners contribute to a business a capital contribution of property in exchange for an interest in the business. A capital contribution is the total amount of cash, other property, services rendered, promissory notes, and/or other obligations contributed to a company for such owners' interest in a company.

As a general rule, the amounts of capital contributions made to an LLC determine the ownership percentages in that LLC. For example, let's assume three women decide to form an LLC. Anne contributes $50,000 in cash, Betty contributes $25,000 in computer equipment, and Cheryl contributes $25,000 in

> **Definition:**
>
> A capital contribution is the total amount of cash, other property, services rendered, promissory note, and/or other obligation contributed to a company by an owner in return for that owner's interests in that company.

services to the LLC. The proportions are easy: Anne's contribution yields her a 50 percent ownership share while Betty and Cheryl each become 25 percent owners. As a general rule, the amount of capital contributions made to an LLC determines the ownership percentages in that LLC.

Sometimes, however, the company organizers will want to divide the percentage ownership differently than their contributions. This is accomplished in various ways. One way is simply to alter the valuation of property contributed to the LLC. In our example above, Betty's computer equipment could be valued at $35,000, thereby entitling her to a larger percentage share in the LLC. Of course, all members must agree to the valuations. (Remember: you'll note each member's contributions in the final operating agreement.) Also, the valuations must have a reasonable basis in fact—members cannot contribute a stapler and claim a contribution of $3,000.

Members' capital contributions should be determined at the planning stage. Each member's capital contributions should be committed to writing in the LLC's operating agreement.

Multiple Classes of Ownership Units

LLCs, by default, have only one class of owners: members with voting privileges. However, they may have one or more additional classes of units. This is yet another notion borrowed from corporation law: corporations can have multiple classes of voting stock and/or additional classes of preferred stock. Secondary classes of voting and nonvoting units appear in infinite varieties. These classes of units can be broadly categorized into three groups: common, preferred, and hybrid. Common units are what are traditionally understood in corporate law as voting stock. All business entities must have one class of ownership with voting power; without a voting class of owners, the business would have no voting authority and could not function.

Small LLCs should hardly ever require multiple classes of ownership units. Multiple classes of ownership can confound even the most experienced attorneys and are used only by a miniscule fraction of business entities. The passages below should give you a basic understanding of multiple classes of ownership. But if, for some reason, you feel that you might want or need multiple classes of ownership units, you should consult an attorney.

Preferred LLC owners are typically entitled to a monetary priority or preference over another class of units. This preference is the source of the term *preferred*. What this means is that owners of preferred units are entitled to receive dividends before other owners and asset distributions upon the business' liquidation before other owners. In other words, preferred owners get paid first and common owners get what remains. Preferred units often carry no voting rights. Sometimes preferred units can be converted to common units.

Hybrid units refer to debt instruments that are convertible into units: they are not true equity ownership instruments. For example, a promissory note—a document evidencing a loan—that is convertible into units of an LLC's ownership is a hybrid unit.

The rights and privileges of all classes of owners in an LLC must be set forth in the articles of organization with a certain degree of particularity. Multiple classes of ownership shares will be appropriate for only less than only percent of all LLCs.

Step 6: File the Articles of Organization

The life of an LLC begins with the preparation and filing of articles of organization. Typically a one-page document, the articles of organization set out the following basic information:

- The name of the LLC
- The name and address of the agent for service of process, the person or entity authorized to receive legal papers on behalf of an LLC
- A statement of the LLC's purpose
- Optionally, the names of initial members or managers

> **Insider Tip:**
>
> Don't file articles of organization in the closing weeks of a fiscal year, such as in the last weeks of December. If you do, you may be required to file tax returns for the entire year. Wait until January 1 to file your organization papers.

- Other optional matters, such as whether the LLC will have an infinite life or be dissolved on some date

To begin the life of an LLC, you file articles of organization with the secretary of state (or other appropriate department) in the state of organization. See Appendix B, State Reference Tables, for contact information and fees for the appropriate department. You must file articles of organization along with a filing fee, which differs in each state.

Don't Disclose the Unnecessary

As a general rule, don't appoint initial members or managers in your articles of organization unless it is required. The states differ on whether appointment of initial members or managers is required in articles of organization. In California, listing the names of initial managers/members is optional. In Nevada, it's required. Members and managers can easily be appointed soon after filing. Articles of organization are public documents and thus could reveal the names of an LLC's members to any member of the public.

Use the Secretary of State's Model Articles of Organization

You will find sample articles of organization for California in Appendix A, Limited Liability Company Forms. These sample articles should be used in California only and are included here as an example. Nearly every secretary of state's web site offers sample articles of organization in either word processor or portable document format (PDF). You should always use the form recommended by the secretary of state, if one is available.

Step 7: Order Your LLC Kit and Seal (Optional)

An LLC kit is little more than an attractive three-ring binder where you maintain LLC records such as articles of organization, operating agreement, minutes of meetings, tax filings, business licenses, membership ledger, etc. LLC kits range in price from $50 to $100. Very fancy kits with luxury features, such as a leather-covered binder, are available for considerably more. LLC kits usually include the following:

- Model operating agreement and minutes of the organizational meeting, with optional provisions
- Blank stock certificates
- An LLC embossing seal
- A blank member ledger and transfer ledger
- LLC forms on CD

LLC kits are not required by law in any state; they are completely optional. The only part of the LLC kit that I feel is totally necessary is the three-ring binder—$1.99 at an office supply store. In my law practice, I offer kits as an option. LLC kits are available from corporation supply companies and some office supply stores. You can obtain an inexpensive LLC kit by visiting www. bizfilings.com.

Whether you elect to purchase a kit or not, you should always maintain the following core LLC documents in a three-ring binder: articles of organization, operating agreement, membership ledger, and business licenses.

> **Insider Tip:**
>
> You can usually pick an exact date for the birth of your LLC. If you would like a special date of organization for your business, such as January 1 or a birthday, contact the secretary of state's office in the state in which you intend to organize. Almost all states will let you designate a special date of organization when you file.

Sample LLC Minutes and Operating Agreement

LLC kits usually include a sample operating agreement and minutes of the LLC's organizational meeting. A sample operating agreement and minutes appear in the Appendix A. The operating agreement sets forth the internal operating rules of an LLC. See "Step 9: Prepare and Approve Your LLC's Operating Agreement" for a description of how to complete this important document.

The LLC Seal

An LLC seal is a hand-operated embossing seal that contains the name of your LLC, state of organization, and date of organization. Seals are used to impress the official company endorsement on important documents, such as recorded minutes of company meetings. LLC seals have a historical ancestor: the corporate seal. Corporate seals, once universally required, are no longer mandated in every state. LLC seals are standard features in almost any LLC kit, but are typically not required by law.

Stock Certificates

A stock certificate is a printed document that evidences ownership of shares in an LLC. LLC kits will include blank stock certificates. You can print the certificates by running them through a printer, typing them, or filling them out by hand.

Stock certificates are historically associated with corporations. However, LLCs operate with less formality than corporations; stock certificates are not as commonly used by LLCs. Still, the function of stock certificates is important: it gives the stockholder written evidence of his or her ownership of the company. I recommend the use of stock certificates because they minimize disputes over ownership.

Membership Ledger

A membership ledger is a written table showing the owners of an LLC. The ledger must also indicate the percentage held by each owner. As new members are added to the LLC through the sale of membership interests, their ownership is recorded on the ledger. The membership ledger should also show transfers of members' ownership interest, as when a member dies and his or her interest is transferred through his or her will.

> **Definition:**
> A membership ledger lists the owners of an LLC, their proportion of ownership, and the transfers or other disposition of such ownership.

The importance of the membership ledger cannot be overstated. It should be maintained diligently. The membership ledger is akin to the deed on a piece of real estate. It is the primary evidence of ownership in an LLC and carries a great degree of weight when presented in court. LLC owners should insist upon receiving updated copies of the membership ledger periodically. See Appendix A for a sample membership ledger.

Step 8: Define the Management Structure and Choose Managers

The next step in organizing your LLC is to decide what type of LLC your company will be: a member-managed LLC or a manager-managed LLC. Your choice is not carved in stone. A member-managed LLC can switch to a manager-managed LLC with a mere vote of its members and a new or revised operating agreement.

Who Will Manage? The Members or Appointed Managers?

Member-managed LLCs are operated by the LLC's owners, much in the manner of a general partnership. Smaller LLCs tend to be member-managed. Member management is simpler because it does not require any voting or appointment of managers—the owners themselves simply go right to work on the LLC's business. Single-member LLCs, in almost all cases, will be member-managed.

Manager-managed LLCs are operated by appointed managers, who may or may not be members. Manager-managed LLCs appear and operate much like limited partnerships or corporations. They are more complex because the appointment of managers requires voting rules to govern the process of appointment. Larger LLCs tend to be managed by appointed managers.

Two pairs of sample operating agreements are included in Appendix A. One pair creates a member-managed LLC and the other pair creates a manager-managed LLC. Each pair consists of a short-form operating agreement and a more complex long-form operating agreement.

If you select a manager-managed format for your LLC, the members will need to agree on a few points at the beginning. First, how many managers will run the LLC? One manager works fine for a small company. Larger companies might want to consider having three managers. Larger companies with more complex challenges benefit from the informed consensus that builds through a multimanager team. Put simply, three people are less likely to make a bad decision collectively than one person acting alone.

Also, multiperson boards are less likely to act in a single manager's personal interest. Managers should always avoid conflicts of interest and abstain from votes in which they have a personal interest. For example, it is improper for an LLC manager to vote on an LLC's purchase of a piece of property if the manager has an ownership interest in the property. Such a vote would obviously create a conflict of interest. A multiperson management team allows a manager with a personal interest in a particular decision to make full disclosure of his or her personal interest to the other managers, thereby ensuring an informed and fair vote.

Finally, odd-numbered manager teams are always preferable to even-numbered manager teams. Even-numbered teams can sometimes encounter deadlock on decisions, when managers split 50-50 on an issue. Extreme cases of deadlock can trigger resignation or removal fights, owner votes, and sometimes even court intervention if the deadlock cannot be resolved according to the LLC's operating rules. Deadlock can occur at the manager/director level in both LLCs and corporations and at the shareholder/member level as well.

Members' Authority Over Managers

Once you determine your LLC's management structure and the number of managers, you simply select appropriate provisions for your operating agreement. If your LLC is to be manager-managed, you will select initial managers and name them in the LLC's operating agreement. LLC managers can, but need not, be LLC members.

Ultimately, LLC managers serve on behalf of an LLC's members. Keep in mind that a proper operating agreement should always give the members the right to oust a manager who is not serving to the satisfaction of members. It is also wise to require that managers be appointed every year or every few years. Managers should not be appointed for indefinite terms.

Typically, the removal of a manager will require some formality. For example, a well-drafted operating agreement will allow the removal of a manager by a vote of the majority of the LLC members—but only after notice and a properly held vote.

Managers' Liability and the Business Judgment Rule

Bear in mind that LLC managers—like directors and officers of corporations—can be held liable for mismanaging the LLCs that they serve. Courts recognize, however, that in a competitive business environment, managers must be given wide latitude in fulfilling their duties. Thus, courts are reluctant to second-guess a manager's management decision. Their rule here is called the business judgment rule. It states that courts will not review manager's business decisions or hold managers liable for errors or mistakes in judgment, so long as the directors meet the following criteria:

- They were independent; in other words, they did not have a personal interest in a transaction underlying the business decision.
- They acted in good faith.
- They were reasonably diligent in informing themselves of the facts.

Step 9: Prepare and Approve Your LLC's Operating Agreement

The operating agreement governs an LLC's internal operations, much like bylaws govern a corporation's internal operations. Operating agreements govern such matters as holding meetings, voting, quorums, elections, and the powers of members and managers. Operating agreements are usually set out in a five- to 20-page document. A sample operating agreement suitable for use in any state appears in Appendix A. Your LLC kit, if you choose to purchase one, may contain a sample operating agreement that may be more appropriate for your particular state. Operating agreements are not filed with the state, like articles of organization. In fact, operating agreements should be kept confidential. Yours should remain with the LLC's core records.

The preparation of your operating agreement takes work. Don't simply sign any sample agreement. You must read through the entire document and make sure that you understand all of its provisions. You and your co-owners should execute the operating agreement only after you have all thoroughly digested its contents.

Is An Operating Agreement Necessary?

Operating agreements are vitally necessary. While many states do not legally require your LLC to have a written operating agreement, it is unwise to operate an LLC without one. The first reason is simple: oral agreements lead to misunderstandings. You are overwhelmingly less likely to have a dispute among members if all parties commit their understandings to a mutual written document.

If your LLC members do not adopt an operating agreement, your LLC will be governed by the state default rules. The default rules are set out in each state's statutes. Naturally, these rules don't cover every possible circumstance; they cover just the basics. You should not rely on the default rules because they might not be right for your company. For example, some states have a default rule that requires LLCs to divide profits into equal shares for each member, regardless of whether each member's ownership is equal. An operating agreement can set forth the manner in which your LLC divides profits and losses among members.

Finally, adopting an operating agreement can protect the members from personal liability in connection with LLC business. Members should always endeavor to give the LLC separate existence, to hold the LLC out to the public. An LLC without a written operating agreement can appear much like a sole proprietorship or partnership. LLCs require fewer formalities than corporations, but that doesn't mean that they require no formalities at all.

Percentage of Ownership

How the ownership percentages of an LLC are divided among its members is one of the most important decisions a company's organizers will face. Choose wisely—in most cases, more than 50.01 percent of the vote of an LLC's members can dictate significant decisions regarding the LLC. This is why many company founders so often jockey for 51 percent ownership—to maintain company control. Furthermore, if an LLC is ever sold, the money received for the LLC will probably be divided among the owners in proportion to their ownership.

The owners' percentage ownership should be set forth in writing as part of the operating agreement. This written record will eliminate any later misunderstandings or disputes with respect to share ownership. All of the sample operating agreements in this book have a table at the end where you should indicate each member's percentage interest.

Distributive Share

A *distributive share* is each owner's percentage share of the LLC profits and losses. Most often, a member's distributive share is equal to that member's percentage ownership share. This is how most people set up their LLC. For example, Nancy is a 55 percent owner and Sheila a 45 percent owner of an LLC. At the end of the year, they have profits of $10,000 to divide between them as owners. They will divide these profits according to their ownership share. Nancy would receive 55 percent of the profits as her distributive share, or $5,500. Sheila would receive 45 percent of the profits as her distributive share, or $4,500.

But what if you want to divide profits in a proportion that is not equal to ownership shares? This is called a *special allocation*. While special allocations are legal, the IRS watches them carefully. It wants to be sure that LLC owners are not using a special allocation to hide income or to allocate losses to the LLC owner in the highest tax bracket. The rules on special allocations are hopelessly complex. If you want to set up a special allocation for profits and losses, you should seek the help of an accountant or attorney.

What Your Operating Agreement Should Cover

Your operating agreement will cover the following matters:

- The powers and duties of members and managers
- The date and time of annual meetings of members and managers
- Procedures for removing managers, if you choose to operate a manager-managed LLC
- Procedures for electing managers
- Quorum requirements for member votes

- Quorum requirements for manager votes, if you choose to operate a manager-managed LLC
- Procedures for voting by written consent without appearing at a formal meeting
- Procedures for giving proxy to other members
- How profits and losses will be allocated among members
- Buy-sell rules, which set forth procedures for transfer when a member wants to sell his interest or dies

The owners of an LLC formally adopt the operating agreement by all signing the agreement and agreeing that it shall govern the operations of the LLC. An operating agreement is a contract among the members of an LLC; once it is executed, the LLC's members are bound by its terms.

Step 10: Obtain a Federal Tax Identification Number for Your LLC

Because your LLC is a legal entity, federal law requires that you obtain a Federal Employer Identification Number (EIN or FEIN). In addition, most banks require you to give an EIN before opening a bank account. You obtain your EIN by filling out Form SS-4, Application for Employer Identification Number, or by applying online. The online application is a recent and welcome simplification of the EIN process. If you mail the form, expect to wait up to six weeks to receive your EIN. If you fax your form to a service center, you will receive your EIN in about five days. You can also obtain an EIN immediately by telephoning an IRS service center during business hours.

How to Apply for an EIN on the Internet

To make an online application of an SS-4, point your web browser to https://sa2.www4.irs.gov/sa_vign/newFormSS4.do. A form will appear in your browser. This clever form will take you step by step through the process of applying online for your SS-4. Simply follow the instructions for filling out the form and you will receive your EIN in a few minutes. Print and save a copy of the form and keep it with your entity's records. You do not need to mail a copy of the form to the IRS.

How to Apply for an EIN over the Telephone

To obtain your EIN immediately, do the following (which works in only some states):

- Either print the blank Form SS-4 in Appendix A or download and print a PDF file of the form from the IRS web site, www.irs.gov.
- Follow the form's instructions and fill in the form's first page.
- Find your state of organization in the "Where to Apply" section of Form SS-4 on pages 2 and 3. There will be a phone number for the IRS service center that handles your region. You must have the form filled out before you call or the representative will ask you to call back.
- The IRS service centers are always busy, so be prepared to get a busy signal or wait on hold. Some service centers will give out EINs over the phone and some will not.
- When you reach a representative, she will ask you to recite the information on the form. The representative will enter the information directly into the IRS computer system. The call will take about ten minutes.
- The representative will then issue you an EIN and give a telephone number to which you must fax your completed form.

Your LLC's Fiscal Year

LLCs must have the same fiscal year-end as their members. While LLCs can have corporations as owners, it's more common for LLCs to be owned by natural persons. Natural persons, like you and me, have fiscal years that end on December 31—our fiscal year is a calendar year. LLCs that are owned by natural persons must select December 31 as their fiscal year. Thus, the LLC's tax returns will be due on April 15 in the year following each fiscal year. See Chapter 5, Operating Your LLC, for more information on filing tax returns with the IRS and with state tax authorities.

FIGURE 4-1. **LLC Organization Worksheet**

1. Proposed name of LLC: _____

   a. Trademark search for name has been completed: _____

   b. Secretary of state's office search for name has been completed: _____

2. Address of principal office: _____

3. State of organization: _____

4. Corporate purpose: [ ] General [ ] Professional practice

5. Organizer name and address: _____

6. LLC will be managed by: [ ] Members [ ] Managers

7. The number of managers will be designated:

     [ ] In the Articles of Organization   [ ] In the Operating Agreement

8. The number of directors that will be authorized: _____

9. Names and addresses of directors: _____

   _____

   _____

10. Name and address of registered agent/local agent/agent for service of process:

    _____

    _____

11. Names and addresses of initial officers:

    a. Chief Executive Officer/President: _____

    _____

    b. Treasurer/Chief Financial Officer: _____

    _____

    c. Secretary: _____

    _____

    d. Vice President(s) (optional): _____

    _____

    _____

12. Authorized number of shares of common stock: _____

13. Shareholders:

Name/Address	Number and Class of Shares of Stock	Type and Amount of Consideration to Be Paid

14. LLC's fiscal year: _____

CHAPTER 5

Operating
Your LLC

N ow you have your LLC fully formed and filed.
But your duties do not end there. All business
entities require some ongoing formalities, responsibilities, and administration. This chapter examines
how to perform the day-to-day operations and
administration of your LLC.

Protecting Yourself from Liability

The most notable feature of an LLC is that an LLC's
individual owners are protected from personal liability for the LLC's debts and obligations. However,
liability protection for owners of LLCs is not

absolute! The doctrines of alter ego liability and piercing the corporate veil (which applies to LLCs as well) give courts the power to disregard the LLC liability shield and impose liability on owners in extraordinary cases of owner and manager misconduct. Because these important doctrines apply equally to LLCs and corporations, we will discuss them together in Chapter 7: LLCs and Personal Liability.

LLC Formalities

LLC organizers and member should never assume that LLCs observe no formalities at all. LLCs observe fewer formalities than corporations, but still must observe certain formalities. After all, an LLC is a business entity and therefore it must observe rules and keep records. The crux of the matter is that LLCs generally do not require periodic formalities such as annual meetings, but must still observe state law and their own operating agreement and maintain adequate records.

- LLCs are not required to have annual meetings of their members.
- LLCs are not required to elect managers periodically. Managers are free to serve year upon year until a vote of the LLC membership decides to change.
- LLCs are not required to have annual meetings of managers.
- Managers need not keep a written record of all significant formal decisions made in the course of managing the LLC—but they should do so.

On the other hand, LLCs should observe other formalities:

- LLCs should have in place a written operating agreement in which the capital contributions and percentage ownership shares of each member are clearly outlined.
- When an LLC member calls a meeting of the LLC members, the LLC must observe all formalities with respect to providing adequate notice to all LLC members.
- All votes of the LLC members, whether by written consent or by formal meeting, must be recorded in written minutes and kept with the LLC's records.

- The LLC managers, when making significant and formal decisions, should record their vote in written minutes and maintain the minutes in the LLC's records.
- LLCs must file all periodic information reports with the secretary of state in their state of organization as well as in any state in which they are qualified as a foreign corporation.
- LLCs must pay all annual state franchise taxes, if required.
- LLCs must file annual tax reports with the IRS and with each state in which they do business.
- Managers and members must respect the boundaries of conflicts of interest when entering personal transactions with the LLC.

Meetings of Members

LLCs are not required by law to hold scheduled annual meetings, so unless the LLC's operating agreement calls for such a meeting, it does not hold them. In such a case, the members must proactively call a meeting if they desire one. This proactive call to hold an annual meeting is akin to a corporation's special meeting. One reason to call a member meeting, for example, would be to make changes to the management—either by removing one, some, or all of the managers or by adding one or more managers.

In order to call a meeting of members, the members must follow several steps. The member or members calling the special meeting must collectively own a minimum percentage of an LLC's outstanding shares. The minimum differs from state to state and from operating agreement to operating agreement; it is typically around 5 to 10 percent. All of the sample documents in this volume allow ten percent or more of the LLC membership to call a meeting. So, if an owner with less than ten percent ownership wishes to call a meeting, he or she will have to find one or more shareholders who agree with the need for the meeting, so these two or more persons can accumulate their ownership percentages to get over the 10 percent minimum.

If the LLC is a manager-managed LLC, the owner calling the meeting typically issues a written document, a *call*, to the LLC manager(s). Thereafter, the LLC manager or managers are charged with the responsibility of sending notice of the meeting to all of the LLC members. See Appendix A, Limited Liability Company Forms, for a sample call letter.

If the LLC is a member-managed LLC, then the owner does not issue a call to the managers. He or she simply proceeds to the next step and notices the other owners of the meeting directly.

Either the manager(s) or the owner prepares a notice of the meeting. Notice must be delivered to all members advising them of the time and place of the meeting and the proposals to be presented. See Appendix A for a sample Notice of Meeting of LLC Members.

> **Definition:**
>
> A call is a written document in which the owner of a manager-managed LLC typically notifies the manager(s) of a meeting. The manager (or managers) are charged with the responsibility of sending notice of the meeting to all the LLC members.

Meetings of Managers

For the most part, appointed managers will conduct their business informally. Managers will not formally adopt resolutions for every small detail that arises in the everyday operation of an LLC. However, some significant decisions will require a meeting of the managers. For example, a decision to acquire a piece of real estate, establish a line of credit with a bank, or shut down a division will require a formal vote. The procedures for calling and noticing meetings of managers parallel the procedures for calling and noticing meetings of members.

Appearance at Member Meetings by Proxy

A proxy is an authorization by one member giving another person the right to vote the member's shares. Proxy also refers to the document granting such authority. Proxy rules are typically outlined in state law and an LLC's operating agreement. See Appendix A for an illustrative sample proxy form. Often proxies are granted when members do not wish to attend member meetings, but want their votes to be counted. They can therefore grant their proxy to another person to attend the meeting and vote their shares on their behalf.

Proxies can state the period of time for which they are effective. If no duration is stated, the proxy will lapse automatically by state law. Proxies tend to be used by corporations that have large numbers of shareholders. Most small corporations and LLCs will not use proxies.

Managers should not vote at meetings of managers by proxy. To do so violates a manager's duty to govern responsibly and to make informed decisions based upon adequate information.

Recording Member and Manager Meetings by Preparing Minutes

Meetings of members and of managers must be recorded. The written record of the actions taken at such meetings is called the minutes. Minutes are very simple to prepare and are often quite short. In Appendix A, there is a simple example of LLC minutes that covers a wide range of LLC actions. Minutes of meetings should always contain the following information:

- The nature of the meeting, i.e., member's or manager's meeting
- That either the meeting was called by notice or the persons voting waived such notice
- Those present at the meeting
- The date, time, and place of the meeting
- Chairperson of the meeting
- Actions taken at the meeting, e.g., election of directors, issuance of units, purchase of real estate, etc.

When in doubt, simply record the foregoing information in plain, conversational English. The person recording the minutes should sign the minutes, attesting to their accuracy. (There is no need to have each member sign the minutes.)

Holding Member and Manager Votes by Written Consent

Subject to certain restrictions, members and managers may take an action without a meeting if their action is memorialized in a document called a written consent. A written consent is simply a formal written document that sets forth a resolution or action to be taken and that is signed by the members or managers consenting to the action. Some members and managers find written consents to be invaluable—they are quicker, easier, cheaper, and more convenient. Actions taken by written consent do not require minutes, because the written consent itself serves as a memorandum of the action. See Appendix A for a sample of an action taken by written consent.

Written consents must be unanimous in some states for some LLC actions, such as the election of managers or to amend the articles of organization. A written consent should include the following information:

- The nature of the action taken, i.e., members' or managers' action
- A statement that the managers or members taking the action waive notice of a meeting
- The actions taken, i.e., election of managers, amendment of operating agreement, purchase of real estate, etc.
- A signature line for each manager or member who contributes a vote to the action

When in doubt, simply record the foregoing information in plain, conversational English.

Maintaining the Membership Ledger and Transferring Shares

One of the most important records you'll maintain for your LLC is the membership ledger. The membership ledger, as explained in Chapter 4, is simply a registry indicating the members who own the LLC, the percentage interest each owns, and the transfers or other disposition of such ownership. For all LLCs, the ledger should begin when the partnership is formed and should be updated diligently when ownership is transferred, gifted, sold, or repurchased by the partnership or when new ownership interests are issued.

Keep in mind that shares in any company are subject to comprehensive state and federal restrictions on sale and transfer unless such shares are registered with the Securities and Exchange Commission and state securities authorities. Registered shares are publicly traded shares that are sold in the public markets. So, if you sell shares in a nonpublic company, you must make sure you carefully follow the exemptions allowed by state and federal law. Unfortunately, a detailed description of such exemptions is beyond the scope of this book. However, exemptions are available for small businesses and can be easily researched by contacting the state securities department in your state.

The sample ledger below shows members Patty Shay and Jane Shay receiving percentage interests upon the formation of a partnership on 1/1/2000, and also shows the transfer of Jane Shay's interest to her daughter Yoko on 12/1/2003. Note the use of plain English.

TABLE 5-1. **Sample LLC Ledger**

Date of Original Issue	Member Name	Percentage Interest	Disposition of Interest
1/1/2000	Patty Shay	72.50%	
1/1/2000	Jane Shay	27.50%	On 12/1/2003, shareholder transferred shares to her daughter, Yoko Shay. Share certificate surrendered and reissued as certificate number 3 to Y. Shay
12/1/2003	Yoko Shay	27.50%	

Annual Reporting Requirements

Nearly all states require LLCs to file periodic reports with the secretary of state's office or its equivalent department. An LLC files such reports in its state of organization and in states in which it is qualified as a foreign LLC. Some states, including California and Alaska, have recently relaxed their reporting requirements; these states have moved to biennial filing of LLC reports (every two years). Annual report filing fees, due dates, late penalties, and information requirements differ from state to state. See Appendix B, State Reference Tables, for information on periodic reporting requirements in your state of organization.

Some states, such as California, Georgia, and Arkansas, now offer online filing of periodic reports. We may reasonably expect that online filing will be offered by more states in the near future. Check the web site of the appropriate office of your state of organization, listed in Appendix B, to see if your state offers an online filing program.

Qualifying as a Foreign LLC

An LLC conducting business in a state other than its state of organization is deemed a foreign LLC in the state in which it is a guest. Conducting business in a foreign state may require you to register your LLC in the state in which you are operating. For example, an Oregon LLC that sells products in California must register as a foreign LLC with the Secretary of State in California. Thereafter, the Oregon LLC must file biennial reports to the California Secretary of State as long as it is doing business in California.

This process of registering in a foreign state is known as *qualification*. In general, you will have to register as a foreign LLC in any state in which you are conducting business. What constitutes conducting business for the purposes of determining the qualification threshold will differ from state to state, but universally states define business activity broadly. Consider California's definition: it defines doing business as "actively engaging in any transaction for the purpose of financial or pecuniary gain or profit." Thus, California interprets a single transaction taking place in California as doing business there.

Qualifying as a foreign LLC closely mirrors the process of organizing an LLC: the LLC must typically file its articles of organization in the foreign state, along with an additional filing that includes information specific to the foreign state, such as the resident agent there. The filing fees for qualification are always at least the same as for filing articles of organization, but often are higher.

But why do states require foreign LLCs to suffer the expensive and burdensome task of filing for qualification as a foreign LLC? There are several reasons.

First, foreign LLCs must pay for the privilege of doing business in a particular state. After all, an Oregon LLC competing for sales in California competes with California LLCs and California corporations—all of which paid organizational fees in California. Thus, requiring uniform registration/qualification for all evens the playing field.

The second reason is for consumer protection. Once an LLC qualifies as a foreign LLC, it admits to jurisdiction in the foreign state and it can be sued there. Also, foreign LLCs must appoint agents for service of process in the foreign state. It is much easier to serve a company in one's home state than in another, especially at a distance. Thus, the consumers in the state where the LLC is qualified are more protected from misdeeds committed by the LLC.

The decision whether to qualify in a foreign state must be made cautiously. Once qualified, an LLC must file periodic information reports in the foreign state, will probably need to file tax returns and pay taxes in the foreign state, and must have a local agent appointed in the foreign state. Also, qualification in a foreign state makes it much easier for creditors to serve process and bring lawsuits against your corporation in the foreign state.

While the requirements of foreign qualification are clear and obvious, in practice smaller companies routinely ignore such requirements. Smaller companies simply lack the resources to register in each state in which they do business. However, this is not to say that such a practice is wise. The law is the law—and you should always endeavor to obey it.

Reporting and Paying Taxes

Internal Revenue Service

The way you report your LLC's income or loss to the Internal Revenue Service depends on how many owners share in the LLC.

If you operate an LLC as a sole owner, your LLC is treated as sole proprietorship for tax purposes. You will file Form 1040, Individual Tax Return, and Schedule C, Profit or Loss from Business.

If your LLC has two or more owners, the IRS automatically treats your LLC as a partnership for tax purposes. LLCs file Form 1065, Partnership Return of Income. LLC management must also furnish copies of Schedule K-1 to each owner at the time the partnership return is due. The Schedule K-1 sets forth the LLC's distribution of profits or losses to each member.

Both single-member and multimember LLCs can elect to be treated as corporations for tax purposes. If you want to treat your LLC as a corporation for tax purposes, you can elect to do so by filing Form 8832, Entity Classification Election. See a qualified accountant before making this election, because it can have potentially undesirable tax consequences.

State Revenue Authorities

Much as you report personal income to both the federal government and your home state, LLCs must report and pay taxes at both the federal and state level. Obviously, state tax forms differ for all 50 states. Some states have separate forms for LLCs and partnerships; some states have one form for both LLCs and partnerships. Organized summaries of each state's taxation and filing reporting requirements are in Appendix B.

But in which state or states does your LLC file a return? Most likely, you must file an LLC tax return in the state in which you are organized—although this depends on the state of organization. Your LLC must also file a tax return in any state in which the LLC is qualified as a foreign LLC. It is presumed that your LLC is doing business in a state in which it is qualified as a foreign LLC. Finally, your LLC must file a tax return in any state in which your LLC is doing business. We discussed above that all states define doing business somewhat differently—but universally states define it broadly.

Amending Articles of Organization and Operating Agreement

Members may amend an LLC's articles of organization. They may vote on proposed amendments at a meeting called for that purpose. Alternatively, the members may approve an amendment by written consent. Any amendment to an LLC's articles of organization must be filed with the secretary of state. In fact, most states have a recommended form for recording and reporting the amendment of the articles. The amendment will not be legally effective until the secretary of state accepts the filing. Some states require either a supermajority vote or a unanimous vote to approve particular amendments. All of the model documents included with this volume require the unanimous vote of members.

Common amendments to articles of incorporation include the following:

- A provision changing the name of the LLC
- A change in the business purpose of the LLC
- A provision adopting an additional class of units

Typically, both members and managers enjoy the right to amend an LLC's operating agreement. This procedure will be outlined in your operating agreement. Because operating agreements are not filed with the state, amendments to operating agreements need not be filed with the state. They become effective immediately upon their adoption by the members or managers. All of the model documents included with this volume require the unanimous vote of members to amend the operating agreement.

Ending the Life of Your LLC: Dissolution

An LLC's life can be cut short by dissolution. A dissolution is the process of shutting down an LLC, settling its affairs, paying its creditors, distributing its remaining assets to its shareholders, and ending its life. A dissolution may be one of three types:

- A *voluntary* dissolution is the intentional dissolution of an LLC by its management.
- An *administrative* dissolution is a dissolution ordered either by the secretary of state or equivalent department or by another authorized state official.
- A *judicial* dissolution is a dissolution ordered by a court of law.

An LLC's members may vote for voluntary dissolution either at a meeting of members or by written consent. A notice of dissolution or application for dissolution form is then filed with the secretary of state. In some states the secretary of state will not approve the voluntary dissolution of LLC that either is not in good standing or has an outstanding tax liability. This is an interesting irony, because the eventual penalty for delinquency in periodic LLC filings is administrative dissolution.

The secretary of state enjoys the power to order an LLC's administrative dissolution. The secretary of state may exercise this power if an LLC becomes seriously delinquent in meeting its statutory requirements such as periodic filing and tax reporting. What constitutes a delinquency serious enough to warrant an administrative dissolution will differ from state to state. Some states allow LLCs to be reinstated in good standing following an administrative dissolution if they apply and pay all overdue fees. Typically, reinstatement may also require the LLC to pay penalties.

A court of law may order the judicial dissolution of an LLC upon the request of a state attorney general, an LLC owner, or a creditor. A member, for example, may bring an action to dissolve an LLC if the LLC is committing a waste of business assets, if other members are abusing the member's rights, or if there is a voting deadlock among members.

You should always endeavor to avoid dissolution. Dissolution can lead to a failure of an LLC's liability protection. See Appendix B, State Reference Tables, for information on periodic reporting requirements and tax requirements in your state of organization. You should always exercise great care when voluntarily dissolving an LLC. If you are a shareholder of an LLC with outstanding liabilities, do not allow it to become dissolved. If your LLC is dissolved while in debt, those liabilities may be attributed to you personally.

CHAPTER 6

Suing and Being Sued as an LLC

Just like a corporation, an LLC is a distinct legal entity. As long as requisite formalitics and mechanics are followed, anyone with a claim against an LLC must look to the LLC for relief. Owners (members), managers, officers, employees, and others are shielded from personal liability by the veil of the LLC. This is true in most instances even though the LLC lacks sufficient assets to pay the claim.

Similarly, when the LLC has a claim against a third party, the LLC, itself, brings the claim. If a supplier fails to deliver promised goods to an LLC in a timely manner according to the terms of an agreement between the supplier and the LLC, the LLC can file a claim against the supplier. If a motorist drives his or her car into the LLC's delivery truck, the LLC may seek relief against the motorist.

The LLC Sues

This part is easy. If an LLC has a claim, it may file a lawsuit in its own name, thus becoming the plaintiff. The complaint must comply with applicable rules of court, the time within which the complaint can be filed, and service of process. The LLC may have to qualify as a foreign LLC in that state prior to filing its complaint.

Of course, an LLC can't act by itself, and therefore, its interests in the complaint must be advanced by an agent. Many states and all the US federal courts require that an LLC be represented by licensed attorneys in court appearances. LLC members, managers, officers, or employees may not appear on behalf of the LLC unless such an individual is licensed as an attorney. This principle applies to judicial proceedings and administrative matters as well.

Unlike individuals who may always represent themselves—known as appearing *pro se* or *in pro per*—LLCs may not represent themselves in many states without an attorney. Check with the local bar association in your state to see if your LLC is required to be represented by an attorney in judicial or administrative proceedings.

The LLC is Sued

Because it is a distinct legal entity, LLCs can be sued. Complaints can be filed and heard against LLCs in courts and in administrative proceedings. These suits and proceedings can be filed in any jurisdiction where the LLC is either chartered or engaged in business regardless of where the LLC's principal place of business is located. Conversely, an LLC cannot be sued in a state where it is neither chartered nor engaged in business. This basic procedural protection shields the LLC from being sued in a place where it has no connection.

For example, TonoSilver LLC, an Oregon LLC, is engaged in business in Oregon, Washington, Idaho, and Maine. Conceivably, a complaint against the LLC could be filed in any of these states. Local court or administrative rules may be used on occasion to dismiss or transfer actions which are filed in one jurisdiction for the sole apparent purpose of inconveniencing the person or entity against which the claim has been filed.

When an LLC is sued or an administrative claim is filed against it, notice of the lawsuit and a copy of the complaint are served upon an LLC manager or owner at the LLC's principal place of business. Service can also be made by serving the LLC's registered agent that is designated in the LLC's articles of organization. State and local court rules govern who can be served with the complaint and the manner and sufficiency of the service.

Owner Suits

It is not uncommon that a partial owner of an LLC finds it necessary to bring a lawsuit against the LLC. These types of actions are generally divided into two classes: individual suits and derivative suits.

Individual Suits

In an individual suit, an owner seeks redress against the LLC for a wrong which has occurred to the owner. For example, if the LLC breached a contract which it had entered into with the owner, the owner could file suit against the LLC. If successful, the owner would recover damages from the LLC for breach of contract.

Similarly, an owner injured as a result of the negligence of an LLC employee engaged in LLC business could sue the LLC.

Individual suits are often maintained to compel an LLC to issue a stock certificate, permit inspection of LLC books and records, or to permit the owner to vote on LLC matters. With individual suits, the right to sue belongs to the individual owner wronged by an LLC action, and any recovery belongs to the owner.

Derivative Suits

Derivative suits are more complex. A derivative suit is civil lawsuit filed by one or more owners on behalf of an LLC asserting rights of the LLC when the

> Derivative suits are always brought by an owner who does not have voting control of the entity. Why? It is because a majority owner with voting control can always protect his personal interests when he controls an entity. Derivative suits are a tool to protect the minority owners from the unfair acts of those controlling an entity.

LLC is refusing to act in a manner to protect the LLC's rights. For example, an owner could bring a derivative suit against an LLC manager who used an LLC's assets for personal gain. When the LLC refuses to act to preserve that LLC's own rights, the owner can step forward and sue as a nominal plaintiff and force the LLC to act.

It is important to note that LLC derivative suits are not universally recognized by the states, although the right of corporate owners to bring equivalent actions is firmly and universally established. The right of LLC owners to bring derivative suits is a fairly active and shifting area of the law. For LLCs, derivative suits involve a legal wrong done to the LLC which the LLC is unable to redress. For example, assume that the officers and directors of TonoSilver, LLC misappropriate funds which belong to the LLC. The LLC has been damaged by this action, but because the officers and directors control the daily operations of the business, the LLC, by itself, is unable to seek relief.

In such a situation, one or more owners could bring a derivative action against the offending owners and managers to seek relief. For procedural purposes, the owner(s) would file a suit against the owners and managers and the LLC as well. Any recovery would be paid to the LLC.

Some states permit successful owners to recover attorney's fees in derivative actions.

Derivative actions can also be maintained when an officer or director breaches any of the duties owed by the officer or director to the LLC or otherwise pursues a course of conduct detrimental to the LLC.

The law imposes a number of additional procedural safeguards to deter the filing of derivative lawsuits by disgruntled owners. Without these safeguards, many more of these suits would be filed at great expense to the LLC.

The safeguards include:

- The owner filing the action must have been an owner at the time of the alleged harm (unless the owner acquired his or her shares by operation of law from a deceased owner who was an owner at the time of the harm).

- The complaint must allege with particularity that the owner has made a demand on the managers or managing members for relief prior to filing the suit and that the demand was refused.
- If no demand was made, the complaint must state in detail why no demand was made or why the owner believes that any such demand would be futile.
- Once filed, the suit may be dismissed or settled only upon approval of the court.
- In some jurisdictions, the owner filing the complaint must maintain his or her status as owner throughout the proceedings.

Final Thoughts on Lawsuits

Suffice it to say, this is a litigious society. Lots of reasons are offered for this unfortunate truth. Many blame it on lawyers; others attribute it to a lottery mentality of a large segment of the population. As with other things in life, there are probably a lot of factors working in combination which cause this situation.

As a lawyer, I often tell my business clients, "Anybody can sue anyone at anytime for anything." And, in my practice I often saw specific, egregious examples of abusive and meritless lawsuits. This viewpoint doesn't bring a smile to many faces. It does, however, focus my client's attention on prevention. What can a business person do to minimize the risk of costly litigation? From an LLC standpoint, the issues described throughout this book provide many answers.

CHAPTER 7

LLCs
and Personal
Liability

The most notable feature of LLCs is that an LLC's owners are protected from personal liability for the company's debts and obligations. This is a valuable tool for businesspersons. LLCs and corporations share this vital feature. In fact, the corporation developed historically as a means by which individuals could pool their investments in order to finance large business projects, while protecting the individual owner from liability. Without this liability shield, individuals would be less likely to invest in companies and the projects they undertake; it would be a very different world without corporations and LLCs.

Consider the following, from California's LLC statute:

no member of a limited liability company shall be personally liable ... for any debt, obligation, or liability of the limited liability company, whether that liability or obligation arises in contract, tort, or otherwise, solely by reason of being a member of the limited liability company.

> "Faithfulness to the formalities is the price paid to the corporation fiction, a relatively small price to pay for limited liability."
>
> -as quoted by the court in *Labadie Coal Co. v. Black*

As you can see, the protection afforded to LLC members in California is strong—and typical of statutes nationwide. Of course, in law there are always exceptions.

Our corporation law has roots in the Roman Empire. But LLCs are a more recent invention. So, where did LLC law come from? Because the LLC lawmakers had no existing law to draw upon, they did the obvious thing: they borrowed doctrines, statutes, and concepts from corporation law. Because the liability shield laws of both corporations and LLCs are so closely related, they are discussed together.

Understand, however, that liability protection for LLC owners is not absolute. In a legal sense, an LLC is a legal entity separate from its owners. This separation, as we will learn, must be vigilantly maintained. Legal errors, personal dealings, ignored formalities, failure to pay taxes, and other misdeeds and missteps can destroy the legal protection afforded to LLC and liability owners, thereby exposing them to liability. There are a number of reasons for concern.

- LLC laws require Articles of Organization and LLC operating agreements and specify actions and duties that must be honored.
- Articles of Organization and LLC operating agreements form a contract between the LLC and its owners, obligating the LLC to act in accordance with the articles and LLC operating agreements.
- Managers and members owe the LLC and co-owners a fiduciary duty to use good faith, exercise due care, and act in the best interests of the LLC.
- Majority owners must act in good faith, in a manner not calculated to oppress the rights of minority owners.

- LLC formality must be respected and observed to pre-serve the integrity of the LLC and to shield members and managers or related businesses from personal liability.

Without question, you want to focus on running your business but paperwork is a part of every business. Like death and taxes, it is unavoidable. Understanding the importance of formality and attention to detail, as well as compliance with applicable statutes, articles, and LLC operating agreements will preserve your LLC status and shield you from personal liability. You must develop good recordkeeping habits from the beginning. This is essential.

> **Expert Tip:**
>
> Separateness is the key to maintaining LLC liability protection. No single concept is more essential than the legal separation between owner and LLC.

This chapter explores several legal theories that have been used to impose liability on individual owners of entities or parent entities. The term most often used to describe this process or concept is "piercing the corporate veil." Don't be confused by the reference to corporations in this section—the doctrine of piercing the corporate veil applies to both corporations and LLCs. Because LLCs have only been around for a few decades, there simply hasn't been time for a thorough body of law to develop around the doctrine of piercing the LLC veil. However, in the past few years some legal cases have emerged, and the phrase is starting to take hold as a doctrine separate from (but by any measure nearly equivalent to) piercing the corporate veil. We'll illustrate this important liability issue with several legal cases later in this chapter. After reading these cases, you may be struck by the absolute lack of demonstrated formality and attention to detail exercised by some owners. Certainly, the cases will illustrate a clear path to proper administration of your LLC, and the preservation of your LLC liability protection.

> **Definition:**
>
> Piercing the LLC veil, as the name implies, means that in some cases a creditor can ask a court to ignore the company liability shield and reach its owners.

The cases presented also highlight the variety of contexts in which piercing the veil cases can arise. In effect, any type of claim which can be asserted against an LLC, whether it is contract, tort, government claim or other, can be the subject of an attempt to pierce the LLC veil.

To help you avoid personal liability for LLC acts, a checklist of do's and don'ts is provided for your convenience at the end of this chapter.

The doctrines of alter ego liability and piercing the LLC veil give courts the power to disregard the LLC liability shield and impose liability on LLC owners in extraordinary cases of owner misconduct. These two doctrines (different in name, but essentially the same) will apply universally to corporations and LLCs. The states offer dozens of differing tests for alter ego liability. One common theme, however, is that a unity of interest and ownership between the entity and its owners can erode liability protection.

Disregarding the LLC Entity

As noted throughout this book, an LLC's separateness must be recognized and acknowledged by the acts of the owners and managers.

Courts recognize the distinct legal status of the LLC, and courts are reluctant to disregard an LLC's separate status to reach an LLC's owner's property. Although reluctant, courts will pierce the LLC veil in appropriate circumstances.

A number of different legal theories have been used to impose personal liability on individuals or parent entities in the case of subsidiaries. Some of these theories require that the court disregard the LLC entity or pierce the LLC veil. Not all claims against individuals require that the LLC status be disregarded, however.

Claims can be asserted against managers and owners without disregarding the LLC veil. For example, federal and state tax laws generally impose personal liability on those individuals responsible for preparing and filing income and sales tax returns. The government agency can bring civil and criminal tax claims against the LLC or the responsible individual, or both. There is no reason to examine LLC formality or attempt to disregard the LLC entity.

The same is true for criminal acts and intentional torts. If the manager or owner knowingly and voluntarily participated in any aspect of the crime or tort, he or she can be personally liable without piercing the LLC veil. Of course, an aggressive plaintiff's attorney will probably bring claims against the individuals and the LLC using a number of legal theories, including ones which would seek to pierce the veil.

It is also important to note that most piercing the veil cases involve corporations and LLCs where the owners are also the owners and managers. Control of the entity is an important concept in these cases. Legal theories commonly used against directors or owners who are not owners or who only own small amounts of stock involve breach of the duties of due care or loyalty.

Instrumentality/Alter Ego

The two most common theories used to justify the imposition of personal liability in disregard of the corporate or LLC entity are the alter ego theory and the instrumentality rule. Historically, the instrumentality rule applied only to parent/subsidiary situations, but it now seems to apply beyond that context as well.

The alter ego theory says, in effect, that if the owners of an LLC disregard the legal separateness of the LLC or disregard proper formalities, then the law will also disregard the LLC form if required to protect individual and LLC creditors. The instrumentality rule has three components, including:

1. The owner(s) must completely dominate the finances, policy, and business practices of the LLC to the extent that the LLC entity at the time of the transaction had no separate mind, will, or existence of its own. Ownership of all or substantially of the stock of the LLC, alone, is not complete domination.

2. The control or domination is used to commit fraud or wrong, to cause the violation of a statute, breach a legal duty, or commit a dishonest or unjust act in violation of the claimant's legal rights.

3. The domination and violation of legal rights must have proximately caused the injury to the claimant.

As noted, the instrumentality rule originally developed as a means to impose liability on a parent LLC for the acts of its

> **Definition:**
>
> Alter ego liability, as the name implies, means that a company's owner or owners have treated the company as indistinct from themselves. Without separation between owner and company, the owner is liable for the company's obligations.

subsidiary. Often, subsidiaries were grossly undercapitalized and effectively judgment proof. To remedy this injustice, creditors of the subsidiary were permitted to pierce the veil of the subsidiary and bring claims against the parent corporation.

Courts have blurred the distinctions between the alter ego and instrumentality theories, and many cases use both terms interchangeably. For the purposes of this discussion, the factors examined by the courts in deciding whether to pierce the LLC veil are the same under either theory. In fact, many of the criteria examined are relevant for claims based on breach of fiduciary duty against managers or owners or on criminal law or tort theories.

Before looking at specific cases to illustrate these theories and the criteria used, it is worth recalling that courts are reluctant to pierce the LLC veil. However, courts will strain to permit the piercing whenever its failure to do so could produce an unjust result. If your undercapitalized business seriously injures a bystander, and your business has no insurance to cover the injuries, a court will work hard to impose personal liability on you personally. It is public policy that businesses should be adequately capitalized to meet the reasonable needs of the business including all foreseeable claims.

Contract and Tort Claims

Courts are more apt to pierce the veil in a tort case than they are in a contract case. A tort is any action or failure to act (when there is a duty to act) that causes damage to another. Examples of tort actions include personal injuries, fraud, misrepresentation, negligence, battery, assault, trespass, and invasion of privacy. In a general sense, any claim not based on a contract could be a tort claim.

Once again, a policy decision of the courts comes into play. It is presumed that contract creditors entered a contract voluntarily with an opportunity to find out for themselves about the LLC. If a contract creditor was not diligent in protecting itself at the time of contract, courts are not likely to pierce the LLC veil in the absence of extreme circumstances. Of course, many contract claimants will include a claim for fraud and seek recovery directly from the individuals involved in the fraud. Unlike contract creditors, tort claimants rarely volunteer or have an opportunity to find out about the LLC in advance. Thus, a stronger argument can be made in tort cases that the LLC veil be set aside.

As you review the cases described below, keep in mind that no single criteria is controlling. In almost every instance, the LLC has failed to satisfy a number of criteria. For example, a single individual owning all of the stock of the LLC alone is not enough to expose that LLC to being pierced. The same is true where one serves as sole officer and director as well. Look for several factors—such as absence of LLC records or minutes, inadequate capitalization, a serious harm to third parties, commingling of personal and LLC assets, etc.—working in combination.

Taxicab Cases

Every law student studies two or three taxicab cases—from the realm of corporation law. These cases were an important part of the early battleground in American corporate veil jurisprudence. Upon first reading, most observers react with a mixture of horror and amazement that businesses could be operated in such a manner. Interestingly, many cab companies still operate in the manner described below.

In *Mull v. Colt*, the plaintiff, Mull, suffered serious injuries when he was struck by a cab driven by Fermaglick. Fermaglick had no assets and was judgment proof, so Mull sued Colt Company, the owner of the cab. At the time of the accident, New York law required that cabs maintain at least $5,000 in liability insurance. The state intended that the $5,000 be a minimum amount, but as might be expected, that's all any cab company carried.

In the course of the discovery phase of the suit, Mull learned that Ackerman and Goodman owned all of the stock of Colt Company. Ackerman and Goodman also owned all of the stock of 100 other corporations, each of which owned two cabs and a $5,000 liability insurance policy. All 200 cabs were garaged, maintained, and dispatched from a single location. Ackerman and

Goodman had obviously devised an inventive plan to shield themselves from liability, but as you'll see, the court saw right through it.

If the court did not permit the corporate veil to be pierced, Mull, who spent 209 days in the hospital and endured 20 surgeries, could have only recovered a wrecked cab and $5,000. The court noted that the use of multiple shell corporations each carrying the minimum statutory insurance clearly perverted the legislative intent, and held, "When the statutory privilege of doing business in the corporate form is employed as a cloak for the evasion of obligations, as a mask behind which to do injustice or invoked to subvert equity, the separate personality of the corporation will be disregarded."

Wallace v. Tulsa Yellow Cab Taxi & Baggage Co. also involved a plaintiff who was injured by a taxi. Wallace sued the cab company and recovered a judgment. Unfortunately for Wallace, by the time he tried to collect on the judgment, the cab company had gone out of business. Or did it? The court permitted Wallace to recover from Tulsa Yellow Cab, a successor corporation. Here are the factors the judge relied upon:

1. The taxi business is hazardous by nature (great potential for harm).

2. The only asset of the new corporation was $1,000 of paid-in stock (inadequate capital).

3. The new corporation leased cabs from the old corporation pursuant to a lease which was terminable on 24 hours notice (an unusual provision).

4. Although the owners of the new corporation were different, the owners were former employees of the old corporation and financed the purchase of their stock by money loaned to them by the owner of the old company (an unusual procedure with no obvious legitimate business purpose).

5. The management of the new corporation was the same as the old corporation, so in effect, the corporations were the same. In both of these cases, the courts relied upon inadequate capitalization and control as key criteria for piercing the corporate veil. The severity of the harm to the claimants was also a significant factor.

Personal Injury Cases and Claims

Of course, all personal injuries aren't the result of taxis. In *Geringer v. Wildhorse Ranch, Inc.*, a widow sued for the wrongful death of her husband and children who were killed in a paddleboat accident at a Colorado ranch. The action was filed against Wildhorse Ranch, Inc., and its principal owner.

The court pierced the corporate veil and attached liability to Wildhorse Ranch's principal owner, noting:

- No corporation stock had been issued in the corporation and no record of the stock existed (absence of records and formality).

- No corporate minutes existed even though the defendant testified that informal board meetings had been conducted (absence of records and formality).

- The principal owner operated several corporations out of one office (absence of separation between corporations).

- Debts of one corporation were frequently paid with funds of another corporation or from the principal owner's personal funds (commingling of funds; no arm's length dealings).

- The principal owner had purchased the paddleboats with funds from another corporation (commingling, related party transaction).

- No record of loans or ledgers existed (no loan documentation).

- Corporate records were so muddled that no clear picture of accountability or organization could be shown (poor recordkeeping).

- Business cards listed the principal owner as the "owner" of the corporation (improper way to hold corporation out to public).

- Employees of the corporation believed that the principal owner was in control (agency, public perception).

- The principal owner knew that the paddleboats leaked and became unstable and overruled employee recommendations that the boats be repaired (active wrongdoing on the part of owner).

Contract Creditors and Contract Claims

Although a court is more likely to pierce a corporate or LLC veil in a tort situation, it will pierce the veil in an appropriate contract situation. *Stone v. Frederick Hobby Associates II LLC* is an illustrative example, and one of the first cases applying the traditional corporation veil test to an LLC. The facts: the Stone family was the dissatisfied purchaser of a $3,300,000 home constructed and sold to them by defendant Frederick Hobby Associates II, LLC. As part of their legal claim, the Stone family asserted that defendant Hobby II's LLC form should be disregarded so as to reach the assets of Hobby II's two owners and a related limited liability company, Hobby I. The Stones charged that the defendant builder had breached the construction contract. The Stones sought to hold Hobby II's two individual members and Hobby I responsible for their losses. They argued that Hobby II was a shell company with no assets and no ability to pay any potential damage award. The court agreed with the Stones on the underlying contract claim against the owners of Hobby II, and against Hobby I. The Connecticut court further recognized that the corporate veil doctrine would also be applicable to the LLC. Connecticut law authorizes individuals to be held personally liable for entity obligations under either the "instrumentality rule" or the "identity rule," and the court held that the criteria for application of both rules had been satisfied.

The facts that the court recognized when applying the instrumentality test were:

- The LLC's two members each held a 50% ownership interest in Hobby II and had full authority to manage Hobby II's affairs;
- Hobby II's office was located in one owner's home, on a rent-free basis;
- Hobby II had no assets other than the residence it sold to the plaintiffs;
- The defendant's attorney had remarked during a meeting that the defendant had no assets;
- Several documents used by Hobby II in connection with the subject premises listed entities or individuals similar to and easily confused with Hobby II as the operative actors (for instance, in the Connecticut real estate conveyance tax return, it is unclear whether the seller is Hobby II or its member Frederick Hobby).

There was also an allegation by plaintiffs that the defendants, shortly following the closing date on the Stones' new residence, had transferred substantially all of Hobby II's assets (including the sale proceeds) to the two members and Hobby I.

The court concluded that the members had complete control over the LLC, that the control was used as a shield to evade contractual obligations to plaintiffs and that the plaintiffs' losses emanated, at least in part, from the control the defendant members exercised over Hobby II, and, accordingly, imposed personal liability on the members.

The case of *Labadie Coal Co. v. Black* is another illustrative example. There, creditors were able to pierce the veil of a trading corporation and recover against controlling owners. The court examined these factors:

> **Expert Tip**
>
> Don't use your name, initials, or other personal reference in the name of your LLC unless there is a good reason to. If liability protection is important to you, you want to appear separate from your LLC, not unified with it.

- The controlling owners owned all of the corporation stock and controlled corporation decisions.
- The corporation failed to maintain corporation minutes or adequate records, including articles of incorporation, corporation operating agreements, or a current list of directors.
- No formalities pertaining to the issuance of corporation stock were followed.
- Funds were commingled with funds and assets of other corporations.
- Corporation funds were diverted to the personal use of the owners.
- The corporation and the owners used the same office for different business activities.
- The corporation was inadequately capitalized. The court noted that fraud was not required to pierce the corporation veil. All that was required was the presence of an unjust situation. The court also stated: "Faithfulness to the formalities is the price paid to the corporation fiction, a relatively small price to pay for limited liability. Furthermore, the formalities are themselves an excellent litmus of the extent to which the individuals involved actually view the corporation as a separate being."

Government Claims

Government agencies can pursue many of the same claims as nongovernmental persons and entities. Tort claims and contract claims are not limited to the private sector. For example, in *United States v. Healthwise-Midtown Convalescent Hospital and Rehabilitation Center, Inc.*, the government sought to recover excess payments of Medicare benefits paid to the hospital.

The hospital's corporate charter had been revoked for failing to pay required state taxes. The action was pursued against the owner of 50% of the hospital's outstanding stock. The court identified the following factors in ruling in favor of the government:

- The principal owner owned 50% of the hospital's stock and 50% of the partnership interests of the partnership which owned the real estate upon which the hospital was built and the furnishings used by the hospital.
- The principal owner served as president, a board member, and administrator of the hospital (control).
- Other board members did not attend board meetings. (Note the potential for a claim of breach of duty of care against the non-attending directors.)
- The principal owner had check writing authority and controlled the affairs of the LLC.
- The corporation was inadequately capitalized, with liabilities in excess of $150,000 and capital of $10,000.
- Regular board meetings were not conducted (lack of formality).
- Funds were commingled.
- Corporation assets were diverted from the corporation.
- The principal owner failed to maintain an arm's length relationship when dealing with the corporation and the partnership.

Here, the partnership was paid amounts due and owing to it by the corporation in full, to the detriment of corporation creditors.

The court in *Securities and Exchange Commission v. Elmas Trading Corp.* provided a detailed list of factors to be considered by the court in determining whether or not to pierce the corporate veil. Presumably, these factors would also apply when analyzing an LLC's liability shield. In this case, 16 separate entities consisting of corporations and partnerships were disregarded. The court noted that no one factor was determinative. Rather, all of the facts and circumstances had to be considered in each case. The criteria listed by the court included:

- Failure to observe corporation formalities;
- Nonpayment of dividends;
- Insolvency of the corporation at the time of the transaction;
- Siphoning funds of the corporation by the dominant owner;
- Nonfunctioning of other officers or directors;
- Absence of corporation records;
- Use of the same office or business location by the corporation and its individual owners;
- Commingling of funds and other assets;
- Unauthorized diversion of corporation assets to other business activities or personal accounts of the owners;
- Failure to maintain minutes or adequate corporation records of separate corporation businesses;
- Common ownership of stock between two or more corporations;
- Identical persons serving as officers and/or directors of two or more corporations;
- The absence of corporation assets;
- The use of a corporation as a mere shell, instrumentality, or conduit for a single venture or the business of an individual or another corporation;
- The concealment and misrepresentation of the identity of the responsible ownership, management and financial interest of a corporation or the concealment of personal business activities;
- Failure to maintain an arm's length relationship in transactions between related entities;
- Use of a corporation entity to procure labor, services, or merchandise for another person or entity to the detriment of creditors;

- The manipulation of assets and liabilities between entities so as to concentrate the assets in one and liabilities in another;
- The contracting with another with the intent to avoid performance by the use of an corporation as a subterfuge of illegal transactions; and
- The formation and use of a corporation to transfer to it the existing liability of another person or entity.

Parent as Alter Ego of Subsidiary

When one LLC owns all or substantially all of the voting stock of another LLC, the LLC owning the stock is the parent corporation, and the other LLC is the subsidiary. Historically, the instrumentality rule has been used to impose liability on the parent for activities of the subsidiary. The veil of the parent and subsidiary could potentially be pierced to impose liability on controlling owners.

In one case, *Miles v. American Telephone & Telegraph Company*, the court refused to pierce the veil and impose liability on the parent corporation. There, the parent and subsidiary maintained their relationship on an arm's length basis. In another, *Sabine Towing & Transportation Co., Inc. v. Merit Ventures, Inc.*, the subsidiary's veil was pierced.

In *Miles v. American Telephone & Telegraph Company*, the plaintiff, Miles, filed a lawsuit against AT&T alleging tortious invasion of plaintiff's privacy by Southwestern Bell, a subsidiary of AT&T. The court granted summary judgment in AT&T's favor, dismissing it from the lawsuit, noting that the subsidiary maintained a great degree of separateness from its parent corporation. Listed below are subsidiary activities deemed to be significant by the court not to pierce the LLC veil. The subsidiary:

- Selected its own banks,
- Selected, trained, and supervised its own personnel,
- Set its own rates with the Federal Communications Commission,
- Prepared its own budget,
- Determined its own construction contracts,
- Prepared its own annual report,

- Had its own employee newsletter,
- Paid its own bills,
- Purchased its own property and equipment, and
- Developed its own sales and marketing procedures.

The court in *Miles* also found that:

- The parent and subsidiary were distinct and adequately capitalized financial units,
- Daily operations of the two corporations were separate with formal barriers between the management of the two corporations, and
- Those dealing with the corporations were apprised of their separate identities.

In *Sabine Towing*, the court reached a different result. There, a suit was filed against the parent corporation for breach of shipping agreements. The factors considered by the court in reaching its decision to pierce the corporate veil were:

- Common stock ownership of the parent and subsidiary corporations existed.
- Parent and subsidiary corporations shared the same owners and managers, making it impossible for the subsidiary board to act independently.
- The same corporate offices were used by both corporations.
- The subsidiary was inadequately capitalized.
- The subsidiary was financed by the parent whenever the subsidiary ran short of capital.
- The parent existed solely as a holding company with no independent active business of its own.
- The parent used the subsidiary's assets and property as its own.
- No formal documentation of loans between the parent and subsidiary existed.
- Subsidiary decisions were made by the parent.
- There were no records of meetings or other corporation records.
- Subsidiary assets were stripped by the parent to the benefit of the parent and the detriment of the subsidiary. For parent/subsidiary LLCs,

the criteria examined in Miles provide a better guide for appropriate behavior than the criteria described in Sabine Towing. Once again, common sense should point you in the right direction, but it is important that you begin good recordkeeping habits early.

How to Sign Documents as an LLC Officer

You must represent yourself as an officer of your entity, not as an individual. When you sign contractual and other documents, use the following form:

> By: Judy Doe (signature)
> Name: Judy Doe
> Title: President of Everclear Waters, LLC

The Seven Most Important Liability Protection Rules

In order to maintain liability protection for you and other owners, you should strictly abide by the following rules:

1. A crucially important rule is to pay creditors before you make distributions to owners. LLCs, like corporations, owe an important obligation to pay creditors before distributing profits to owners. Universally, state law will force an LLC owner to give back distributions of profits made to entity owners in lieu of paying creditors.

2. Always hold yourself out as an officer/manager of the entity—not as an individual. Sign documents in your capacity as a representative of the entity, not personally, i.e., "John Jones, President, OldeCraft, LLC." You should always endeavor to prevent a creditor from arguing that you personally guaranteed an obligation. Identify your LLC in advertisements, correspondence, invoices, statements, business cards, your web site, etc.

3. Follow your LLC operating agreements. A crafty creditor's attorney can have an easy time asserting alter ego liability if you do not follow your own entity's written procedures.

4. Keep proper records. When owners and managers/officers meet, be sure to prepare minutes of the meetings. If the owners or managers/officers reach a decision, even informally, commit that decision to writing in the form of a written consent. Creditors wishing to pierce the liability veil will always seek to discover improper record keeping.

5. Obtain and maintain a business checking account in the name of the entity. Furthermore, always keep your personal assets and entity assets separate. Also, if you operate more than one entity (many people do), keep each entity's assets separate. Keep accurate business records for your entity.

6. Always keep your company in good standing with the Secretary of State. An LLC is subject to administrative dissolution if it fails to meet its ongoing responsibilities. This means that you must always file all tax returns, including franchise tax returns, and file all periodic reporting forms. Also, maintain close contact with your registered agent and always pay their bills on time.

7. Never dissolve a company that has debts outstanding. These debts can be imputed to you personally if the company is dissolved.

A Dead Company Offers Little Liability Protection

If an LLC is not in good standing or has been dissolved, the entity's ability to shield its owners from liability can be undermined. An LLC is in good standing when it is in full compliance with the law, its taxes are paid, and all periodic reports have been filed on time. An LLC can be subject to an administrative dissolution by the secretary of state if its taxes are not paid and its periodic filings are not made on time. A dissolution is the end of an LLC's life. Such an entity offers significantly reduced liability protection to its owners.

The following oversights by management can threaten an LLC's ability to shield its owners from liability:

• Managers or members fail to pay LLC and franchise taxes in the state of organization.

- Managers or members fail to file annual and periodic reports in the state of organization.
- Managers or members fail to notify the secretary of state of a change of address.
- Managers or members fail to pay the annual fees of the resident agent or fail to advise the resident agent of a change of address.

Liability Protection: Corporation Versus LLC

Does an LLC offer greater liability protection than a corporation? In short—but this is a generalization—yes. Of course, the LLC wins by just a hair. The reason is that LLCs do not require such intensive periodic formalities, such as annual meetings, as LLCs do. Such formalities consume time and resources. Although it is not recommended, many small corporations fall behind on their formalities, especially annual meetings and elections of directors. Failing to observe these formalities weakens the corporation liability shield. Because LLCs are not subject to such intensive formalities, LLC liability protection cannot be weakened by failure to follow formalities.

Final Thoughts on Liability Protection

Attention to detail, common sense, good recordkeeping are three characteristics that will go a long way toward preserving your LLC and protecting your personal assets. As many of these cases illustrated, you can't escape personal liability if you don't treat your LLC as a separate legal entity. Don't use your LLC as your personal playground. Use common sense, maintain good records, and pay attention to detail.

LLC Do's and Don'ts Checklist

DO:

- Maintain capital reserves sufficient to meet reasonably foreseeable needs of the LLC, including liability insurance coverage.

- Maintain active and independent managers or managing members.

- If asked to serve as a manager or managing member, be active and use your best independent business judgment even if that requires you to disagree with management.

- Use business cards and letterhead which reflect the LLC name.

- Make certain that LLC letters and agreements are signed by the LLC.

- Distinguish pre-organizational LLC activities by a promoter from post-organizational LLC activities by officers or directors.

- Use formal loan documents, including notes and security agreements, for LLC loans, especially to owners and managers and be sure to have a written resolution authorizing the transaction.

- Use written leases, purchase and sale agreements, and bills of sale in transactions involving owners and managers and be sure to have a member or manager resolution authorizing the transaction.

- Use separate offices for activities of separate businesses.

- Use separate telephone lines for each business.

- Use separate employees for each business.

- Allow each LLC to own its own assets or equipment or lease them pursuant to written lease agreements.

- Apply for all required permits, licenses, and identification numbers in the LLC name.

- Obtain necessary business insurance in the LLC name.

DON'T:

- Commingle personal and LLC assets or assets among related LLCs.

- Divert LLC assets for personal use.

- Engage in any act for an illegal or improper purpose such as to defraud creditors or oppress minority owners.

- Hold yourself out as the owner of the LLC; you may be an owner, officer, or director, but the LLC should be held out as the legal entity for the action.

- Engage in transactions between LLCs and their owners and managers on any basis other than on an arm's length basis.

- If you operate several LLCs, don't use the same people as owners and managers of each LLC.

Parent/Subsidiary/Successor Considerations Checklist

In addition to the do's and don'ts outlined in the previous checklist, parent/subsidiary or successor LLCs should be sensitive to the following issues:

Parent/Subsidiary LLCs

To avoid liability by the parent, the subsidiary should be as independent as possible. Answer these questions.

Who makes decisions for the other? _____

Who finances the subsidiary? _____

Does the parent have its own active business?   ❑ Yes   ❑ No

   Or Is it merely a holding company for other businesses?   ❑ Yes   ❑ No

Who prepares the budget? _____

Is there an identity of owners and managers?   ❑ Yes   ❑ No

Is there common stock ownership?   ❑ Yes   ❑ No

If a parent LLC controls the decision-making processes of the subsidiary, finances the subsidiary, prepares the subsidiary's budget, shares a complete or partial overlap of officers or directors, and engages in no active business of its own, the parent LLC is more likely to be responsible for the acts of the subsidiary.

Successor Employer or Corporation

If you can answer yes to the first three questions below, the successor LLC may retain liability for acts of its predecessor.

Is there continuity in the work force?   ❑ Yes   ❑ No

Is there continuity in the management?   ❑ Yes   ❑ No

Is there continuity in the stock ownership?   ❑ Yes   ❑ No

What other items carry over? _____

Appendix A
Limited Liability Company Forms

LLC Form 1: **LLC-1, California LLC Articles of Organization**

LIMITED LIABILITY COMPANIES

California Tax Information

Registration of a limited liability company with the California Secretary of State will obligate a limited liability company that is not taxed as a corporation to pay to the Franchise Tax Board an annual minimum tax of $800.00 and a fee based on the annual total income of the entity. The tax and fee are required to be paid for the taxable year of registration and each taxable year, or part thereof, until a Certificate of Cancellation is filed with the California Secretary of State. (Rev. and Tax. Code §§ 17941 and 17942.) A limited liability company is not subject to the taxes and fees imposed by Revenue and Taxation Code sections 17941 and 17942 if the limited liability company did no business in California during the taxable year and the taxable year was 15 days or less. (Rev. and Tax. Code § 17946.) For further information, please contact the Franchise Tax Board at:

From within the United States (toll free).. (800) 852-5711

From outside the United States (not toll free).. (916) 845-6500

Automated Toll Free Phone Service... (800) 338-0505

PROFESSIONAL SERVICES INFORMATION

Pursuant to California Corporations Code section 17375, a domestic or foreign limited liability company may not render professional services, as defined in Corporations Code sections 13401(a) and 13401.3. Professional services are defined as: Any type of professional services that may be lawfully rendered only pursuant to a license, certification, or registration authorized by the Business and Professions Code, the Chiropractic Act, the Osteopathic Act or the Yacht and Ship Brokers Act. If your business is required to be licensed, registered or certified, it is recommended that you contact the appropriate licensing authority before filing with the Secretary of State's office in order to determine whether your services are considered professional.

LLC FORM 2: **Sample Letter to Secretary of State Accompanying Articles of Organization**

Note: This letter is a version appropriate for use in Delaware, but can be modified for use in any state.

Laura Spader
123 Elm Street
San Francisco, CA 94107
415-555-1212

September 28, 2007

State of Delaware
Division of Corporations
401 Federal Street, Suite 4
Dover, DE 19901

To whom it may concern,

Enclosed you will find articles of organization for 17 Reasons, LLC. Please file the enclosed articles.

I have enclosed five copies of the filing and a check for $_____ to cover filing fees. Please return any necessary papers in the envelope that I have provided.

Yours truly,

Laura Spader

LLC FORM 3: **Sample Letter to Registered Agent Accompanying Articles of Organization**

Laura Spader
123 Elm Street
San Francisco, CA 94107
415-555-1212

September 28, 2007

Harvard Business Services, Inc.
25 Greystone Manor
Lewes, DE 19958

To whom it may concern,

I have enclosed a copy of articles of organization I am filing today. As you can see, I have used you as our registered agents in the state of Delaware.

Please use the following contact information:

17 Reasons, LLC
c/o Laura Spader
123 Elm Street
San Francisco, CA 94107

I have enclosed a check for $50 to cover the first year's services.

Yours truly,

Laura Spader

LLC FORM 4: **Short-Form Operating Agreement for Member-Managed LLC**

OPERATING AGREEMENT OF [Insert full name of LLC]

THIS OPERATING AGREEMENT (the "Agreement") is hereby entered into by the undersigned, who are owners and shall be referred to as Member or Members.

RECITALS

The Members desire to form [insert full name of LLC], a limited liability company (the "Company"), for the purposes set forth herein, and, accordingly, desire to enter into this Agreement in order to set forth the terms and conditions of the business and affairs of the Company and to determine the rights and obligations of its Members.

NOW, THEREFORE, the Members, intending to be legally bound by this Agreement, hereby agree that the limited liability company operating agreement of the Company shall be as follows:

ARTICLE I: DEFINITIONS

When used in this Agreement, the following terms shall have the meanings set forth below.

1.1 "Act" means the Limited Liability Company Law of the State in which the Company is organized or chartered, including any amendments or the corresponding provision(s) of any succeeding law.

1.2 "Capital Contribution(s)" means the amount of cash and the agreed value of property, services rendered, or a promissory note or other obligation to contribute cash or property or to perform services contributed by the Members for such Members' Interest in the Company, equal to the sum of the Members' initial Capital Contributions plus the Members' additional Capital Contributions, if any, made pursuant to Sections 4.1 and 4.2, respectively, less payments or distributions made pursuant to Section 5.1.

1.3 "Code" means the Internal Revenue Code of 1986 and the regulations promulgated thereunder, as amended from time to time (or any corresponding provision or provisions of succeeding law).

1.4 "Interest" or "Interests" means the ownership Interest, expressed as a number, percentage, or fraction, set forth in Table A, of a Member in the Company.

1.5 "Person" means any natural individual, partnership, firm, corporation, limited liability company, joint-stock company, trust, or other entity.

1.6 "Secretary of State" means the Office of the Secretary of State or the office charged with accepting articles of organization in the Company's state of organization.

LLC FORM 4: Short-Form Operating Agreement for Member-Managed LLC (continued)

ARTICLE II: FORMATION

2.1 Organization. The Members hereby organize the Company as a limited liability company pursuant to the provisions of the Act.

2.2 Effective Date. The Company shall come into being on, and this Agreement shall take effect from, the date the Articles of Organization of the Company are filed with the Secretary of State in the state of organization or charter.

2.3 Agreement: Invalid Provisions and Saving Clause. The Members, by executing this Agreement, hereby agree to the terms and conditions of this Agreement. To the extent any provision of this Agreement is prohibited or ineffective under the Act, this Agreement shall be deemed to be amended to the least extent necessary in order to make this Agreement effective under the Act. In the event the Act is subsequently amended or interpreted in such a way to validate any provision of this Agreement that was formerly invalid, such provision shall be considered to be valid from the effective date of such amendment or interpretation.

ARTICLE III: PURPOSE; NATURE OF BUSINESS

3.1 Purpose; Nature of Business. The purpose of the Company shall be to engage in any lawful business that may be engaged in by a limited liability company organized under the Act, as such business activities may be determined by the Member or Members from time to time.

3.2 Powers. The Company shall have all powers of a limited liability company under the Act and the power to do all things necessary or convenient to accomplish its purpose and operate its business as described in Section 3.1 here.

ARTICLE IV: MEMBERS AND CAPITAL CONTRIBUTIONS

4.1 Members and Initial Capital Contribution. The name, address, Interest, and value of the initial Capital Contribution of the Members shall be set forth on Table A attached hereto.

4.2 Additional Capital Contributions. The Members shall have no obligation to make any additional Capital Contributions to the Company. The Members may make additional Capital Contributions to the Company as the Members unanimously determine are necessary, appropriate, or desirable.

ARTICLE V: DISTRIBUTIONS AND ALLOCATIONS

5.1 Distributions and Allocations. All distributions of cash or other assets of the Company shall be made and paid to the Members at such time and in such amounts as the majority of the Members may determine. All items of income, gain, loss, deduction, and credit shall be allocated to the Members in proportion to their Interests.

LLC FORM 4: Short-Form Operating Agreement for Member-Managed LLC (continued)

ARTICLE VI: TAXATION

6.1 Income Tax Reporting. Each Member is aware of the income tax consequences of the allocations made by Article V here and agrees to be bound by the provisions of Article V here in reporting each Member's share of Company income and loss for federal and state income tax purposes.

6.2 Tax Treatment. Notwithstanding anything contained herein to the contrary and only for purposes of federal and, if applicable, state income tax purposes, the Company shall be classified as a partnership for such federal and state income tax purposes unless and until the Members unanimously determine to cause the Company to file an election under the Code to be classified as an association taxable as a corporation.

ARTICLE VII: MANAGEMENT BY MEMBERS

7.1 Management by Members. The Company shall be managed by its Members, who shall have full and exclusive right, power, and authority to manage the affairs of the Company and to bind the Company to contracts and obligations, to make all decisions with respect thereto, and to do or cause to be done any and all acts or things deemed by the Members to be necessary, appropriate, or desirable to carry out or further the business of the Company.

7.2 Voting Power in Proportion to Interest. The Members shall enjoy voting power and authority in proportion to their Interests. Unless expressly provided otherwise in this Agreement or the Articles of Organization, Company decisions shall be made by majority vote.

7.3 Duties of Members. The Members shall manage and administer the day-to-day operations and business of the Company and shall execute any and all reports, forms, instruments, documents, papers, writings, agreements, and contracts, including but not limited to deeds, bills of sale, assignments, leases, promissory notes, mortgages, and security agreements, and any other type or form of document by which property or property rights of the Company are transferred or encumbered, or by which debts and obligations of the Company are created, incurred, or evidenced.

ARTICLE VIII: BOOKS AND RECORDS

8.1 Books and Records. The Members shall keep, or cause to be kept, at the principal place of business of the Company true and correct books of account, in which shall be entered fully and accurately each and every transaction of the Company. The Company's taxable and fiscal years shall end on December 31. All Members shall have the right to inspect the Company's books and records at any time, for any reason.

ARTICLE IX: LIMITATION OF LIABILITY; INDEMNIFICATION

9.1 Limited Liability. Except as otherwise required by law, the debts, obligations, and liabilities of the Company, whether arising in contract, tort, or otherwise, shall be solely the debts, obligations, and liabilities of the Company, and the Members shall not be obligated personally for any such debt, obligation, or liability of the Company solely by reason of being Members. The failure of the Company to observe any formalities or requirements relating to the exercise of its powers or the management of its business or affairs under this Agreement or by law shall not be grounds for imposing personal liability on the Members for any debts, liabilities, or obligations of the Company. Except as otherwise expressly required by law, the Members, in such Members' capacity as such, shall have no liability in excess of (a) the amount of such Members' Capital Contributions, (b) such Members' share of any assets and undistributed profits of the Company, and (c) the amount of any distributions required to be returned according to law.

9.2 Indemnification. The Company shall, to the fullest extent provided or allowed by law, indemnify, save harmless, and pay all judgments and claims against the Members, and each of the Company's or Members' agents, affiliates, heirs, legal representatives, successors, and assigns (each, an "Indemnified Party") from, against, and in respect of any and all liability, loss, damage, and expense incurred or sustained by the Indemnified Party in connection with the business of the Company or by reason of any act performed or omitted to be performed in connection with the activities of the Company or in dealing with third parties on behalf of the Company, including costs and attorneys' fees before and at trial and at all appellate levels, whether or not suit is instituted (which attorneys' fees may be paid as incurred), and any amounts expended in the settlement of any claims of liability, loss, or damage, to the fullest extent allowed by law.

9.3. Insurance. The Company shall not pay for any insurance covering liability of the Members or the Company's or Members' agents, affiliates, heirs, legal representatives, successors, and assigns for actions or omissions for which indemnification is not permitted hereunder, provided, however, that nothing contained here shall preclude the Company from purchasing and paying for such types of insurance, including extended coverage liability and casualty and worker's compensation, as would be customary for any Person owning, managing, and/or operating comparable property and engaged in a similar business, or from naming the Members and any of the Company's or Members' agents, affiliates, heirs, legal representatives, successors, or assigns or any Indemnified Party as additional insured parties thereunder.

9.4 Non-Exclusive Right. The provisions of this Article IX shall be in addition to and not in limitation of any other rights of indemnification and reimbursement or limitations of liability to which an Indemnified Party may be entitled under the Act, common law, or otherwise.

LLC FORM 4: **Short-Form Operating Agreement for Member-Managed LLC** (continued)

ARTICLE X: AMENDMENT

10.1 Amendment. This Agreement may not be altered or modified except by the unanimous written consent or agreement of the Members as evidenced by an amendment hereto whereby this Agreement is amended or amended and restated.

ARTICLE XI: WITHDRAWAL

11.1 Withdrawal of a Member. No Member may withdraw from the Company except by written request of the Member given to each of the other Members and with the unanimous written consent of the other Members, the effective date of withdrawal being the date on which the unanimous written consent of all of the other Members is given or upon the effective date of any of the following events:

(a) the Member makes an assignment of his or her property for the benefit of creditors;

(b) the Member files a voluntary petition of bankruptcy;

(c) the Member is adjudged bankrupt or insolvent or there is entered against the Member an order for relief in any bankruptcy or insolvency proceeding;

(d) the Member seeks, consents to, or acquiesces in the appointment of a trustee or receiver for, or liquidation of the Member or of all or any substantial part of the Member's property;

(e) the Member files an answer or other pleading admitting or failing to contest the material allegations of a petition filed against the Member in any proceeding described in Subsections 11.1 (a) through (d);

(f) if the Member is a corporation, the dissolution of the corporation or the revocation of its articles of incorporation or charter;

(g) if the Member is an estate, the distribution by the fiduciary of the estate's Interest in the Company;

(h) if the Member is an employee of the Company and he or she resigns, retires, or for any reason ceases to be employed by the Company in any capacity; or

(i) if the other Members owning more than fifty percent (50%) of the Interests vote or request in writing that a Member withdraw and such request is given to the Member (the effective date of withdrawal being the date on which the vote or written request of the other Members is given to the Member).

11.2 Valuation of Interest. The value of the withdrawing Member's Interest in all events shall be equal to the greater of the following: (a) the amount of the Member's Capital Contribution or (b) the amount of the Member's share of the Members' equity in the Company, plus the amount of any unpaid and outstanding loans or advances made by the Member to the Company (plus any due and unpaid interest thereon, if interest on the loan or advance has been agreed to between the Company and the Member), calculated as of the end of the fiscal quarter immediately preceding the effective date of the Member's withdrawal.

11.3 Payment of Value. The value shall be payable as follows: (a) If the value is equal to or less than $500, at closing, and (b) If the value is greater than $500, at the option of the Company, $500 at closing with the balance of the purchase price paid by delivering a promissory note of the Company dated as of the closing date and bearing interest at the prime rate published in The Wall Street Journal as of the effective date of withdrawal, with the principal amount being payable in five (5) equal annual installments beginning one (1) year from closing and with the interest on the accrued and unpaid balance being payable at the time of payment of each principal installment.

11.4 Closing. Payment of the value of the departing Member's Interest shall be made at a mutually agreeable time and date on or before thirty (30) days from the effective date of withdrawal. Upon payment of the value of the Interest as calculated in Section 11.3 above: (a) the Member's right to receive any and all further payments or distributions on account of the Member's ownership of the Interest in the Company shall cease; (b) the Member's loans or advances to the Company shall be paid and satisfied in full; and (c) the Member shall no longer be a Member or creditor of the Company on account of the Capital Contribution or the loans or advances.

11.5 Limitation on Payment of Value. If payment of the value of the Interest would be prohibited by any statute or law prohibiting distributions that would

(a) render the Company insolvent; or

(b) be made at a time that the total Company liabilities (other than liabilities to Members on account of their Interests) exceed the value of the Company's total assets;

then the value of the withdrawing Member's Interest in all events shall be $1.00.

ARTICLE XII: MISCELLANEOUS PROVISIONS

12.1 Assignment of Interest and New Members. No Member may assign such person's Interest in the Company in whole or in part except by the vote or written consent of the other Members owning more than fifty percent (50%) of the Interests. No additional Person may be admitted as a Member except by the vote or written consent of the Members owning more than fifty percent (50%) of the Interests.

12.2 Determinations by Members. Except as required by the express provisions of this Agreement or of the Act:

LLC FORM 4: Short-Form Operating Agreement for Member-Managed LLC (continued)

(a) Any transaction, action, or decision which requires or permits the Members to consent to, approve, elect, appoint, adopt, or authorize or to make a determination or decision with respect thereto under this Agreement, the Act, the Code, or otherwise shall be made by the Members owning more than fifty percent (50%) of the Interests.

(b) The Members shall act at a meeting of Members or by consent in writing of the Members. Members may vote or give their consent in person or by proxy.

(c) Meetings of the Members may be held at any time, upon call of any Member or Members owning, in the aggregate, at least ten percent (10%) of the Interests.

(d) Unless waived in writing by the Members owning more than fifty percent (50%) of the Interests (before or after a meeting), at least two (2) business days' prior notice of any meeting shall be given to each Member. Such notice shall state the purpose for which such meeting has been called. No business may be conducted or action taken at such meeting that is not provided for in such notice.

(e) Members may participate in a meeting of Members by means of conference telephone or similar communications equipment by means of which all Persons participating in the meeting can hear each other, and such participation shall constitute presence in person at such meeting.

(f) The Members shall cause to be kept a book of minutes of all meetings of the Members in which there shall be recorded the time and place of such meeting, by whom such meeting was called, the notice thereof given, the names of those present, and the proceedings thereof. Copies of any consents in writing shall also be filed in such minute book.

12.3 Binding Effect. This Agreement shall be binding upon and inure to the benefit of the undersigned Members, their legal representatives, heirs, successors, and assigns. This Agreement and the rights and duties of the Members hereunder shall be governed by, and interpreted and construed in accordance with, the laws of the Company's state of organization or charter, without regard to principles of choice of law.

12.4 Headings. The article and section headings in this Agreement are inserted as a matter of convenience and are for reference only and shall not be construed to define, limit, extend, or describe the scope of this Agreement or the intent of any provision.

12.5 Number and Gender. Whenever required by the context here, the singular shall include the plural, and vice versa and the masculine gender shall include the feminine and neuter genders, and vice versa.

12.6 Entire Agreement and Binding Effect. This Agreement constitutes the sole operating agreement among the Members and supersedes and cancels any prior agreements, representations, warranties, or

LLC FORM 4: **Short-Form Operating Agreement for Member-Managed LLC** (continued)

communications, whether oral or written, between the Members relating to the affairs of the Company and the conduct of the Company's business. No amendment or modification of this Agreement shall be effective unless approved in writing as provided in Section 10.1. The Articles of Organization and this Agreement are binding upon and shall inure to the benefit of the Members and Agent(s) and shall be binding upon their successors, assigns, affiliates, subsidiaries, heirs, beneficiaries, personal representatives, executors, administrators, and guardians, as applicable and appropriate.

IN WITNESS WHEREOF, this Agreement has been made and executed by the Members effective as of the date first written above.

_____ (member)

_____ (member)

_____ (member)

LLC FORM 4: **Short-Form Operating Agreement for Member-Managed LLC** (continued)

TABLE A: **NAME, ADDRESS, AND INITIAL CAPITAL CONTRIBUTION OF THE MEMBERS**

Name and Address of Member	Value of Initial Capital Contribution	Nature of Member's Initial Capital Contribution (i.e., cash, services, property)	Percentage Interest of Member

OPERATING AGREEMENT OF [insert name of LLC], LLC

THIS OPERATING AGREEMENT (the "Agreement") is made and entered into on _____, 20__, and those persons whose names, addresses, and signatures are set forth below, being the Members of [insert name of LLC], LLC (the "Company"), represent and agree that they have caused or will cause to be filed, on behalf of the Company, Articles of Organization, and that they desire to enter into an operating agreement.

The Members agree as follows:

ARTICLE I: DEFINITIONS

1.1. **"Act"** means the Limited Liability Company Law of the State in which the Company is organized or chartered, including any amendments or the corresponding provision(s) of any succeeding law.

1.2. **"Affiliate" or "Affiliate of a Member"** means any Person under the control of, in common control with, or in control of a Member, whether that control is direct or indirect. The term "control," as used herein, means, with respect to a corporation or limited liability company, the ability to exercise more than fifty percent (50%) of the voting rights of the controlled entity, and with respect to an individual, partnership, trust, or other entity or association, the ability, directly or indirectly, to direct the management of policies of the controlled entity or individual.

1.3. **"Agreement"** means this Operating Agreement, in its original form and as amended from time to time.

1.4. **"Articles"** means the Articles of Organization or other charter document filed with the Secretary of State in the state of organization forming this limited liability company, as initially filed and as they may be amended from time to time.

1.5. **"Capital Account"** means the amount of the capital interest of a Member in the Company, consisting of the amount of money and the fair market value, net of liabilities, of any property initially contributed by the Member, as (1) increased by any additional contributions and the Member's share of the Company's profits; and (2) decreased by any distribution to that Member as well as that Member's share of Company losses.

1.6. **"Code"** means the Internal Revenue Code of 1986, as amended from time to time, the regulations promulgated thereunder, and any corresponding provision of any succeeding revenue law.

1.7. **"Company Minimum Gain"** shall have the same meaning as set forth for the term "Partnership Minimum Gain" in the Regulations section 1.704-2(d) (26 CFR Section1.704-2(d)).

LLC FORM 5: **Long-Form Operating Agreement for Member-Managed LLC** (continued)

1.8. "Departing Member" means any Member whose conduct results in a Dissolution Event or who withdraws from or is expelled from the Company in accordance with Section 4.3, where such withdrawal does not result in dissolution of the Company.

1.9. "Dissolution Event" means, with respect to any Member, one or more of the following: the death, resignation, retirement, expulsion, bankruptcy, or dissolution of any Member.

1.10. "Distribution" means the transfer of money or property by the Company to the Members without consideration.

1.11. "Member" means each Person who has been admitted into membership in the Company, executes this Agreement and any subsequent amendments, and has not engaged in conduct resulting in a Dissolution Event or terminated membership for any other reason.

1.12. "Member Nonrecourse Debt" shall have the same meaning as set forth for the term "Partnership Nonrecourse Debt" in the Code.

1.13. "Member Nonrecourse Deductions" means items of Company loss, deduction, or Code Section 705(a)(2)(B) expenditures which are attributable to Member Nonrecourse Debt.

1.14. "Membership Interest" means a Member's rights in the Company, collectively, including the Member's economic interest, right to vote and participate in management, and right to information concerning the business and affairs of the Company provided in this Agreement or under the Act.

1.15. "Net Profits" and **"Net Losses"** mean the Company's income, loss, and deductions computed at the close of each fiscal year in accordance with the accounting methods used to prepare the Company's information tax return filed for federal income tax purposes.

1.16. "Nonrecourse Liability" has the meaning provided in the Code.

1.17. "Percentage Interest" means the percentage ownership of the Company of each Member as set forth in the column entitled "Member's Percentage Interest" contained in Table A as recalculated from time to time pursuant to this Agreement.

1.18. "Person" means an individual, partnership, limited partnership, corporation, limited liability company, registered limited liability partnership, trust, association, estate, or any other entity.

1.19. "Remaining Members" means, upon the occurrence of a Dissolution Event, those members of the Company whose conduct did not cause its occurrence.

LLC FORM 5: Long-Form Operating Agreement for Member-Managed LLC (continued)

ARTICLE II: FORMATION AND ORGANIZATION

2.1. Initial Date and Initial Parties. This Agreement is deemed entered into upon the date of the filing of the Company's Articles.

2.2. Subsequent Parties. No Person may become a Member of the Company without agreeing to and without becoming a signatory of this Agreement, and any offer or assignment of a Membership Interest is contingent upon the fulfillment of this condition.

2.3. Term. The Company shall commence upon the filing of its Articles and it shall continue in existence until December 31, 2050, unless terminated earlier under the provisions of this Agreement.

2.4. Principal Place of Business. The Company will have its principal place of business at [insert address of principal place of business], or at any other address upon which the Members agree. The Company shall maintain its principal executive offices at its principal place of business, as well as all required records and documents.

2.5. Authorization and Purpose. The purpose of the Company is to engage in any lawful business activity that is permitted by the Act.

ARTICLE III: CAPITAL CONTRIBUTIONS AND ACCOUNTS

3.1. Initial Capital Contributions. The initial capital contribution of each Member is listed in Table A attached hereto. Table A shall be revised to reflect any additional contributions pursuant to Section 3.2.

3.2. Additional Contributions. No Member shall be required to make any additional contributions to the Company. However, upon agreement by the Members that additional capital is desirable or necessary, any Member may, but shall not be required to, contribute additional capital to the Company on a pro rata basis consistent with the Percentage Interest of each of the Members.

3.3. Interest Payments. No Member shall be entitled to receive interest payments in connection with any contribution of capital to the Company, except as expressly provided herein.

3.4. Right to Return of Contributions. No Member shall be entitled to a return of any capital contributed to the Company, except as expressly provided in the Agreement.

3.5. Capital Accounts. A Capital Account shall be created and maintained by the Company for each Member, in conformance with the Code, which shall reflect all Capital Contributions to the Company. Should any Member transfer or assign all or any part of his or her Membership Interest in accordance with this Agreement, the successor shall receive that portion of the Member's Capital Account attributable to the interest assigned or transferred.

LLC FORM 5: Long-Form Operating Agreement for Member-Managed LLC (continued)

ARTICLE IV: MEMBERS

4.1. Limitation of Liability. No Member shall be personally liable for the debts, obligations, liabilities, or judgments of the Company solely by virtue of his or her Membership in the Company, except as expressly set forth in this Agreement or required by law.

4.2. Additional Members. The Members may admit additional Members to the Company only if approved by a two-thirds majority in interest of the Company Membership. Additional Members shall be permitted to participate in management at the discretion of the existing Members. Likewise, the existing Members shall agree upon an Additional Member's participation in Net Profits, Net Losses, and Distributions, as those terms are defined in this Agreement. Table A shall be amended to include the name, present mailing address, taxpayer identification number, and percentage ownership of any Additional Members.

4.3. Withdrawal or Expulsion from Membership. Any Member may withdraw at any time after sixty (60) days' written notice to the company, without prejudice to the rights of the Company or any Member under any contract to which the withdrawing Member is a party. Such withdrawing Member shall have the rights of a transferee under this Agreement and the remaining Members shall be entitled to purchase the withdrawing Member's Membership Interest in accordance with this Agreement. Any Member may be expelled from the Company upon a vote of two-thirds majority in interest of the Company Membership. Such expelled Member shall have the rights of a transferee under this Agreement and the remaining Members shall be entitled to purchase the expelled Member's Membership Interest in accordance with this Agreement.

4.4. Competing Activities. The Members and their officers, directors, shareholders, partners, managers, agents, employees, and Affiliates are permitted to participate in other business activities which may be in competition, direct or indirect, with those of the Company. The Members further acknowledge that they are under no obligation to present to the Company any business or investment opportunities, even if the opportunities are of such a character as to be appropriate for the Company's undertaking. Each Member hereby waives the right to any claim against any other Member or Affiliate on account of such competing activities.

4.5. Compensation of Members. No Member or Affiliate shall be entitled to compensation for services rendered to the Company, absent agreement by the Members. However, Members and Affiliates shall be entitled to reimbursement for the actual cost of goods and services provided to the Company, including, without limitation, reimbursement for any professional services required to form the Company.

4.6. Transaction with the Company. The Members may permit a Member to lend money to and transact business with the Company, subject to any limitations contained in this Agreement or in the Act. To the extent permitted by applicable laws, such a Member shall be treated like any other Person with respect to transactions with the Company.

4.7. Meetings.

(a) There will be no regular or annual meeting of the Members. However, any Member(s) with an aggregate Percentage Interest of ten percent (10%) or more may call a meeting of the Members at any time. Such meeting shall be held at a place to be agreed upon by the Members.

(b) Minutes of the meeting shall be made and maintained along with the books and records of the Company.

(c) If any action on the part of the Members is to be proposed at the meeting, then written notice of the meeting must be provided to each Member entitled to vote not less than ten (10) days or more than sixty (60) days prior to the meeting. Notice may be given in person, by fax, by first class mail, or by any other written communication, charges prepaid, at the Members' address listed in Table A. The notice shall contain the date, time, and place of the meeting and a statement of the general nature of this business to be transacted there.

4.8. Actions at Meetings.

(a) No action may be taken at a meeting that was not proposed in the notice of the meeting, unless there is unanimous consent among all Members entitled to vote.

(b) No action may be taken at a meeting unless a quorum of Members is present, either in person or by proxy. A quorum of Members shall consist of Members holding a majority of the Percentage Interest in the Company.

(c) A Member may participate in, and is deemed present at, any meeting by clearly audible conference telephone or other similar means of communication.

(d) Any meeting may be adjourned upon the vote of the majority of the Membership Interests represented at the meeting.

(e) Actions taken at any meeting of the Members have full force and effect if each Member who was not present, in person or by proxy, signs a written waiver of notice and consent to the holding of the meeting or approval of the minutes of the meeting. All such waivers and consents shall become Company records.

(f) Presence at a meeting constitutes a waiver of the right to object to notice of a meeting, unless the Member expresses such an objection at the start of the meeting.

4.9. Actions Without Meetings.
Any action that may be taken at a meeting of the Members may be taken without a meeting and without prior notice, if written consents to the action are submitted to the Company within sixty (60) days of the record date for the taking of the action, executed by Members

LLC FORM 5: Long-Form Operating Agreement for Member-Managed LLC (continued)

holding a sufficient number of votes to authorize the taking of the action at a meeting at which all Members entitled to vote thereon are present and vote. All such consents shall be maintained as Company records.

4.10. Record Date. For the purposes of voting, notices of meetings, distributions, or any other rights under this Agreement, the Articles, or the Act, the Members representing in excess of ten percent (10%) of the Percentage Interests in the Company may fix, in advance, a record date that is not more than sixty (60) or less than ten (10) days prior to the date of such meeting or sixty (60) days prior to any other action. If no record date is fixed, the record date shall be determined in accordance with the Act.

4.11. Voting Rights. Except as expressly set forth in this Agreement, all actions requiring the vote, approval, or consent of the Members may be authorized upon the vote, approval, or consent of those Members holding a majority of the Percentage Interests in the Company. The following actions require the unanimous vote, approval, or consent of all Members who are neither the subjects of a dissolution event nor the transferors of a Membership Interest:

(a) Approval of the purchase by the Company or its nominee of the Membership Interest of a transferor Member;

(b) Approval of the sale, transfer, exchange, assignment, or other disposition of a Member's interest in the Company and admission of the transferee as a Member;

(c) A decision to make any amendment to the Articles or to this Agreement; and

(d) A decision to compromise the obligation of any Member to make a Capital Contribution or return money or property distributed in violation of the Act.

ARTICLE V: MANAGEMENT

5.1. Management by Members. The Company shall be managed by the Members. Each Member has the authority to manage and control the Company and to act on its behalf, except as limited by the Act, the Articles, or this Agreement.

5.2. Limitation on Exposing Members to Personal Liability. Neither the Company nor any Member may take any action that will have the effect of exposing any Member of the Company to personal liability for the obligations of the Company, without first obtaining the consent of the affected Member.

5.3. Limitation on Powers of Members. The Members shall not be authorized to permit the Company to perform the following acts or to engage in the following transactions without first obtaining

LLC FORM 5: Long-Form Operating Agreement for Member-Managed LLC (continued)

the affirmative vote or written consent of the Members holding a majority Interest or such greater Percentage Interest as may be indicated below:

(a) The sale or other disposition of all or a substantial part of the Company's assets, whether occurring as a single transaction or a series of transactions over a 12-month period, except if the same is part of the orderly liquidation and winding up of the Company's affairs upon dissolution;

(b) The merger of the Company with any other business entity without the affirmative vote or written consent of all members;

(c) Any alteration of the primary purpose or business of the Company shall require the affirmative vote or written consent of Members holding at least sixty-six percent (66%) of the Percentage Interest in the Company;

(d) The establishment of different classes of Members;

(e) Transactions between the Company and one or more Members or one or more of any Member's Affiliates, or transactions in which one or more Members or Affiliates thereof have a material financial interest;

(f) Without limiting subsection (e) of this section, the lending of money to any Member or Affiliate of the Company;

(g) Any act which would prevent the Company from conducting its duly authorized business;

(h) The confession of a judgment against the Company.

Notwithstanding any other provisions of this Agreement, the written consent of all of the Members is required to permit the Company to incur an indebtedness or obligation greater than one hundred thousand dollars ($100,000). All checks, drafts, or other instruments requiring the Company to make payment of an amount less than fifty thousand dollars ($50,000) may be signed by any Member, acting alone. Any check, draft, or other instrument requiring the Company to make payment in the amount of fifty thousand dollars ($50,000) or more shall require the signature of two (2) Members acting together.

5.4. Fiduciary Duties. The fiduciary duties a Member owes to the Company and to the other Members of the Company are those of a partner to a partnership and to the partners of a partnership.

5.5. Liability for Acts and Omissions. As long as a Member acts in accordance with Section 5.4, no Member shall incur liability to any other Member or to the Company for any act or omission which occurs while in the performance of services for the Company.

ARTICLE VI: ALLOCATION OF PROFIT AND LOSS

6.1. Compliance with the Code. The Company intends to comply with the Code and all applicable Regulations, including without limitation the minimum gain chargeback requirements, and intends that the provisions of this Article be interpreted consistently with that intent.

6.2. Net Profits. Except as specifically provided elsewhere in this Agreement, Distributions of Net Profit shall be made to Members in proportion to their Percentage Interest in the Company.

6.3. Net Losses. Except as specifically provided elsewhere in this Agreement, Net Losses shall be allocated to the Members in proportion to their Percentage Interest in the Company. However, the foregoing will not apply to the extent that it would result in a Negative Capital Account balance for any Member equal to the Company Minimum Gain which would be realized by that Member in the event of a foreclosure of the Company's assets. Any Net Loss which is not allocated in accordance with the foregoing provision shall be allocated to other Members who are unaffected by that provision. When subsequent allocations of profit and loss are calculated, the losses reallocated pursuant to this provision shall be taken into account such that the net amount of the allocation shall be as close as possible to that which would have been allocated to each Member if the reallocation pursuant to this section had not taken place.

6.4. Regulatory Allocations. Notwithstanding the provisions of Section 6.3, the following applies:

(a) Should there be a net decrease in Company Minimum Gain in any taxable year, the Members shall specially allocate to each Member items of income and gain for that year (and, if necessary, for subsequent years) as required by the Code governing minimum gain chargeback requirements.

(b) Should there be a net decrease in Company Minimum Gain based on a Member Nonrecourse Debt in any taxable year, the Members shall first determine the extent of each Member's share of the Company Minimum Gain attributable to Member Nonrecourse Debt in accordance with the Code. The Members shall then specially allocate items of income and gain for that year (and, if necessary, for subsequent years) in accordance with the Code to each Member who has a share of the Company Nonrecourse Debt Minimum Gain.

(c) The Members shall allocate Nonrecourse Deductions for any taxable year to each Member in proportion to his or her Percentage Interest.

(d) The Members shall allocate Member Nonrecourse Deductions for any taxable year to the Member who bears the risk of loss with respect to the Nonrecourse Debt to which the Member Nonrecourse Deduction is attributable, as provided in the Code.

(e) If a Member unexpectedly receives any allocation of loss or deduction, or item thereof, or distributions which result in the Member's having a Negative Capital Account balance at the end of the taxable year greater than the Member's share of Company Minimum Gain, the Company shall specially allocate items of income and gain to that Member in a manner designed to eliminate the excess Negative Capital Account balance as rapidly as possible. Any allocations made in accordance with this provision shall taken into consideration in determining subsequent allocations under Article VI, so that, to the extent possible, the total amount allocated in this and subsequent allocations equals that which would have been allocated had there been no unexpected adjustments, allocations, and distributions and no allocation pursuant to Section 6.4(e).

(f) In accordance with Code Section 704(c) and the Regulations promulgated pursuant thereto, and notwithstanding any other provision in this Article, income, gain, loss, and deductions with respect to any property contributed to the Company shall, solely for tax purposes, be allocated among Members, taking into account any variation between the adjusted basis of the property to the Company for federal income tax purposes and its fair market value on the date of contribution. Allocations pursuant to this subsection are made solely for federal, state, and local taxes and shall not be taken into consideration in determining a Member's Capital Account or share of Net Profits or Net Losses or any other items subject to Distribution under this agreement.

6.5. Distributions. The Members may elect, by unanimous vote, to make a Distribution of assets at any time that would not be prohibited under the Act or under this Agreement. Such a Distribution shall be made in proportion to the unreturned capital contributions of each Member until all contributions have been paid, and thereafter in proportion to each Member's Percentage Interest in the Company. All such Distributions shall be made to those Persons who, according to the books and records of the Company, were the holders of record of Membership Interests on the date of the Distribution. Subject to Section 6.6, neither the Company nor any Members shall be liable for the making of any Distributions in accordance with the provisions of this section.

6.6. Limitations on Distributions.

(a) The Members shall not make any Distribution if, after giving effect to the Distribution, (1) the Company would not be able to pay its debts as they become due in the usual course of business, or (2) the Company's total assets would be less than the sum of its total liabilities plus, unless this Agreement provides otherwise, the amount that would be needed, if the Company were to be dissolved at the time of Distribution, to satisfy the preferential rights of other Members upon dissolution that are superior to the rights of the Member receiving the Distribution.

(b) The Members may base a determination that a Distribution is not prohibited under this section on any of the following: (1) financial statements prepared on the basis of accounting practices and principles that are reasonable under the circumstances, (2) a fair valuation, or (3) any other method that is reasonable under the circumstances.

LLC FORM 5: Long-Form Operating Agreement for Member-Managed LLC (continued)

6.7. Return of Distributions. Members shall return to the Company any Distributions received which are in violation of this Agreement or the Act. Such Distributions shall be returned to the account or accounts of the Company from which they were taken in order to make the Distribution. If a Distribution is made in compliance with the Act and this Agreement, a Member is under no obligation to return it to the Company or to pay the amount of the Distribution for the account of the Company or to any creditor of the Company.

6.8. Members Bound by These Provisions. The Members understand and acknowledge the tax implications of the provisions of this Article of the Agreement and agree to be bound by these provisions in reporting items of income and loss relating to the Company on their federal and state income tax returns.

ARTICLE VII: TRANSFERS AND TERMINATIONS OF MEMBERSHIP INTERESTS

7.1. Restriction on Transferability of Membership Interests. A Member may not transfer, assign, encumber, or convey all or any part of his or her Membership Interest in the Company, except as provided herein. In entering into this Agreement, each of the Members acknowledges the reasonableness of this restriction, which is intended to further the purposes of the Company and the relationships among the Members.

7.2. Permitted Transfers. In order to be permitted, a transfer or assignment of all or any part of a Membership Interest must have the approval of a two-thirds majority of the Members of the Company. Each Member, in his or her sole discretion, may proffer or withhold approval. In addition, the following conditions must be met:

(a) The transferee must provide a written agreement, satisfactory to the Members, to be bound by all of the provisions of this Agreement;

(b) The transferee must provide the Company with his or her taxpayer identification number and initial tax basis in the transferred interest;

(c) The transferee must pay the reasonable expenses incurred in connection with his or her admission to Membership;

(d) The transfer must be in compliance with all federal and state securities laws;

(e) The transfer must not result in the termination of the Company pursuant to Code Section 708.

(f) The transfer must not render the Company subject to the Investment Company Act of 1940, as amended; and

(g) The transferor must comply with the provisions of this Agreement.

LLC FORM 5: Long-Form Operating Agreement for Member-Managed LLC (continued)

7.3. Company's Right to Purchase Transferor's Interest and Valuation of Transferor's Interest. Any Member who wishes to transfer all or any part of his or her interest in the Company shall immediately provide the Company with written notice of his or her intention. The notice shall fully describe the nature of the interest to be transferred. Thereafter, the Company, or its nominee, shall have the option to purchase the transferor's interest at the Repurchase Price (as defined below).

(a) The "Repurchase Price" shall be determined as of the date of the event causing the transfer or dissolution event (the "Effective Date"). The date that the Company receives notice of a Member's intention to transfer his or her interest pursuant to this paragraph shall be deemed to be the Effective Date. The Repurchase Price shall be determined as follows:

    i. The Repurchase Price of a Member's Percentage Interest shall be computed by the independent certified public accountant (CPA) regularly used by the Company or, if the Company has no CPA or if the CPA is unavailable, then by a qualified appraiser selected by the Company for this purpose. The Repurchase Price of a Member's Percentage Interest shall be the sum of the Company's total Repurchase Price multiplied by the Transferor's Percentage Interest as of the Effective Date.

    ii. The Repurchase Price shall be determined by the book value method, as more further described herein. The book value of the interests shall be determined in accordance with the regular financial statements prepared by the Company and in accordance with generally accepted accounting principles, applied consistently with the accounting principles previously applied by the Company, adjusted to reflect the following:

        (1) All inventory, valued at cost.

        (2) All real property, leasehold improvements, equipment, and furnishings and fixtures valued at their fair market value.

        (3) The face amount of any accounts payable.

        (4) Any accrued taxes or assessments, deducted as liabilities.

        (5) All usual fiscal year-end accruals and deferrals (including depreciation), prorated over the fiscal year.

        (6) The reasonable fair market value of any good will or other intangible assets.

The cost of the assessment shall be borne by the Company.

(b) The option provided to the Company shall be irrevocable and shall remain open for thirty (30) days from the Effective Date, except that if notice is given by regular mail, the option shall remain open for thirty-five (35) days from the Effective Date.

(c) At any time while the option remains open, the Company (or its nominee) may elect to exercise the option and purchase the transferor's interest in the Company. The transferor Member shall not vote on the question of whether the Company should exercise its option.

(d) If the Company chooses to exercise its option to purchase the transferor Member's interest, it shall provide written notice to the transferor within the option period. The notice shall specify a "Closing Date" for the purchase, which shall occur within thirty (30) days of the expiration of the option period.

(e) If the Company declines to exercise its option to purchase the transferor Member's interest, the transferor Member may then transfer his or her interest in accordance with Section 7.2. Any transfer not in compliance with the provisions of Section 7.2 shall be null and void and have no force or effect.

(f) In the event that the Company chooses to exercise its option to purchase the transferor Member's interest, the Company may elect to purchase the Member's interest on the following terms:

  i. The Company may elect to pay the Repurchase Price in cash, by making such cash payment to the transferor Member upon the Closing Date.

  ii. The Company may elect to pay any portion of the Repurchase Price by delivering to the transferor Member, upon the Closing Date, all of the following:

  (1) An amount equal to at least 10% of the Repurchase Price in cash or in an immediately negotiable draft, and

  (2) A Promissory Note for the remaining amount of the Repurchase Price, to be paid in 12 successive monthly installments, with such installments beginning 30 days following the Closing Date, and ending one year from the Closing Date, and

  (3) A security agreement guaranteeing the payment of the Promissory Note by offering the Transferor's former membership interest as security for the payment of the Promissory Note.

7.4. Occurrence of Dissolution Event. Upon the death, withdrawal, resignation, retirement, expulsion, insanity, bankruptcy, or dissolution of any Member (a Dissolution Event), the Company shall be dissolved, unless all of the Remaining Members elect by a majority in interest within 90 days thereafter to continue the operation of the business. In the event that the Remaining Members to agree, the Company and the Remaining Members shall have the right to purchase the interest of the Member whose actions caused the occurrence of the Dissolution Event. The interest shall be sold in the manner described in Section 7.6.

LLC FORM 5: Long-Form Operating Agreement for Member-Managed LLC (continued)

7.5. Withdrawal from Membership. Notwithstanding Section 7.4, in the event that a Member withdraws in accordance with Section 4.3 and such withdrawal does not result in the dissolution of the Company, the Company and the Remaining Members shall have the right to purchase the interest of the withdrawing Member in the manner described in Section 7.6.

7.6. Purchase of Interest of Departing Member. The purchase price of a Departing Member's interest shall be determined in accordance with the procedure provided in Section 7.3.

(a) Once a value has been determined, each Remaining Member shall be entitled to purchase that portion of the Departing Member's interest that corresponds to his or her percentage ownership of the Percentage Interests of those Members electing to purchase a portion of the Departing Member's interest in the Company.

(b) Each Remaining Member desiring to purchase a share of the Departing Member's interest shall have thirty (30) days to provide written notice to the Company of his or her intention to do so. The failure to provide notice shall be deemed a rejection of the opportunity to purchase the Departing Member's Interest.

(c) If any Member elects not to purchase all of the Departing Member's interest to which he or she is entitled, the other Members may purchase that portion of the Departing Member's interest. Any interest which is not purchased by the Remaining Members may be purchased by the Company.

(d) The Members shall assign a closing date within 60 days after the Members' election to purchase is completed. At that time, the Departing Member shall deliver to the Remaining Members an instrument of title, free of any encumbrances and containing warranties of title, duly conveying his or her interest in the Company and, in return, he or she shall be paid the purchase price for his or her interest in cash. The Departing Member and the Remaining Members shall perform all acts reasonably necessary to consummate the transaction in accordance with this agreement.

7.7. No Release of Liability. Any Member or Departing Member whose interest in the Company is sold pursuant to Article VII is not relieved thereby of any liability he or she may owe the Company.

ARTICLE VIII: BOOKS, RECORDS, AND REPORTING

8.1. Books and Records. The Members shall maintain at the Company's principal place of business the following books and records: a current list of the full name and last known business or residence address of each Member, together with the Capital Contribution, Capital Account, and Membership Interest of each Member; a copy of the Articles and all amendments thereto, copies of the Company's federal, state, and local income tax or information returns and reports, if any, for the six (6) most recent taxable years, a copy of this Agreement and any amendments to it; copies of the Company's financial statements, if any; the books and records of the Company as they relate to its internal affairs for at least the current and past four (4) fiscal years; and true and correct copies of all relevant documents and records indicating the amount, cost, and value of all the property and assets of the Company.

8.2. Accounting Methods. The books and records of the Company shall be maintained in accordance with the accounting methods utilized for federal income tax purposes.

8.3. Reports. The Members shall cause to be prepared and filed in a timely manner all reports and documents required by any governmental agency. The Members shall cause to be prepared at least annually all information concerning the Company's operations that is required by the Members for the preparation of their federal and state tax returns.

8.4. Inspection Rights. For purposes reasonably related to their interests in the Company, all Members shall have the right to inspect and copy the books and records of the Company during normal business hours, upon reasonable request.

8.5. Bank Accounts. The Members shall maintain all of the funds of the Company in a bank account or accounts in the name of the Company, at a depository institution or institutions to be determined by a majority of the Members. The Members shall not permit the funds of the Company to be commingled in any manner with the funds or accounts of any other Person. The Members shall have the powers enumerated in Section 5.3 with respect to endorsing, signing, and negotiating checks, drafts, or other evidence of indebtedness to the Company or obligating the Company money to a third party.

ARTICLE IX: DISSOLUTION, LIQUIDATION, AND WINDING UP

9.1. Conditions Under Which Dissolution Shall Occur. The Company shall dissolve and its affairs shall be wound up upon the happening of the first of the following: at the time specified in the Articles; upon the happening of a Dissolution Event and the failure of the Remaining Members to elect to continue, in accordance with Section 7.4; upon the vote of all of the Members to dissolve; upon the entry of a decree of judicial dissolution pursuant to the Act; upon the happening of any event specified in the Articles as causing or requiring dissolution; or upon the sale of all or substantially all of the Company's assets.

9.2. Winding Up and Dissolution. If the Company is dissolved, the Members shall wind up its affairs, including the selling of all of the Company's assets and the provision of written notification to all of the Company's creditors of the commencement of dissolution proceedings.

9.3. Order of Payment. After determining that all known debts and liabilities of the Company in the process of winding up have been paid or provided for, including, without limitation, debts and liabilities to Members who are creditors of the Company, the Members shall distribute the remaining assets among the Members in accordance with their Positive Capital Account balances, after taking into consideration the profit and loss allocations made pursuant to Section 6.4. Members shall not be required to restore Negative Capital Account Balances.

ARTICLE X: INDEMNIFICATION

10.1. Indemnification. The Company shall indemnify any Member and may indemnify any Person to the fullest extent permitted by law on the date such indemnification is requested for any judgments, settlements, penalties, fines, or expenses of any kind incurred as a result of the Person's performance in the capacity of Member, officer, employee, or agent of the Company, as long as the Member or Person did not behave in violation of the Act or this Agreement.

ARTICLE XI: MISCELLANEOUS PROVISIONS

11.1. Assurances. Each Member shall execute all documents and certificates and perform all acts deemed appropriate by the Members and the Company or required by this Agreement or the Act in connection with the formation and operation of the Company and the acquisition, holding, or operation of any property by the Company.

11.2. Complete Agreement. This Agreement and the Articles constitute the complete and exclusive statement of the agreement among the Members with respect to the matters discussed herein and therein and they supersede all prior written or oral statements among the Members, including any prior statement, warranty, or representation.

11.3. Section Headings. The section headings which appear throughout this Agreement are provided for convenience only and are not intended to define or limit the scope of this Agreement or the intent of subject matter of its provisions.

11.4. Binding Effect. Subject to the provisions of this Agreement relating to the transferability of Membership Interests, this Agreement is binding upon and shall inure to the benefit of the parties hereto and their respective heirs, administrators, executors, successors, and assigns.

11.5. Interpretation. All pronouns and common nouns shall be deemed to refer to the masculine, feminine, neuter, singular, and plural, as the context may require. In the event that any claim is made by any Member relating to the drafting and interpretation of this Agreement, no presumption, inference, or burden of proof or persuasion shall be created or implied solely by virtue of the fact that this Agreement was drafted by or at the behest of a particular Member or his or her counsel.

LLC FORM 5: **Long-Form Operating Agreement for Member-Managed LLC** (continued)

11.6. Applicable Law. Each Member agrees that all disputes arising under or in connection with this Agreement and any transactions contemplated by this Agreement shall be governed by the internal law, and not the law of conflicts, of the state of organization.

11.7. Specific Performance. The Members acknowledge and agree that irreparable injury shall result from a breach of this Agreement and that money damages will not adequately compensate the injured party. Accordingly, in the event of a breach or a threatened breach of this Agreement, any party who may be injured shall be entitled, in addition to any other remedy which may be available, to injunctive relief to prevent or to correct the breach.

11.8. Remedies Cumulative. The remedies described in this Agreement are cumulative and shall not eliminate any other remedy to which a Person may be lawfully entitled.

11.9. Notice. Any notice or other writing to be served upon the Company or any Member thereof in connection with this Agreement shall be in writing and shall be deemed completed when delivered to the address specified in Table A, if to a Member, and to the resident agent, if to the Company. Any Member shall have the right to change the address at which notices shall be served upon ten (10) days' written notice to the Company and the other Members.

11.10. Amendments. Any amendments, modifications, or alterations to this Agreement or the Articles must be in writing and signed by all of the Members.

11.11. Severability. Each provision of this Agreement is severable from the other provisions. If, for any reason, any provision of this Agreement is declared invalid or contrary to existing law, the inoperability of that provision shall have no effect on the remaining provisions of the Agreement which shall continue in full force and effect.

11.12. Counterparts. This Agreement may be executed in counterparts, each of which shall be deemed an original and all of which shall, when taken together, constitute a single document.

IN WITNESS WHEREOF, this Agreement has been made and executed by the Members effective as of the date first written above.

_____ (member)

_____ (member)

_____ (member)

LLC FORM 5: **Long-Form Operating Agreement for Member-Managed LLC** (continued)

TABLE A: **NAME, ADDRESS, AND INITIAL CAPITAL CONTRIBUTION OF THE MEMBERS**

Name and Address of Member	Taxpayer Identification Number	Number Value of Initial Capital Contribution	Nature of Member's Initial Capital Contribution (i.e., cash, services, property)	Member's Percentage Interest

TABLE B: **MANAGER(S)**

Name of Manager	Address of Manager

LLC FORM 6: **Short Short-Form Operating Agreement for Manager-Managed LLC**

OPERATING AGREEMENT OF [Insert full name of LLC]

THIS OPERATING AGREEMENT (the "Agreement") is hereby entered into by the undersigned, who are owners and shall be referred to as Member or Members.

RECITALS

The Members desire to form [insert full name of LLC], a limited liability company (the "Company"), for the purposes set forth herein, and, accordingly, desire to enter into this Agreement in order to set forth the terms and conditions of the business and affairs of the Company and to determine the rights and obligations of its Members.

NOW, THEREFORE, the Members, intending to be legally bound by this Agreement, hereby agree that the limited liability company operating agreement of the Company shall be as follows:

ARTICLE I: DEFINITIONS

When used in this Agreement, the following terms shall have the meanings set forth below.

1.1 "Act" means the Limited Liability Company Law of the State in which the Company is organized or chartered, including any amendments or the corresponding provision(s) of any succeeding law.

1.2 "Capital Contribution(s)" means the amount of cash and the agreed value of property, services rendered, or a promissory note or other obligation to contribute cash or property or to perform services contributed by the Members for such Members' Interest in the Company, equal to the sum of the Members' initial Capital Contributions plus the Members' additional Capital Contributions, if any, made pursuant to Sections 4.1 and 4.2, respectively, less payments or distributions made pursuant to Section 5.1.

1.3 "Code" means the Internal Revenue Code of 1986 and the regulations promulgated thereunder, as amended from time to time (or any corresponding provision or provisions of succeeding law).

1.4 "Interest" or "Interests" means the ownership Interest, expressed as a number, percentage, or fraction, set forth in Table A, of a Member in the Company.

1.5 "Manager" or "Managers" means the natural person or person who have authority to govern the Company according to the terms of this Agreement.

1.6 "Person" means any natural individual, partnership, firm, corporation, limited liability company, joint-stock company, trust or other entity.

LLC FORM 6: **Short Short-Form Operating Agreement for Manager-Managed LLC**

1.7 "Secretary of State" means the Office of the Secretary of State or the office charged with accepting articles of organization in the Company's state of organization.

ARTICLE II: FORMATION

2.1 Organization. The Members hereby organize the Company as a limited liability company pursuant to the provisions of the Act.

2.2 Effective Date. The Company shall come into being on, and this Agreement shall take effect from, the date the Articles of Organization of the Company are filed with the Secretary of State in the state of organization or charter.

2.3 Agreement: Invalid Provisions and Saving Clause. The Members, by executing this Agreement, hereby agree to the terms and conditions of this Agreement. To the extent any provision of this Agreement is prohibited or ineffective under the Act, this Agreement shall be deemed to be amended to the least extent necessary in order to make this Agreement effective under the Act. In the event the Act is subsequently amended or interpreted in such a way to validate any provision of this Agreement that was formerly invalid, such provision shall be considered to be valid from the effective date of such amendment or interpretation.

ARTICLE III: PURPOSE; NATURE OF BUSINESS

3.1 Purpose; Nature of Business. The purpose of the Company shall be to engage in any lawful business that may be engaged in by a limited liability company organized under the Act, as such business activities may be determined by the Manager or Managers from time to time.

3.2 Powers. The Company shall have all powers of a limited liability company under the Act and the power to do all things necessary or convenient to accomplish its purpose and operate its business as described in Section 3.1 here.

ARTICLE IV: MEMBERS AND CAPITAL CONTRIBUTIONS

4.1 Members and Initial Capital Contribution. The name, address, Interest, type of property, and value of the initial Capital Contribution of the Members shall be set forth on Table A attached hereto.

4.2 Additional Capital Contributions. The Members shall have no obligation to make any additional Capital Contributions to the Company. The Members may make additional Capital Contributions to the Company as the Members unanimously determine are necessary, appropriate or desirable.

LLC FORM 6: **Short Short-Form Operating Agreement for Manager-Managed LLC** (continued)

ARTICLE V: DISTRIBUTIONS AND ALLOCATIONS

5.1 Distributions and Allocations. All distributions of cash or other assets of the Company shall be made and paid to the Members at such time and in such amounts as a majority of the Managers may determine. All items of income, gain, loss, deduction and credit shall be allocated to the Members in proportion to their Interests.

ARTICLE VI: TAXATION

6.1 Income Tax Reporting. Each Member is aware of the income tax consequences of the allocations made by Article V here and agrees to be bound by the provisions of Article V here in reporting each Members' share of Company income and loss for federal and state income tax purposes.

6.2 Tax Treatment. Notwithstanding anything contained herein to the contrary and only for purposes of federal and, if applicable, state income tax purposes, the Company shall be classified as a partnership for such federal and state income tax purposes unless and until the Members determine to cause the Company to file an election under the Code to be classified as an association taxable as a corporation.

ARTICLE VII: MANAGERS AND AGENTS

7.1 Management by Manager(s). The Members shall elect and appoint the Manager(s) who shall have the full and exclusive right, power and authority to manage the affairs of the Company and to bind the Company, to make all decisions with respect thereto and to do or cause to be done any and all acts or things deemed by the Members to be necessary, appropriate or desirable to carry out or further the business of the Company. All decisions and actions of the Manager(s) shall be made by majority vote of the Manager(s) as provided in Section 12.3. No annual meeting shall be required to reappoint Manager(s). Such Person(s) shall serve in such office(s) at the pleasure of the Members and until his, her or their successors and are duly elected and appointed by the Members. Until further action of the Members as provided herein, the Manager(s) whose names appear on Table B, below are the Manager(s) of the Company.

7.2 Agents. Without limiting the rights of the Members or the Manager(s), or the Company, the Manager(s) shall appoint the Person(s) who is (are) to act as the agent(s) of the Company to carry out and further the decisions and actions of the Members or the Manager(s), to manage and the administer the day-to-day operations and business of the Company and to execute any and all reports, forms, instruments, documents, papers, writings, agreements and contracts, including but not limited to deeds, bills of sale, assignments, leases, promissory notes, mortgages and security agreements and any other type or form of document by which property or property rights of the Company are transferred or encumbered, or by which debts and obligations of the Company are created, incurred or evidenced, which are necessary, appropriate or beneficial to carry out or further such decisions or actions and to manage and administer the day-to-day operations and business.

ARTICLE VIII: BOOKS AND RECORDS

8.1 Books and Records. The Managers shall keep, or cause to be kept, at the principal place of business of the Company true and correct books of account, in which shall be entered fully and accurately each and every transaction of the Company. The Company's taxable and fiscal years shall end on December 31. All Members shall have the right to inspect the Company's books and records at any time, for any reason.

ARTICLE IX: LIMITATION OF LIABILITY; INDEMNIFICATION

9.1 Limited Liability. Except as otherwise required by law, the debts, obligations and liabilities of the Company, whether arising in contract, tort or otherwise, shall be solely the debts, obligations and liabilities of the Company, and the Members shall not be obligated personally for any such debt, obligation or liability of the Company solely by reason of being Members. The failure of the Company to observe any formalities or requirements relating to the exercise of its powers or the management of its business or affairs under this Agreement or by law shall not be grounds for imposing personal liability on the Members for any debts, liabilities or obligations of the Company. Except as otherwise expressly required by law, the Members, in such Members' capacity as such, shall have no liability in excess of (a) the amount of such Members' Capital Contributions, (b) such Members' share of any assets and undistributed profits of the Company, and (c) the amount of any distributions required to be returned according to law.

9.2 Indemnification. The Company shall, to the fullest extent provided or allowed by law, indemnify, save harmless and pay all judgments and claims against the Members or Manager(s), and each of the Company's, Members' or Manager(s)' agents, affiliates, heirs, legal representatives, successors and assigns (each, an "Indemnified Party") from, against and in respect of any and all liability, loss, damage and expense incurred or sustained by the Indemnified Party in connection with the business of the Company or by reason of any act performed or omitted to be performed in connection with the activities of the Company or in dealing with third parties on behalf of the Company, including costs and attorneys' fees before and at trial and at all appellate levels, whether or not suit is instituted (which attorneys' fees may be paid as incurred), and any amounts expended in the settlement of any claims of liability, loss or damage, to the fullest extent allowed by law.

9.3. Insurance. The Company shall not pay for any insurance covering liability of the Members or the Manager(s) or the Company's, Members' or Manager(s)' agents, affiliates, heirs, legal representatives, successors and assigns for actions or omissions for which indemnification is not permitted hereunder; provided, however, that nothing contained here shall preclude the Company from purchasing and paying for such types of insurance, including extended coverage liability and casualty and worker's compensation, as would be customary for any Person owning, managing and/or operating comparable property and engaged in a similar business or from naming the Members or the Manager(s) and any of

LLC FORM 6: Short Short-Form Operating Agreement for Manager-Managed LLC (continued)

the Company's, Members' or Manager(s)' agents, affiliates, heirs, legal representatives, successors or assigns or any Indemnified Party as additional insured parties thereunder.

9.4 Non-Exclusive Right. The provisions of this Article IX shall be in addition to and not in limitation of any other rights of indemnification and reimbursement or limitations of liability to which an Indemnified Party may be entitled under the Act, common law, or otherwise.

ARTICLE X: AMENDMENT

10.1 Amendment. This Agreement may not be altered or modified except by the unanimous written consent or agreement of the Members as evidenced by an amendment hereto whereby this Agreement is amended or amended and restated.

ARTICLE XI: WITHDRAWAL

11.1 Withdrawal of a Member. No Member may withdraw from the Company except by written request of the Member given to each of the other Members and with the unanimous written consent of the other Members (the effective date of withdrawal being the date on which the unanimous written consent of all of the other Members is given), or upon the effective date of any of the following events:

(a)   the Member makes an assignment of his or her property for the benefit of creditors;

(b)   the Member files a voluntary petition of bankruptcy;

(c)   the Member is adjudged bankrupt or insolvent or there is entered against the Member an order for relief in any bankruptcy or insolvency proceeding;

(d)   the Member seeks, consents to, or acquiesces in the appointment of a trustee or receiver for, or liquidation of the Member or of all or any substantial part of the Member's property;

(e)   the Member files an answer or other pleading admitting or failing to contest the material allegations of a petition filed against the Member in any proceeding described in Subsections 11.1 (a) through (d);

(f)   if the Member is a corporation, the dissolution of the corporation or the revocation of its articles of incorporation or charter;

(g)   if the Member is an estate, the distribution by the fiduciary of the estate's Interest in the Company;

(h)   if the Member is an employee of the Company and he or she resigns, retires or for any reason ceases to be employed by the Company in any capacity; or

(i)   if the other Members owning more than fifty percent (50%) of the Interests vote or request in writing that a Member withdraw and such request is given to the Member (the effective date of

LLC FORM 6: Short Short-Form Operating Agreement for Manager-Managed LLC (continued)

withdrawal being the date on which the vote or written request of the other Members is given to the Member).

11.2 Valuation of Interest. The value of the withdrawing Member's Interest in all events shall be equal to the greater of the following: (a) the amount of the Member's Capital Contribution or (b) the amount of the Member's share of the Members' equity in the Company, plus the amount of any unpaid and outstanding loans or advances made by the Member to the Company (plus any due and unpaid interest thereon, if interest on the loan or advance has been agreed to between the Company and the Member), calculated as of the end of the fiscal quarter immediately preceding the effective date of the Member's withdrawal.

11.3 Payment of Value. The value shall be payable as follows:

(i)   If the value is equal to or less than $500, at closing, and

(ii) If the value is greater than $500, at the option of the Company, $500 at closing with the balance of the purchase price paid by delivering a promissory note of the Company dated as of the closing date and bearing interest at the prime rate published in the Wall Street Journal as of the effective date of withdrawal with the principal amount being payable in five (5) equal annual installments beginning one (1) year from closing and with the interest on the accrued and unpaid balance being payable at the time of payment of each principal installment.

11.4 Closing. Payment of the value of the departing Member's Interest shall be made at a mutually agreeable time and date on or before thirty (30) days from the effective date of withdrawal. Upon payment of the value of the Interest as calculated in Section 11.3 above:

(a) the Member's right to receive any and all further payments or distributions on account of the Member's ownership of the Interest in the Company shall cease;

(b) the Member's loans or advances to the Company shall be paid and satisfied in full; and

(c) the Member shall no longer be a Member or creditor of the Company on account of the Capital Contribution or the loans or advances.

11.5 Limitation on Payment of Value. If payment of the value of the Interest would be prohibited by any statute or law prohibiting distributions that would

(a) render the Company insolvent; or

(b) be made at a time that the total Company liabilities (other than liabilities to Members on account of their Interests) exceed the value of the Company's total assets;

then the value of the withdrawing Member's Interest in all events shall be $1.00.

LLC FORM 6: **Short Short-Form Operating Agreement for Manager-Managed LLC** (continued)

ARTICLE XII: MISCELLANEOUS PROVISIONS

12.1 Assignment of Interest and New Members. No Member may assign such person's Interest in the Company in whole or in part except by the vote or written consent of the other Members owning more than fifty percent (50%) of the Interests. No additional Person may be admitted as a Member except by the vote or written consent of the Members owning more than fifty percent (50%) of the Interests.

12.2 Determinations by Members: Except as required by the express provisions of this Agreement or of the Act:

(a) Any transaction, action or decision which requires or permits the Members to consent to, approve, elect, appoint, adopt or authorize or to make a determination or decision with respect thereto under this Agreement, the Act, the Code or otherwise shall be made by the Members owning more than fifty percent (50%) of the Interests.

(b) The Members shall act at a meeting of Members or by consent in writing of the Members. Members may vote or give their consent in person or by proxy.

(c) Meetings of the Members may be held at any time, upon call of any Manager or a Member or Members owning, in the aggregate, at least ten percent (10 %) of the Interests.

(d) Unless waived in writing by the Members owning more than fifty percent (50%) of the Interests (before or after a meeting), at least two (2) business days prior notice of any meeting shall be given to each Member. Such notice shall state the purpose for which such meeting has been called. No business may be conducted or action taken at such meeting that is not provided for in such notice.

(e) Members may participate in a meeting of Members by means of conference telephone or similar communications equipment by means of which all Persons participating in the meeting can hear each other, and such participation shall constitute presence in person at such meeting.

(f) The Managers shall cause to be kept a book of minutes of all meetings of the Members in which there shall be recorded the time and place of such meeting, by whom such meeting was called, the notice thereof given, the names of those present, and the proceedings thereof. Copies of any consents in writing shall also be filed in such minute book.

12.3 Determinations by Managers. Except as required by the express provisions of this Agreement or of the Act and if there shall be more than one Manager:

(a) Any transaction, action or decision which requires or permits the Managers to consent to, approve, elect, appoint, adopt or authorize or to make a determination or decision with respect thereto under this Agreement, the Act, the Code or otherwise shall be made by a majority of the Managers.

LLC FORM 6: Short Short-Form Operating Agreement for Manager-Managed LLC (continued)

(b) The Managers shall act at a meeting of the Managers or by consent in writing of the Managers. Managers may vote or give their consent in person only and not by proxy.

(c) Meetings of the Managers may be held at any time, upon call of any agent of the Company appointed pursuant to Section 7.2 of this Agreement or any Manager.

(d) Notice of any meeting shall be given to a majority of the Managers at any time prior to the meeting, in writing or by verbal communication. Such notice need not state the purpose for which such meeting has been called.

(e) The Managers may participate in a meeting of the Managers by means of conference telephone or similar communications equipment by means of which all Persons participating in the meeting can hear each other, and such participation shall constitute presence in person at such meeting.

(f) The Managers may cause to be kept a book of minutes of all meetings of the Managers in which there shall be recorded the time and place of such meeting, by whom such meeting was called, the notice thereof given, the names of those present, and the proceedings thereof. Copies of any consents in writing shall also be filed in such minute book.

12.4 Binding Effect. This Agreement shall be binding upon and inure to the benefit of the undersigned, their legal representatives, heirs, successors and assigns. This Agreement and the rights and duties of the Members hereunder shall be governed by, and interpreted and construed in accordance with, the laws of the State of Florida, without regard to principles of choice of law.

12.5 Headings. The article and section headings in this Agreement are inserted as a matter of convenience and are for reference only and shall not be construed to define, limit, extend or describe the scope of this Agreement or the intent of any provision.

12.6 Number and Gender. Whenever required by the context here, the singular shall include the plural, and vice versa and the masculine gender shall include the feminine and neuter genders, and vice versa.

12.7 Entire Agreement and Binding Effect. This Agreement constitutes the sole operating agreement among the Members and supersedes and cancels any prior agreements, representations, warranties or communications, whether oral or written, between the Members relating to the affairs of the Company and the conduct of the Company's business. No amendment or modification of this Agreement shall be effective unless approved in writing as provided in Section 10.1. The Articles of Organization and this Agreement are binding upon and shall inure to the benefit the Members and Agent(s) and shall be binding upon their successors, assigns, affiliates, subsidiaries, heirs, beneficiaries, personal representatives, executors, administrators and guardians, as applicable and appropriate.

LLC FORM 6: **Short Short-Form Operating Agreement for Manager-Managed LLC** (continued)

IN WITNESS WHEREOF, this Agreement has been made and executed by the Members effective as of the date first written above.

_____ (member)

_____ (member)

_____ (member)

TABLE A: **NAME, ADDRESS AND INITIAL CAPITAL CONTRIBUTION OF THE MEMBERS**

Name and Address of Member	Value of Initial Capital Contribution	Nature of Member's Initial Capital Contribution (i.e., cash, services, property)	Percentage Interest of Member

TABLE B: **MANAGER(S)**

Name of Manager	Address of Manager

LLC FORM 7: Long-Form Operating Agreement For Manager-Managed LLC

OPERATING AGREEMENT OF [Insert Name of LLC], LLC

THIS OPERATING AGREEMENT (the "Agreement") is made and entered into on _____, 20__, and those persons whose names, addresses and signatures are set forth below, being the Members of [Insert name of LLC], LLC (the "Company"), represent and agree that they have caused or will cause to be filed, on behalf of the Company, Articles of Organization, and that they desire to enter into an operating agreement.

The Members agree as follows:

ARTICLE I: DEFINITIONS

1.1. "Act" means the Limited Liability Company Law of the State in which the Company is organized or chartered, including any amendments or the corresponding provision(s) of any succeeding law.

1.2. "Affiliate" or "Affiliate of a Member" means any Person under the control of, in common control with, or in control of a Member, whether that control is direct or indirect. The term "control," as used herein, means, with respect to a corporation or limited liability company, the ability to exercise more than fifty percent (50%) of the voting rights of the controlled entity, and with respect to an individual, partnership, trust, or other entity or association, the ability, directly or indirectly, to direct the management of policies of the controlled entity or individual.

1.3. "Agreement" means this Operating Agreement, in its original form and as amended from time to time.

1.4. "Articles" means the Articles of Organization or other charter document filed with the Secretary of State in the state of organization forming this limited liability company, as initially filed and as they may be amended from time to time.

1.5. "Capital Account" means the amount of the capital interest of a Member in the Company, consisting of the amount of money and the fair market value, net of liabilities, of any property initially contributed by the Member, as (1) increased by any additional contributions and the Member's share of the Company's profits; and (2) decreased by any distribution to that Member as well as that Member's share of Company losses.

1.6. "Code" means the Internal Revenue Code of 1986, as amended from time to time, the regulations promulgated thereunder, and any corresponding provision of any succeeding revenue law.

1.7. "Company Minimum Gain" shall have the same meaning as set forth for the term "Partnership Minimum Gain" in the Regulations section 1.704-2(d) (26 CFR Section1.704-2(d)).

LLC FORM 7: **Long-Form Operating Agreement For Manager-Managed LLC** (continued)

1.8. "Departing Member" means any Member whose conduct results in a Dissolution Event or who withdraws from or is expelled from the Company in accordance with Section 4.3, where such withdrawal does not result in dissolution of the Company.

1.9. "Dissolution Event" means, with respect to any Member, one or more of the following: the death, resignation, retirement, expulsion, bankruptcy, or dissolution of any Member.

1.10. "Distribution" means the transfer of money or property by the Company to the Members without consideration.

1.11 "Manager" means each Person who has been appointed to serve as a Manager of the Company in accordance with the Act, the Articles, and this Agreement.

1.12. "Member" means each Person who has been admitted into membership in the Company; executes this Agreement and any subsequent amendments, and has not engaged in conduct resulting in a Dissolution Event or terminated membership for any other reason.

1.13. "Member Nonrecourse Debt" shall have the same meaning as set forth for the term "Partnership Nonrecourse Debt" in the Code.

1.14. "Member Nonrecourse Deductions" means items of Company loss, deduction, or Code Section 705(a)(2)(B) expenditures which are attributable to Member Nonrecourse Debt.

1.15. "Membership Interest" means a Member's rights in the Company, collectively, including the Member's economic interest, right to vote and participate in management, and right to information concerning the business and affairs of the Company provided in this Agreement or under the Act.

1.16. "Net Profits" and "Net Losses" mean the Company's income, loss, and deductions computed at the close of each fiscal year in accordance with the accounting methods used to prepare the Company's information tax return filed for federal income tax purposes.

1.17. "Nonrecourse Liability" has the meaning provided in the Code.

1.18. "Percentage Interest" means the percentage ownership of the Company of each Member as set forth in the column entitled "Member's Percentage Interest" contained in Table A as recalculated from time to time pursuant to this Agreement.

1.19. "Person" means an individual, partnership, limited partnership, corporation, limited liability company, registered limited liability partnership, trust, association, estate, or any other entity.

1.20. "Remaining Members" means, upon the occurrence of a Dissolution Event, those members of the Company whose conduct did not cause its occurrence.

LLC FORM 7: Long-Form Operating Agreement For Manager-Managed LLC (continued)

ARTICLE II: FORMATION AND ORGANIZATION

2.1. Initial Date and Initial Parties. This Agreement is deemed entered into upon the date of the filing of the Company's Articles.

2.2. Subsequent Parties. No Person may become a Member of the Company without agreeing to and without becoming a signatory of this Agreement, and any offer or assignment of a Membership Interest is contingent upon the fulfillment of this condition.

2.3. Term. The Company shall commence upon the filing of its Articles and it shall continue in existence until December 31, 2050, unless terminated earlier under the provisions of the Act this Agreement.

2.4. Principal Place of Business. The Company will have its principal place of business at [insert address of principal place of business], or at any other address upon which the Members agree. The Company shall maintain its principal executive offices at its principal place of business, as well as all required records and documents.

2.5. Authorization and Purpose. The purpose of the Company is to engage in any lawful business activity that is permitted by the Act.

ARTICLE III: CAPITAL CONTRIBUTIONS AND ACCOUNTS

3.1. Initial Capital Contributions. The initial capital contribution of each Member is listed in Table A attached hereto. Table A shall be revised to reflect and additional contributions pursuant to Section 3.2.

3.2. Additional Contributions. No Member shall be required to make any additional contributions to the Company. However, upon agreement by the Members that additional capital is desirable or necessary, any Member may, but shall not be required to, contribute additional capital to the Company on a pro rata basis consistent with the Percentage Interest of each of the Members.

3.3. Interest Payments. No Member shall be entitled to receive interest payments in connection with any contribution of capital to the Company, except as expressly provided herein.

3.4. Right to Return of Contributions. No Member shall be entitled to a return of any capital contributed to the Company, except as expressly provided in the Agreement.

3.5. Capital Accounts. A Capital Account shall be created and maintained by the Company for each Member, in conformance with the Code, which shall reflect all Capital Contributions to the Company. Should any Member transfer or assign all or any part of his or her membership interest in accordance with this Agreement, the successor shall receive that portion of the Member's Capital Account attributable to the interest assigned or transferred.

LLC FORM 7: **Long-Form Operating Agreement For Manager-Managed LLC** (continued)

ARTICLE IV: MEMBERS

4.1. Limitation of Liability. No Member shall be personally liable for the debts, obligations, liabilities, or judgments of the Company solely by virtue of his or her Membership in the Company, except as expressly set forth in this Agreement or required by law.

4.2. Additional Members. The Members may admit additional Members to the Company only if approved by a two-thirds majority in interest of the Company Membership. Additional Members shall be permitted to participate in management at the discretion of the existing Members. Likewise, the existing Members shall agree upon an Additional Member's participation in "Net Profits," "Net Losses," and distributions, as those terms are defined in this Agreement. Table A shall be amended to include the name, present mailing address, taxpayer identification number, and percentage ownership of any Additional Members.

4.3. Withdrawal or Expulsion From Membership. Any Member may withdraw at any time after sixty (60) days written notice to the company, without prejudice to the rights of the Company or any Member under any contract to which the withdrawing Member is a party. Such withdrawing Member shall have the rights of a transferee under this Agreement and the remaining Members shall be entitled to purchase the withdrawing Member's Membership Interest in accordance with this Agreement. Any Member may be expelled from the Company upon a vote of two-thirds majority in interest of the Company Membership. Such expelled Member shall have the rights of a transferee under this Agreement and the remaining Members shall be entitled to purchase the withdrawing Member's Membership Interest in accordance with this Agreement.

4.4. Competing Activities. The Members and their officers, directors, shareholders, partners, managers, agents, employees and Affiliates are permitted to participate in other business activities which may be in competition, direct or indirect, with those of the Company. The Members further acknowledge that they are under no obligation to present to the Company any business or investment opportunities, even if the opportunities are of such a character as to be appropriate for the Company's undertaking. Each Member hereby waives the right to any claim against any other Member or Affiliate on account of such competing activities.

4.5. Compensation of Members. No Member or Affiliate shall be entitled to compensation for services rendered to the Company, absent agreement by the Members. However, Members and Affiliates shall be entitled to reimbursement for the actual cost of goods and services provided to the Company, including, without limitation, reimbursement for any professional services required to form the Company.

4.6. Transaction with the Company. The Members may permit a Member to lend money to and transact business with the Company, subject to any limitations contained in this Agreement or in the

LLC FORM 7: **Long-Form Operating Agreement For Manager-Managed LLC** (continued)

Act. To the extent permitted by applicable laws, such a Member shall be treated like any other Person with respect to transactions with the Company.

4.7. Meetings.

(a) There will be no regular or annual meeting of the Members. However, any Member(s) with an aggregate Percentage Interest of ten percent (10%) or more may call a meeting of the Members at any time. Such meeting shall be held at a place to be agreed upon by the Members.

(b) Minutes of the meeting shall be made and maintained along with the books and records of the Company.

(c) If any action on the part of the Members is to be proposed at the meeting, then written notice of the meeting must be provided to each Member entitled to vote not less than ten (10) days or more than sixty (60) days prior to the meeting. Notice may be given in person, by fax, first class mail, or any other written communication, charges prepaid, at the Members' address listed in Table A. The notice shall contain the date, time, and place of the meeting and a statement of the general nature of this business to be transacted there.

4.8. Actions at Meetings.

(a) No action may be taken at a meeting that was not proposed in the notice of the meeting, unless there is unanimous consent among all Members entitled to vote.

(b) No action may be taken at a meeting unless a quorum of Members is present, either in person or by proxy. A quorum of Members shall consist of Members holding a majority of the Percentage Interest in the Company.

(c) A Member may participate in, and is deemed present at, any meeting by clearly audible conference telephone or other similar means of communication,

(d) Any meeting may be adjourned upon the vote of the majority of the Membership Interests represented at the meeting.

(e) Actions taken at any meeting of the Members have full force and effect if each Member who was not present in person or by proxy, signs a written waiver of notice and consent to the holding of the meeting, or approval of the minutes of the meeting. All such waivers and consents shall become Company records.

(f) Presence at a meeting constitutes a waiver of the right to object to notice of a meeting, unless the Member expresses such an objection at the start of the meeting.

LLC FORM 7: Long-Form Operating Agreement For Manager-Managed LLC (continued)

4.9. Actions Without Meetings. Any action that may be taken at a meeting of the Members may be taken without a meeting and without prior notice, if written consents to the action are submitted to the Company within sixty (60) days of the record date for the taking of the action, executed by Members holding a sufficient number of votes to authorize the taking of the action at a meeting at which all Members entitled to vote thereon are present and vote. All such consents shall be maintained as Company records.

4.10. Record Date. For the purposes of voting, notices of meetings, distributions, or any other rights under this Agreement, the Articles, or the Act, the Members representing in excess of then percent (10%) of the Percentage Interests in the Company may fix, in advance, a record date that is not more than sixty (60) or less than ten (10) days prior to the date of such meeting or sixty (60) days prior to any other action. If no record date is fixed, the record date shall be determined in accordance with the Act.

4.11. Voting Rights. Except as expressly set forth in this Agreement, all action requiring the vote, approval, or consent of the Members may be authorized upon the vote, approval, or consent of those Members holding a majority of the Percentage Interests in the Company. The following actions require the unanimous vote, approval, or consent of all Members who are neither the subjects of a dissolution event nor the transferors of a Membership Interest:

(a) Approval of the purchase by the Company or its nominee of the Membership Interest of a transferor Member;

(b) Approval of the sale, transfer, exchange, assignment, or other disposition of a Member's interest in the Company, and admission of the transferee as a Member;

(c) A decision to make any amendment to the Articles or to this Agreement; and

(d) A decision to compromise the obligation to any Member to make a Capital Contribution or return money or property distributed in violation of the Act.

ARTICLE V: MANAGEMENT

5.1. Management by Appointed Managers. The Company shall be managed by one or more appointed Managers. The number of Managers, and the identity of each Manager is set forth in Table B, below. The Members shall elect and appoint the Managers (and also determine the number of managers) who shall have the full and exclusive right, power and authority to manage the affairs of the Company and to bind the Company, to make all decisions with respect thereto and to do or cause to be done any and all acts or things deemed by the Members to be necessary, appropriate or desirable to carry out or further the business of the Company. All decisions and actions of the Managers shall be made by majority vote of the Managers as provided in this Agreement. There shall be no annual meetings of the

LLC FORM 7: **Long-Form Operating Agreement For Manager-Managed LLC** (continued)

Members or Managers; Managers shall serve at the pleasure of the Members and until his or her successors and are duly elected and appointed by the Members.

5.2. Limitation on Powers of Managers; Member Vote Required for Some Actions. The Managers shall not be authorized to permit the Company to perform the following acts or to engage in the following transactions without first obtaining the affirmative vote or written consent of the Members holding a majority Interest or such greater Percentage Interest as may be indicated below:

(a)   The sale or other disposition of all or a substantial part of the Company's assets, whether occurring as a single transaction or a series of transactions over a 12-month period, except if the same is part of the orderly liquidation and winding up of the Company's affairs upon dissolution.

(b)   The merger of the Company with any other business entity without the affirmative vote or written consent of all members;

(c)   Any alteration of the primary purpose or business of the Company shall require the affirmative vote or written consent of Members holding at least sixty-six percent (66%) of the Percentage Interest in the Company.

(d)   The establishment of different classes of Members:

(e)   Transactions between the Company and one or more Members or one or more of any Member's Affiliates, or transactions in which one or more Members or Affiliates thereof have a material financial interest;

(f)   Without limiting subsection (e) of this section, the lending of money to any Member or Affiliate of the Company.

(g)   Any act which would prevent the Company from conducting its duly authorized business;

(h)   The confession of a judgment against the Company;

Notwithstanding any other provisions of this Agreement, the written consent of all of the Members is required to permit the Company to incur an indebtedness or obligation greater than One Hundred Thousand Dollars ($100,000.00). All checks, drafts, or other instruments requiring the Company to make payment of an amount less than Fifty Thousand dollars ($50,000.00) may be signed by any Member, acting alone. Any check, draft, or other instrument requiring the Company to make payment in the amount of Fifty Thousand dollars ($50,000.00) or more shall require the signature of two (2) Members acting together.

5.3. Fiduciary Duties. The fiduciary duties a Member owes to the Company and to the other Members of the Company are those of a partner to a partnership and to the partners of a partnership.

5.4. Liability for Acts and Omissions. As long as a Member acts in accordance with Section 5.3, no Member shall incur liability to any other Member or to the Company for any act or omission which occurs while in the performance of services for the Company.

ARTICLE VI: ALLOCATION OF PROFIT AND LOSS

6.1. Compliance with the Code. The Company intends to comply with the Code and all applicable Regulations, including without limitation the minimum gain chargeback requirements, and intends that the provisions of this Article be interpreted consistently with that intent.

6.2. Net Profits. Except as specifically provided elsewhere in this Agreement, Distributions of Net Profit shall be made to Members in proportion to their Percentage interest in the Company.

6.3. Net Losses. Except as specifically provided elsewhere in this Agreement, Net Losses shall be allocated to the Members in proportion to their Percentage Interest in the Company. However, the foregoing will not apply to the extent that it would result in a Negative Capital Account balance for any Member equal to the Company Minimum Gain which would be realized by that Member in the event of a foreclosure of the Company's assets. Any Net Loss which is not allocated in accordance with the foregoing provision shall be allocated to other Members who are unaffected by that provision. When subsequent allocations of profit and loss are calculated, the losses reallocated pursuant to this provision shall be taken into account such that the net amount of the allocation shall be as close as possible to that which would have been allocated to each Member if the reallocation pursuant to this section had not taken place.

6.4. Regulatory Allocations. Notwithstanding the provisions of Section 6.3, the following applies:

(a) Should there be a net decrease in Company Minimum Gain in any taxable year, the Members shall specially allocate to each Member items of income and gain for that year (and, if necessary, for subsequent years) as required by the Code governing "minimum gain chargeback" requirements.

(b) Should there be a net decrease in Company Minimum Gain based on a Member Nonrecourse Debt in any taxable year, the Members shall first determine the extent of each Member's share of the Company Minimum Gain attributable to Member Nonrecourse Debt in accordance with the Code. The Members shall then specially allocate items of income and gain for that year (and, if necessary, for subsequent years) in accordance with the Code to each Member who has a share of the Company Nonrecourse Debt Minimum Gain.

(c) The Members shall allocate Nonrecourse deductions for any taxable year to each Member in proportion to his or her Percentage Interest.

LLC FORM 7: Long-Form Operating Agreement For Manager-Managed LLC (continued)

(d) The Members shall allocate Member Nonrecourse Deductions for any taxable year to the Member who bears the risk of loss with respect to the Nonrecourse debt to which the Member Nonrecourse Deduction is attributable, as provided in the Code.

(e) If a Member unexpectedly receives any allocation of loss or deduction, or item thereof, or distributions which result in the Member's having a Negative Capital Account balance at the end of the taxable year greater than the Member's share of Company Minimum Gain, the Company shall specially allocate items of income and gain to that Member in a manner designed to eliminate the excess Negative Capital Account balance as rapidly as possible. Any allocations made in accordance with this provision shall taken into consideration in determining subsequent allocations under Article VI, so that, to the extent possible, the total amount allocated in this and subsequent allocations equals that which would have been allocated had there been no unexpected adjustments, allocations and distributions and no allocation pursuant to Section 6.4(e).

(f) In accordance with Code Section 704(c) and the Regulations promulgated pursuant thereto, and notwithstanding any other provision in this Article, income, gain, loss, and deductions with respect to any property contributed to the Company shall, solely for tax purposes, be allocated among Members taking into account any variation between the adjusted basis of the property to the Company for federal income tax purposes and its fair market value on the date of contribution. Allocations pursuant to this subsection are made solely for federal, state, and local taxes and shall not be taken into consideration in determining a Member's Capital Account or share of Net Profits or Net Losses or any other items subject to Distribution under this agreement.

6.5. Distributions. The Members may elect, by unanimous vote, to make a Distribution of assets at any time that would not be prohibited under the Act or under this Agreement. Such a Distribution shall be made in proportion to the unreturned capital contributions of each Member until all contributions have been paid, and thereafter in proportion to each Member's Percentage Interest in the Company. All such Distributions shall be made to those Persons who, according to the books and records of the Company, were the holders of record of Membership Interests on the date of the Distribution. Subject to Section 6.6, neither the Company nor any Members shall be liable for the making of any Distributions in accordance with the provisions of this section.

6.6. Limitations on Distributions.

(a) The Members shall not make any Distribution if, after giving effect to the distribution: (1) The Company would not be able to pay its debts as they become due in the usual course of business; or (2) The Company's total assets would be less than the sum of its total liabilities plus, unless this Agreement provides otherwise, the amount that would be needed, of the Company were to

LLC FORM 7: Long-Form Operating Agreement For Manager-Managed LLC (continued)

be dissolved at the time of Distribution, to satisfy the preferential rights of other Members upon dissolution that are superior to the rights of the Member receiving the Distribution.

(b) The Members may base a determination that a Distribution is not prohibited under this section on any of the following: (1) Financial statements prepared on the basis of accounting practices and principles that are reasonable under the circumstances; (2) A fair valuation; or (3) Any other method that is reasonable under the circumstances.

6.7. Return of Distributions. Members shall return to the Company any Distributions received which are in violation of this Agreement or the Act. Such Distributions shall be returned to the account or accounts of the Company from which they were taken in order to make the Distribution. If a Distribution is made in compliance with the Act and this Agreement, a Member is under no obligation to return it to the Company or to pay the amount of the Distribution for the account of the Company or to any creditor of the Company.

6.8. Members Bound by These Provisions. The Members understand and acknowledge the tax implications of the provisions of this Article of the Agreement and agree to be bound by these provisions in reporting items of income and loss relating to the Company on their federal and state income tax returns.

ARTICLE VII: TRANSFERS AND TERMINATIONS OF MEMBERSHIP INTERESTS

7.1. Restriction on Transferability of Membership Interests. A Member may not transfer, assign, encumber, or convey all or any part of his or her Membership Interest in the Company, except as provided herein. In entering into this Agreement, each of the Members acknowledges the reasonableness of this restriction, which is intended to further the purposes of the Company and the relationships among the Members.

7.2. Permitted Transfers. In order to be permitted, a transfer or assignment of all or any part of a Membership interest must have the approval of a two-thirds majority of the Members of the Company. Each Member, in his or her sole discretion, may proffer or withhold approval. In addition, the following conditions must be met:

(a) The transferee must provide a written agreement, satisfactory to the Members, to be bound by all of the provisions of this Agreement;

(b) The transferee must provide the Company with his or her taxpayer identification number and initial tax basis in the transferred interest;

(c) The transferee must pay the reasonable expenses incurred in connection with his or her admission to Membership;

LLC FORM 7: Long-Form Operating Agreement For Manager-Managed LLC (continued)

(d) The transfer must be in compliance with all federal and state securities laws;

(e) The transfer must not result in the termination of the Company pursuant to Code Section 708.

(f) The transfer must not render the Company subject to the Investment Company Act of 1940, as amended; and

(g) The transferor must comply with the provisions of this Agreement.

7.3. Company's Right to Purchase Transferor's Interest and Valuation of Transferor's Interest. Any Member who wishes to transfer all or any part of his or her interest in the Company shall immediately provide the Company with written notice of his or her intention. The notice shall fully describe the nature of the interest to be transferred. Thereafter, the Company, or its nominee, shall have the option to purchase the transferor's interest at the Repurchase Price (as defined below).

(a) The "Repurchase Price" shall be determined as of the date of the event causing the transfer or dissolution event (the "Effective Date"). The date that the Company receives notice of a Member's intention to transfer its interest pursuant to this paragraph shall be deemed to be the Effective Date. The Repurchase Price shall be determined as follows:

  i. The Repurchase Price of a Member's Percentage Interest shall be computed by the independent certified public accountant (CPA) regularly used by the Company or, if the Company has no CPA or if the CPA is unavailable, then by a qualified appraiser selected by the Company for this purpose. The Repurchase Price of a Member's Percentage Interest shall be the sum of the Company's total Repurchase Price multiplied by the Transferor's Percentage Interest as of the Effective Date.

  ii. The Repurchase Price shall be determined by the book value method, as more further described herein. The book value of the interests shall be determined in accordance with the regular financial statements prepared by the Company and in accordance with generally accepted accounting principles, applied consistently with the accounting principles previously applied by the Company, adjusted to reflect the following:

   (1) All inventory, valued at cost.

   (2) All real property, leasehold improvements, equipment, and furnishings and fixtures valued at their fair market value.

   (3) The face amount of any accounts payable.

   (4) Any accrued taxes or assessments, deducted as liabilities.

LLC FORM 7: Long-Form Operating Agreement For Manager-Managed LLC (continued)

    (5)   All usual fiscal year-end accruals and deferrals (including depreciation), prorated over the fiscal year.

    (6)   The reasonable fair market value of any good will or other intangible assets.

    The cost of the assessment shall be borne by the Company.

(b)   The option provided to the Company shall be irrevocable and shall remain open for (30) days from the Effective Date, except that if notice is given by regular mail, the option shall remain open for thirty-five (35) days from the Effective Date.

(c)   At any time while the option remains open, the Company (or its nominee) may elect to exercise the option and purchase the transferor's interest in the Company. The transferor Member shall not vote on the question of whether the Company should exercise its option.

(d)   If the Company chooses to exercise its option to purchase the transferor Member's interest, it shall provide written notice to the transferor within the option period. The notice shall specify a "Closing Date" for the purchase, which shall occur within thirty (30) days of the expiration of the option period.

(e)   If the Company declines to exercise its option to purchase the transferor Member's interest, the transferor Member may then transfer his or her interest in accordance with Section 7.2. Any transfer not in compliance with the provisions of Section 7.2 shall be null and void and have no force or effect.

(f)   In the event that the Company chooses to exercise its option to purchase the transferor Member's interest, the Company may elect to purchase the Member's interest on the following terms:

    i.   The Company may elect to pay the Repurchase Price in cash, by making such cash payment to the transferor Member upon the Closing Date.

    ii.   The Company may elect to pay any portion of the Repurchase Price by delivering to the transferor Member, upon the Closing Date, all of the following:

        (1).   An amount equal to at least 10% of the Repurchase Price in cash or in an immediately negotiable draft, and

        (2)   A Promissory Note for the remaining amount of the Repurchase Price, to be paid in 12 successive monthly installments, with such installments beginning 30 days following the Closing Date, and ending one year from the Closing Date, and

        (3)   A security agreement guaranteeing the payment of the Promissory Note by offering the Transferor's former membership interest as security for the payment of the Promissory Note.

LLC FORM 7: Long-Form Operating Agreement For Manager-Managed LLC (continued)

7.4. Occurrence of Dissolution Event. Upon the death, withdrawal, resignation, retirement, expulsion, insanity, bankruptcy, or dissolution of any Member (a Dissolution Event), the Company shall be dissolved, unless all of the Remaining Members elect by a majority in interest within 90 days thereafter to continue the operation of the business. In the event that the Remaining Members to agree, the Company and the Remaining Members shall have the right to purchase the interest of the Member whose actions caused the occurrence of the Dissolution Event. The interest shall be sold in the manner described in Section 7.6.

7.5. Withdrawal from Membership. Notwithstanding Section 7.4, in the event that a Member withdraws in accordance with Section 4.3, and such withdrawal does not result in the dissolution of the Company, the Company and the Remaining Members shall have the right to purchase the interest of the withdrawing Member in the manner described in Section 7.6.

7.6. Purchase of Interest of Departing Member. The purchase price of a Departing Member's interest shall be determined in accordance with the procedure provided in Section 7.3.

(a) Once a value has been determined, each Remaining Member shall be entitled to purchase that portion of the Departing Member's interest that corresponds to his or her percentage ownership of the Percentage Interests of those Members electing to purchase a portion of the Departing Member's interest in the Company.

(b) Each Remaining Member desiring to purchase a share of the Departing Member's interest shall have thirty (30) days to provide written notice to the Company of his or her intention to do so. The failure to provide notice shall be deemed a rejection of the opportunity to purchase the Departing Member's interest.

(c) If any Member elects not to purchase all of the Departing Member's interest to which he or she is entitled, the other Members may purchase that portion of the Departing Member's interest. Any interest which is not purchased by the Remaining Members may be purchased by the Company.

(d) The Members shall assign a closing date within 60 days after the Members' election to purchase is completed. At that time, the Departing Member shall deliver to the Remaining Members an instrument of title, free of any encumbrances and containing warranties of title, duly conveying his or her interest in the Company and, in return, he or she shall be paid the purchase price for his or her interest in cash. The Departing Member and the Remaining Members shall perform all acts reasonably necessary to consummate the transaction in accordance with this agreement.

7.7. No Release of Liability. Any Member or Departing Member whose interest in the Company is sold pursuant to Article VII is not relieved thereby of any liability he or she may owe the Company.

LLC FORM 7: **Long-Form Operating Agreement For Manager-Managed LLC** (continued)

ARTICLE VIII: BOOKS, RECORDS AND REPORTING

8.1. Books and Records. The Members shall maintain at the Company's principal place of business the following books and records: a current list of the full name and last known business or residence address of each Member is set forth, together with the Capital Contribution, Capital Account, and Membership Interest of each Member; a copy of the Articles and all amendments thereto, copies of the Company's federal, state, and local income tax or information returns and reports, if any, for the six (6) most recent taxable years, a copy of this Agreement and any amendments to it, copies of the Company's financial statements, if any, the books and records of the Company as they relate to its internal affairs for at least the current and past four (4) fiscal years, and true and correct copies of all relevant documents and records indicating the amount, cost and value of all the property and assets of the Company.

8.2. Accounting Methods. The books and records of the Company shall be maintained in accordance with the accounting methods utilized for federal income tax purposes.

8.3. Reports. The Members shall cause to be prepared and filed in a timely manner all reports and documents required by any governmental agency. The Members shall cause to be prepared at least annually all information concerning the Company's operations that is required by the Members for the preparation of their federal and state tax returns.

8.4. Inspection Rights. For purposes reasonably related to their interests in the Company, all Members shall have the right to inspect and copy the books and records of the Company during normal business hours, upon reasonable request.

8.5. Bank Accounts. The Managers shall maintain all of the funds of the Company in a bank account or accounts in the name of the Company, at a depository institution or institutions to be determined by a majority of the Members. The Managers shall not permit the funds of the Company to be commingled in any manner with the funds or accounts of any other Person. The Managers shall have the powers enumerated in Section 5.2 with respect to endorsing, signing, and negotiating checks, drafts, or other evidence of indebtedness to the Company or obligating the Company money to a third party.

ARTICLE IX: DISSOLUTION, LIQUIDATION, AND WINDING UP

9.1. Conditions Under Which Dissolution Shall Occur. The Company shall dissolve and its affairs shall be wound up upon the happening the first of the following: at the time specified in the Articles, upon the happening of a Dissolution Event, and the failure of the Remaining Members to elect to continue, in accordance with Section 7.4, upon the vote of all of the Members to dissolve, upon the entry of a decree of judicial dissolution pursuant to the Act, upon the happening of any event specified in the Articles as causing or requiring dissolution, or upon the sale of all or substantially all of the Company's assets.

9.2. Winding Up and Dissolution. If the Company is dissolved, the Members shall wind up its affairs, including the selling of all of the Company's assets and the provision of written notification to all of the Company's creditors of the commencement of dissolution proceedings.

9.3. Order of Payment. After determining that all known debts and liabilities of the Company in the process of winding up have been paid or provided for, including, without limitation, debts and liabilities to Members who are creditors of the Company, the Members shall distribute the remaining assets among the Members in accordance with their Positive Capital Account balances, after taking into consideration the profit and loss allocations made pursuant to Section 6.4. Members shall not be required to restore Negative Capital Account Balances.

ARTICLE X: INDEMNIFICATION

10.1. Indemnification. The Company shall indemnify any Member and may indemnify any Person to the fullest extent permitted by law on the date such indemnification is requested for any judgments, settlements, penalties, fines, or expenses of any kind incurred as a result of the Person's performance in the capacity of Member, officer, employee, or agent of the Company, as long as the Member, or Person did not behave in violation of the Act or this Agreement.

ARTICLE XI: MISCELLANEOUS PROVISIONS

11.1. Assurances. Each Member shall execute all documents and certificates and perform all acts deemed appropriate by the Members and the Company or required by this Agreement or the Act in connection with the formation and operation of the Company and the acquisition, holding, or operation of any property by the Company.

11.2. Complete Agreement. This Agreement and the Articles constitute the complete and exclusive statement of the agreement among the Members with respect to the matters discussed herein and therein and they supersede all prior written or oral statements among the Members, including and prior statement, warranty, or representation.

11.3. Section Headings. The section headings which appear throughout this Agreement are provided for convenience only and are not intended to define or limit the scope of this Agreement or the intent of subject matter of its provisions.

11.4. Binding Effect. Subject to the provisions of this Agreement relating to the transferability of Membership Interests, this Agreement is binding upon and shall inure to the benefit of the parties hereto and their respective heirs, administrators, executors, successors, and assigns.

LLC FORM 7: **Long-Form Operating Agreement For Manager-Managed LLC** (continued)

11.5. Interpretation. All pronouns and common nouns shall be deemed to refer to the masculine, feminine, neuter, singular, and plural, as the context may require. In the event that any claim is made by any Member relating to the drafting and interpretation of this Agreement, no presumption, inference, or burden of proof or persuasion shall be created or implied solely by virtue of the fact that this Agreement was drafted by or at the behest of a particular Member or his or her counsel.

11.6. Applicable Law. Each Member agrees that all disputes arising under or in connection with this Agreement and any transactions contemplated by this Agreement shall be governed by the internal law, and not the law of conflicts, of the state of organization.

11.7. Specific Performance. The Members acknowledge and agree that irreparable injury shall result from a breach of this Agreement and that money damages will not adequately compensate the injured party. Accordingly, in the event of a breach or a threatened breach of this Agreement, any party who may be injured shall be entitled, in addition to any other remedy which may be available, to injunctive relief to prevent or to correct the breach.

11.8. Remedies Cumulative. The remedies described in this Agreement are cumulative and shall not eliminate any other remedy to which a Person may be lawfully entitled.

11.9. Notice. Any notice or other writing to be served upon the Company or any Member thereof in connection with this Agreement shall be in writing and shall be deemed completed when delivered to the address specified in Table A, if to a Member, and to the resident agent, if to the Company. Any Member shall have the right to change the address at which notices shall be served upon ten (10) days' written notice to the Company and the other Members.

11.10. Amendments. Any amendments, modifications, or alterations to this Agreement or the Articles must be in writing and signed by all of the Members.

11.11. Severability. Each provision of this Agreement is severable from the other provisions. If, for any reason, any provision of this Agreement is declared invalid or contrary to existing law, the inoperability of that provision shall have no effect on the remaining provisions of the Agreement which shall continue in full force and effect.

11.12. Counterparts. This Agreement may be executed in counterparts, each of which shall be deemed an original and all of which shall, when taken together, constitute a single document.

LLC FORM 7: **Long-Form Operating Agreement For Manager-Managed LLC** (continued)

IN WITNESS WHEREOF, this Agreement has been made and executed by the Members effective as of the date first written above.

_____ (member)

_____ (member)

_____ (member)

TABLE A: **NAME, ADDRESS AND INITIAL CAPITAL CONTRIBUTION OF THE MEMBERS**

Name and Address of Member	Value of Initial Capital Contribution	Nature of Member's Initial Capital Contribution (i.e., cash, services, property)	Percentage Interest of Member

TABLE B: **MANAGER(S)**

Name of Manager	Address of Manager

LLC FORM 8: **Membership Ledger**

Date of Original Issue	Member Name	Percentage Interest	Disposition of Shares (transferred or surrendered stock certificate)

LLC FORM 9: **Investment Representation Letter**

Note: The following Investment Representation Letter should be executed by each LLC member and delivered to the company. The Representation Letter seeks to ensure company compliance with securities laws, by asking owners to certify that they are joining the LLC as an investment and not to trade shares in the LLC.

[insert date]

To whom it may concern,

I am delivering this letter to Olde Craft, LLC in connection with my purchase of a 25% interest in Olde Craft, LLC for a total sum of $75,000. I represent the following:

I am purchasing the shares in my own name and for my own account, for investment and not with an intent to sell or for sale in connection with any distribution of such stock; and no other person has any interest in or right with respect to the shares; nor have I agreed to give any person any such interest or right in the future.

I recognize that the shares have not been registered under the Federal Securities Act of 1933, as amended, or qualified under any state securities law, and that any sale or transfer of the shares is subject to restrictions imposed by federal and state law.

I also recognize that I cannot dispose of the shares absent registration and qualification or an available exemption from registration and qualification. I understand that no federal or state securities commission or other government body has approved of the fairness of the shares offered by the LLC and that the Commissioner has not and will not recommend or endorse the shares.

I have not seen or received any advertisement or general solicitation with respect to the sale of the shares.

I have a preexisting personal or business relationship with the Company or one or more of its officers, directors, or controlling persons, and I am aware of its character and general financial and business circumstances.

I acknowledge that during the course of this transaction and before purchasing the shares I have been provided with financial and other written information about the Company. I have been given the opportunity by the Company to obtain any information and ask questions concerning the Company, the shares, and my investment that I felt necessary; and to the extent I availed myself of that opportunity, I have received satisfactory information and answers.

In reaching the decision to invest in the shares, I have carefully evaluated my financial resources and investment position and the risks associated with this investment, and I acknowledge that I am able to bear the economic risks of this investment.

John Miller

LLC FORM 10: **Appointment of Proxy for Members' Meeting**

Note: Use the following form when a Member wants to give his or her vote to another person at a meeting of an LLC's membership.

APPOINTMENT OF PROXY FOR (ANNUAL/SPECIAL) MEETING
MADHATTER, LLC

SHAREHOLDER: John Miller

PERCENTAGE INTEREST HELD BY SHAREHOLDER: 32%

I, the undersigned, as record holder of a 32% interest in MadHatter, LLC, revoke any previous proxies and appoint the person whose name appears just below this paragraph as my proxy to attend the member's meeting on _____ and any adjournment of that meeting.

The person I want to appoint as my proxy is _____

The proxy holder is entitled to cast a total number of votes equal to but not exceeding the number of shares that I would be entitled to cast if I were personally present.

I authorize my proxy holder to vote and otherwise represent me with regard to any business that may come before this meeting in the same manner and with the same effect as if I were personally present.

I may revoke this proxy at any time. This proxy will lapse three months after the date of its execution.

Date [*important!*] _____

_____
Name

_____
Title

Note: All proxies must be signed. Sign exactly as your name appears on your stock certificate. If you are signing for a business entity, state your title. Joint shareholders must each sign this proxy. If signed by an attorney in fact, the power of attorney must be attached.

LLC FORM 11: **Call for Meeting of Members**

Note: This "call" is an instruction by LLC members to the managers that the members want to call a meeting of members. This serves as official notice. This call is required only in manager-managed LLCs; if a member in a member-managed LLC wants to call a meeting of members, he or she would skip the call and simply send a notice of meeting of members to all other members. The next form, LLC Form 12, is a notice of meeting of members.

CALL FOR MEETING OF LLC MEMBERS

TO: The Managers of MadHatter, LLC

[Insert date]

The party or parties whose name appears below are members of MadHatter, LLC, and own percentage interests entitled to cast not less than 10 percent of MadHatter's votes. We hereby call a meeting of the members of MadHatter to be held _____ (date), at _____ (time), for the purpose of considering and acting upon the following matters:

[Insert matters to be considered, such as "A proposal that John Jones be removed as a manager of MadHatter."]

You are directed to give notice of this meeting of the members, in the manner prescribed by MadHatter's operating agreement and by law, to all members entitled to receive notice of the meeting.

Date: _____

Name _____

Name _____

Name _____

LLC FORM 12: **Notice of Meeting of LLC Members**

Note: This form is an LLC's announcement to its members that a meeting of members has been called.

NOTICE OF MEETING OF MEMBERS OF OLDE CRAFT, LLC

Certain members of Olde Craft, LLC, have called a meeting of the members of Olde Craft pursuant to Olde Craft's operating agreement.

Therefore, this is your official notice as an Olde Craft member that a meeting of members of Olde Craft, LLC will be held on _____ (date), at _____ (time), at _____ (address), to consider and act on the following matters:

[Insert matters to be considered, such as "A proposal that John Jones be removed from the board of directors."]

If you do not expect to be present at the meeting and wish your shares to be voted, you may complete the attached form of proxy and mail it in the enclosed addressed envelope.

Date: _____

_____

John Wilson, Manager

LLC FORM 13: **Minutes of Meeting of LLC Members**

Note: While LLC members and managers enjoy far fewer corporate formalities than corporation owners, an LLC must still maintain records of its meetings. When an LLC's members meet to formally vote on any matter, the results of that vote should be committed to written minutes.

MINUTES OF MEETING OF MEMBERS OF OLDE CRAFT, LLC

The members of Olde Craft, LLC held a meeting on _____ (date), at _____ (time), at _____ (place). The meeting was called by John Miller and the company managers mailed notice to all members that the meeting would take place.

The following members were present at the meeting, in person or by proxy, representing membership interests as indicated:

John Jones, 50%

John Smith, 30%

John Miller, 20%

Also present were Laura Spader, attorney to the company, and Lisa Jones, wife of John Jones, and the company's president and sole manager.

The company's president called the meeting to order and announced that she would chair the meeting, that a quorum was present, and that the meeting was held pursuant to a written notice of meeting given to all members of the company. A copy of the notice was ordered inserted in the minute book immediately preceding the minutes of this meeting.

The minutes of the previous meeting of shareholders were then read and approved.

The chairperson then announced that the election of a manager was in order. Lisa Jones stated that she could no longer serve as manager of the company. John Smith was then elected to serve until the next meeting of members, and until the manager's successor was duly elected and qualified.

There being no further business to come before the meeting, on motion duly made, seconded, and adopted, the meeting was adjourned.

_____

John Smith, Manager

LLC FORM 14: **Action by Written Consent of LLC Members**

Note: In the real world, most company votes are taken by written consent rather than by notice and meeting and an in-person vote. Use the following form when you wish to take a company action in writing, rather than by a noticed meeting. Keep in mind, however, that your operating agreement and articles may require more than a simple majority to pass certain actions. Written consents are important company records and should be maintained in the record books.

ACTION BY WRITTEN CONSENT OF SHAREHOLDERS OF OLDE CRAFT, LLC

The undersigned members of Olde Craft, LLC owning of record the number of shares entitled to vote as set forth, hereby consent to the following company actions. The vote was unanimous. (For actions where a unanimous vote is not required: "A vote of 66% was required to take the actions listed below, and 80% of the membership interest in the company have given their consent."):

1. Pete Wilson is hereby removed as manager of the company.

2. The number of managers of the company is increased from one to two.

John Smith and John Miller, both also members, are hereby elected to serve as company managers until the next meeting of members.

Dated: _____   Percentage Owned: _____

_____
John Miller

Dated: _____   Percentage Owned: _____

_____
John Miller

LLC FORM 15: Written Consent of Members Approving a Certificate of Amendment of Articles of Organization Changing an LLC's Name

ACTION OF MEMBERS BY WRITTEN CONSENT TO APPROVE
AN AMENDMENT TO ARTICLES OF ORGANIZATION CHANGING LLC NAME

The undersigned, who comprise all the members of PLASTICWORLD, LLC, agree unanimously to the following:

RESOLVED, that the Certificate of Amendment of Articles of Organization presented to the undersigned members, specifically changing the name of the company to PLASTICUNIVERSE, LLC, is approved.

Dated: _____

_____

Scott Bess

_____

Brian Bess

LLC FORM 16: **Written Consent of Members Approving a Conversion from LLC to Corporation**

ACTION OF MEMBERS BY WRITTEN CONSENT
TO APPROVE A CONVERSION OF LLC TO CORPORATION

The undersigned, who comprise all the members of PLASTICWORLD, LLC, agree unanimously to the following:

RESOLVED, that the members, following consultation, have agreed that it is in the best interests of PLASTICWORLD, LLC to convert the legal status of the entity from an LLC to a Corporation, to be entitled PLASTICWORLD CORP.

To facilitate the tax reporting of the LLC, it is agreed that the conversion shall be filed so that it takes place on January 1, 2008.

The managers of PLASTICWORLD, LLC are authorized and directed to file an appropriate Articles of Conversion with the Secretary of State of _____ to accomplish the conversion.

Dated: _____

_____

Scott Bess

_____

Brian Bess

LLC FORM 17: Sample Certificate/Articles of Conversion from an LLC to a Corporation, State of Delaware

STATE OF DELAWARE
CERTIFICATE OF CONVERSION FROM A LIMITED LIABILITY COMPANY TO A CORPORATION
PURSUANT TO SECTION 265 OF THE DELAWARE GENERAL CORPORATION LAW

1. The jurisdiction where the Limited Liability Company first formed is Delaware.

2. The jurisdiction immediately prior to filing this Certificate is Delaware.

3. The date the Limited Liability Company first formed is 21/15/2002.

4. The name of the Limited Liability Company immediately prior to filing this Certificate is PlasticWorld, LLC.

5. The name of the Corporation as set forth in the new Certificate of Incorporation is PlasticWorld Corp.

IN WITNESS WHEREOF, the undersigned being duly authorized to sign on behalf of the converting Limited Liability Company have executed this Certificate on the 12th day of November, 2007

By: _____
　　　　　Scott Bess, President

LLC FORM 18: Notice to Remaining Members by a Member Desiring to Withdraw from an LLC

Scott Bess
123 Elm Street
San Francisco, CA 94107
415-555-1212

September 28, 2007

Dear Brian,

This is my formal notice that I will be withdrawing from my ownership and membership of PLASTICWORLD, LLC. Section 11 of the operating agreement states that:

"No Member may withdraw from the Company except by written request of the Member given to each of the other Members and with the unanimous written consent of the other Members, the effective date of withdrawal being the date on which the unanimous written consent of all of the other Members is given."

In accordance with that Section, I hereby give such notice. As required by our operating agreement, I hereby ask that you, as the remaining member, consent to my withdrawal.

Assuming you consent to my withdrawal, we must next discuss the valuation of my interest. I suggest that we speak informally first, and if we can't come to some resolution, we can then trigger the appraisal rights under the operating agreement. I'll await your response.

Yours,

Scott Bess

LLC FORM 19: **Notice to Withdrawing Member**

Brian Bess
801 Minnesota Street
San Francisco, CA 94107
415-555-1212

September 30, 2007

Dear Scott,

I received your letter, your notice of your desire to withdraw your ownership and membership of PLASTICWORLD, LLC.

As you requested, I consent to your withdrawal.

I also agree that we should discuss the valuation of your interest before we seek an expensive appraisal.

Yours,

Brian Bess

LLC FORM 20: **Written Consent of Members to Expel Member From LLC**

WRITTEN CONSENT OF MEMBERS TO EXPEL MEMBER FROM LLC

The undersigned members of 17 REASONS, LLC owning of record the number of shares entitled to vote as set forth, hereby consent to the following company actions.

The purpose of this consent is to expel member David Canaan from 17 REASONS, LLC. The standard by which a member can be expelled from 17 REASONS, LLC is set forth in the operating agreement of the LLC:

> A Member may be expelled from the Company upon a vote of two-thirds majority in interest of the Company Membership. Such expelled Member shall have the rights of a transferee under this Agreement and the remaining Members shall be entitled to purchase the expelled Member's Membership Interest in accordance with this Agreement.

Three of the four members have agreed that Mr. Canaan should be expelled from the LLC. As such, three-fourths of the LLC membership meets the requirements of expulsion set forth in the governing documents.

The governing documents do not set forth any cause or reason that the voting members need to have to expel a member. Nevertheless, the undersigned members wish to expel Mr. Canaan for the following reasons:

> *Mr. Canaan has not met his employment responsibilities with the LLC; he has preferred to devote his time to other businesses.

> *Mr. Canaan failed to make a required capital contribution.

This written consent is effective as of the date set forth below.

_____

John Farnsworth

_____

Lisa Knowles

_____

David Stapleton

LLC FORM 21: **Notice to Member of Expulsion From LLC**

17 REASONS, LLC
1010 Mission Street
San Francisco, CA 94107

September 30, 2007

David Canaan
48 Sanchez Street
Austin, TX 7875

Dear Mr. Canaan,

This is an important notice that concerns your ownership and membership of 17 Reasons, LLC. As you know, the operating agreement that governs 17 Reasons, LLC contains a provision allowing for a two-thirds majority of the owners of 17 Reasons to expel a member. The section reads:

A Member may be expelled from the Company upon a vote of two-thirds majority in interest of the Company Membership. Such expelled Member shall have the rights of a transferee under this Agreement and the remaining Members shall be entitled to purchase the expelled Member's Membership Interest in accordance with this Agreement.

On September 29, 2007, three of the four members of 17 Reasons voted, by written consent, to expel you from 17 Reasons.

Within the next 30 days, we will order an appraisal to value your interest in 17 Reasons so that you may be compensated for your terminated interest. We wish you the best in the future.

_____

John Farnsworth

_____

Lisa Knowles

_____

David Stapleton

LLC FORM 22: **Resolution Authorizing Manager to Transfer Property**

RESOLUTION BY WRITTEN CONSENT OF THE MEMBERS OF 17 REASONS, LLC

The undersigned, who constitute the entire membership of 17 Reasons, LLC, a Michigan LLC (the "LLC"), acting pursuant to the operating agreement of the LLC, and pursuant to the Laws of the state of Michigan, hereby adopt and approve the recitals and resolutions set forth below, which shall have the same force and effect as if adopted and approved at a duly held meeting.

RESOLVED, that the Manager for the LLC, Michael Heskett, a member in good standing of the bar of the State of Michigan, is hereby authorized to transfer, and is furthermore authorized to execute all instruments and documents to effect such transfer such as deeds, stock powers, etc., all of the following property:

- The LLC's interest in shares of stock of Initech Corporation.

- The LLC's interest in a parcel of real property known as 123 14th Street in Dearborn Michigan

Witness our Signatures to be effective the 5th day of February, 2008

_____

John Farnsworth

_____

Lisa Knowles

_____

David Stapleton

LLC FORM 23: Resolution Authorizing a One-Time Mandatory Capital Contribution From LLC Members

RESOLUTION OF THE MEMBERS OF 17 REASONS, LLC
REQUIRING A ONE-TIME MANDATORY CAPITAL CONTRIBUTION FROM LLC MEMBERSHIP

The undersigned, who constitute the entire membership of 17 Reasons, LLC, a Michigan LLC (the "LLC"), acting pursuant to the operating agreement of the LLC, and pursuant to the Laws of the state of Michigan, hereby adopt and approve the recitals and resolutions set forth below, which shall have the same force and effect as if adopted and approved at a duly held meeting.

WHEREAS, the operating agreement of the LLC states the following, concerning the members' obligations to make capital contributions:

4.2 Additional Capital Contributions. The Members shall have no obligation to make any additional Capital Contributions to the Company. The Members may make additional Capital Contributions to the Company as the Members unanimously determine are necessary, appropriate, or desirable.

RESOLVED, that after careful deliberation, the members have unanimously determined and resolved hereby that it is in the interest of the LLC and its members if the members made a one-time mandatory capital contribution to the LLC as follows:

• Each member shall pay a capital contribution based upon his or her percentage ownership in the LLC.

• As such, each 1% of LLC ownership shall obligate a member for a $100 capital contribution.

RESOLVED, therefore, that each member (each member owns equal shares of 33.33% each) shall contribute $3,333.00 as a capital contribution to the LLC.

RESOLVED, that the articles of organization are not amended or modified in any way by these resolutions.

_____

John Farnsworth

_____

Lisa Knowles

_____

David Stapleton

LLC FORM 24: **Notice of Year-End Distribution**

December 31, 2007

To:
John Farnsworth
993b Hayes Street
San Francisco, CA 92110

This notice concerns your (25%) membership interest in 17 Reasons, LLC. As you know, it is the policy of 17 Reasons, LLC to distribute year-end profits to members in proportion to their membership interests.

As such, your membership interest entitles you to a pro-rata share of the year-end distribution of profits. A check for your distribution is included.

_____

Lisa Knowles, LLC Manager

LLC FORM 25: **Resolution of Members Converting Member-Managed LLC Into Manager-Managed LLC**

RESOLUTION OF THE MEMBERS OF 17 REASONS, LLC CONVERTING MEMBER-MANAGED LLC INTO MANAGER-MANAGED LLC AND ADOPTING CHANGES TO LLC OPERATING AGREEMENT

The undersigned, who constitute the entire membership of 17 Reasons, LLC, a Michigan LLC (the "LLC"), acting pursuant to the operating agreement of the LLC, and pursuant to the Laws of the state of Michigan, hereby adopt and approve the recitals and resolutions set forth below, which shall have the same force and effect as if adopted and approved at a duly held meeting.

RESOLVED, that the LLC is hereby converted from a member-managed LLC into a Manager-Managed LLC.

RESOLVED, that the following paragraph is hereby stricken from the operating agreement of the LLC:

7.1 Management by Members. The Company shall be managed by its Members, who shall have full and exclusive right, power, and authority to manage the affairs of the Company and to bind the Company to contracts and obligations, to make all decisions with respect thereto, and to do or cause to be done any and all acts or things deemed by the Members to be necessary, appropriate, or desirable to carry out or further the business of the Company.

RESOLVED, that the following paragraph is hereby inserted into the operating agreement of the LLC:

7.1 Management by Manager(s). The Members shall elect and appoint the Manager(s) who shall have the full and exclusive right, power and authority to manage the affairs of the Company and to bind the Company, to make all decisions with respect thereto and to do or cause to be done any and all acts or things deemed by the Members to be necessary, appropriate or desirable to carry out or further the business of the Company. All decisions and actions of the Manager(s) shall be made by majority vote of the Manager(s) as provided in Section 12.3. No annual meeting shall be required to reappoint Manager(s). Such Person(s) shall serve in such office(s) at the pleasure of the Members and until his, her or their successors and are duly elected and appointed by the Members. Until further action of the Members as provided herein, the Manager(s) whose names appear on Table B, below are the Manager(s) of the Company.

_____

John Farnsworth

_____

Lisa Knowles

_____

David Stapleton

LLC FORM 26: **Internal Revenue Service Tax Form SS-4**

| Form **SS-4** (Rev. February 2006) Department of the Treasury Internal Revenue Service | **Application for Employer Identification Number** (For use by employers, corporations, partnerships, trusts, estates, churches, government agencies, Indian tribal entities, certain individuals, and others.) ▶ **See separate instructions for each line.** ▶ **Keep a copy for your records.** | OMB No. 1545-0003 EIN |

Type or print clearly.

1 Legal name of entity (or individual) for whom the EIN is being requested

2 Trade name of business (if different from name on line 1)

3 Executor, administrator, trustee, "care of" name

4a Mailing address (room, apt., suite no. and street, or P.O. box)

5a Street address (if different) (Do not enter a P.O. box.)

4b City, state, and ZIP code

5b City, state, and ZIP code

6 County and state where principal business is located

7a Name of principal officer, general partner, grantor, owner, or trustor

7b SSN, ITIN, or EIN

8a **Type of entity** (check only one box)
☐ Sole proprietor (SSN) _____
☐ Partnership
☐ Corporation (enter form number to be filed) ▶ _____
☐ Personal service corporation
☐ Church or church-controlled organization
☐ Other nonprofit organization (specify) ▶ _____
☐ Other (specify) ▶

☐ Estate (SSN of decedent) _____
☐ Plan administrator (SSN) _____
☐ Trust (SSN of grantor) _____
☐ National Guard   ☐ State/local government
☐ Farmers' cooperative   ☐ Federal government/military
☐ REMIC   ☐ Indian tribal governments/enterprises
Group Exemption Number (GEN) ▶ _____

8b If a corporation, name the state or foreign country (if applicable) where incorporated | State | Foreign country

9 **Reason for applying** (check only one box)
☐ Started new business (specify type) ▶_____
☐ Hired employees (Check the box and see line 12.)
☐ Compliance with IRS withholding regulations
☐ Other (specify) ▶

☐ Banking purpose (specify purpose) ▶ _____
☐ Changed type of organization (specify new type) ▶ _____
☐ Purchased going business
☐ Created a trust (specify type) ▶ _____
☐ Created a pension plan (specify type) ▶ _____

10 Date business started or acquired (month, day, year). See instructions.

11 Closing month of accounting year

12 First date wages or annuities were paid (month, day, year). **Note.** If applicant is a withholding agent, enter date income will first be paid to nonresident alien. (month, day, year) . . . . ▶

13 Highest number of employees expected in the next 12 months (enter -0- if none).
Do you expect to have $1,000 or less in employment tax liability for the calendar year? ☐ **Yes** ☐ **No.** (If you expect to pay $4,000 or less in wages, you can mark yes.) | Agricultural | Household | Other

14 Check **one** box that best describes the principal activity of your business. ☐ Health care & social assistance ☐ Wholesale agent/broker
☐ Construction ☐ Rental & leasing ☐ Transportation & warehousing ☐ Accommodation & food service ☐ Wholesale-other ☐ Retail
☐ Real estate ☐ Manufacturing ☐ Finance & insurance ☐ Other (specify)

15 Indicate principal line of merchandise sold, specific construction work done, products produced, or services provided.

16a Has the applicant ever applied for an employer identification number for this or any other business? . . . . . ☐ **Yes** ☐ **No**
Note. If "Yes," please complete lines 16b and 16c.

16b If you checked "Yes" on line 16a, give applicant's legal name and trade name shown on prior application if different from line 1 or 2 above.
Legal name ▶   Trade name ▶

16c Approximate date when, and city and state where, the application was filed. Enter previous employer identification number if known.
Approximate date when filed (mo., day, year) | City and state where filed | Previous EIN

Third Party Designee	Complete this section **only** if you want to authorize the named individual to receive the entity's EIN and answer questions about the completion of this form.
	Designee's name	Designee's telephone number (include area code) ( )
	Address and ZIP code	Designee's fax number (include area code) ( )

Under penalties of perjury, I declare that I have examined this application, and to the best of my knowledge and belief, it is true, correct, and complete. | Applicant's telephone number (include area code) ( )

Name and title (type or print clearly) ▶

Signature ▶   Date ▶ | Applicant's fax number (include area code) ( )

For Privacy Act and Paperwork Reduction Act Notice, see separate instructions.   Cat. No. 16055N   Form **SS-4** (Rev. 2-2006)

LLC FORM 27: **Internal Revenue Service Tax Form 2553**

Form **2553**	**Election by a Small Business Corporation**	
(Rev. March 2005)	(Under section 1362 of the Internal Revenue Code)	OMB No. 1545-0146
Department of the Treasury Internal Revenue Service	▶ See Parts II and III on back and the separate instructions. ▶ The corporation may either send or fax this form to the IRS. See page 2 of the instructions.	

Notes: 1. *Do not file Form 1120S*, U.S. Income Tax Return for an S Corporation, for any tax year before the year the election takes effect.

2. *This election to be an S corporation can be accepted only if all the tests are met under **Who May Elect** on page 1 of the instructions; all shareholders have signed the consent statement; an officer has signed this form; and the exact name and address of the corporation and other required form information are provided.*

Part I   Election Information

Please Type or Print	Name (see instructions)	**A** Employer identification number
	Number, street, and room or suite no. (If a P.O. box, see instructions.)	**B** Date incorporated
	City or town, state, and ZIP code	**C** State of incorporation

D Check the applicable box(es) if the corporation, after applying for the EIN shown in **A** above, changed its name ☐ or address ☐

E Election is to be effective for tax year beginning (month, day, year) . . . . ▶

F Name and title of officer or legal representative who the IRS may call for more information

G Telephone number of officer or legal representative
(   )

H If this election takes effect for the first tax year the corporation exists, enter month, day, and year of the **earliest** of the following: (1) date the corporation first had shareholders, (2) date the corporation first had assets, or (3) date the corporation began doing business . . . . ▶   /   /

I Selected tax year: Annual return will be filed for tax year ending (month and day) ▶

If the tax year ends on any date other than December 31, except for a 52-53-week tax year ending with reference to the month of December, complete Part II on the back. If the date you enter is the ending date of a 52-53-week tax year, write "52-53-week year" to the right of the date.

J Name and address of each shareholder or former shareholder required to consent to the election. (See the instructions for column K)	**K** Shareholders' Consent Statement. Under penalties of perjury, we declare that we consent to the election of the above-named corporation to be an S corporation under section 1362(a) and that we have examined this consent statement, including accompanying schedules and statements, and to the best of our knowledge and belief, it is true, correct, and complete. We understand our consent is binding and may not be withdrawn after the corporation has made a valid election. (Sign and date below.)		**L** Stock owned or percentage of ownership (see instructions)		**M** Social security number or employer identification number (see instructions)	**N** Share-holder's tax year ends (month and day)
	Signature	Date	Number of shares or percentage of ownership	Date(s) acquired		

Under penalties of perjury, I declare that I have examined this election, including accompanying schedules and statements, and to the best of my knowledge and belief, it is true, correct, and complete.

Signature of officer ▶   Title ▶   Date ▶

For Paperwork Reduction Act Notice, see page 4 of the instructions.   Cat. No. 18629R   Form **2553** (Rev. 3-2005)

Appendix B
State Reference Tables

The following tables set forth a wealth of contact information, as well as summaries of corporation law (for both LLCs and for Corporations) for each of the 50 states and the District of Columbia. Please keep in mind that the information in these tables is subject to the whim of each state's legislature, so the information is constantly changing. It is a good idea to do a reality check with the Secretary of State's office to confirm that the information is still current.

ALABAMA	
Contact Information for Business Formation Assistance	Alabama Secretary of State Attn: Corporations Division P.O. Box 5616 Montgomery, AL 36104 (334) 242-5324
Web Site Address	www.sos.state.al.us
Incorporation Information and Fees	The fee for filing Articles of Incorporation is $40 payable to the Alabama Secretary of State; Articles of Incorporation must be filed in the county where the corporation's registered office is located. There are additional local fees payable to the Probate Judge and the County.
LLC Organization Information and Fees	The fee for filing Articles of Organization is $40 payable to the Alabama Secretary of State but filed with the probate judge in the county of organization; Articles of Organization must be filed in the county where the LLCs registered office is located. There are additional local fees payable to the Probate Judge and the County (a minimum of $35, and the fees vary by county). Foreign LLCs must may a filing fee of $75 for qualification in Alabama.
Corporate Name Reservation Information	For Domestic Corporations: To reserve a corporate name, call the Alabama Corporations Call Center at (334) 242-5324 or fax (334) 240-3138 your request to the Corporations Division. If the name is available, you will be issued a "certificate of name reservation," and you will have 120 days to file the certificate with your Articles of Incorporation. If you do not incorporate within the 120 days, your name reservation will expire and you owe the Secretary of State a $10 cancellation fee for the name reservation that was issued. After 120 days, you may renew ($10) the name reservation for an additional 120 days. For Foreign Corporations: To reserve a corporate name, you must submit an "Application for Registration of Foreign Corporate Name" with a fee of between $5 and $12 dollars (see the form for an explanation).
LLC Name Reservation Information	Alabama does not reserve names for Limited Liability Companies, only for corporations.
Where to Get Corporate & LLC Formation Forms	www.sos.state.al.us/business/corpdl.cfm
Periodic Corporation Reporting Requirements	Alabama corporations and qualified foreign corporations must file an Alabama Business Privilege Tax Return, which also serves as an annual report. This form is due by March 15.

Periodic LLC Reporting Requirements	Alabama LLCs and qualified foreign LLCs must file an Alabama Business Privilege Tax Return, which also serves as an annual report. This form is due by March 15.
Where to Get Corporate & LLC Formation Tax Forms	www.ador.state.al.us/incometax/BPT_INDEX.htm
Corporate Tax Summary	Alabama's Corporate Franchise Tax was ruled unconstitutional in 1999. Alabama recently repealed the following business taxes: Corporate Entrance Fee and the Corporate Permit Fee. Alabama has unified its business entity tax under the Business Privilege Tax, to which Alabama corporations, and foreign corporations operating in Alabama are subject. The Privilege Tax ranges from .25% up to 1.75%, with a maximum Privilege Tax of $15,000 for LLCs. There is a helpful summary of Alabama's taxation scheme at www.ador.state.al.us/gensum.pdf.
"S" Corporation Information	Alabama requires the filing of Form 20S to qualify as an S corporation.
LLC Tax Summary	Alabama's Corporate Franchise Tax was ruled unconstitutional in 1999. Alabama recently repealed the following business taxes: Corporate Entrance Fee and the Corporate Permit Fee. Alabama has unified its business entity tax under the Business Privilege Tax, to which Alabama LLCs, and foreign LLCs operating in Alabama are subject. The Privilege Tax ranges from .25% up to 1.75%, with a maximum Privilege Tax of $15,000 for LLCs. There is a helpful summary of Alabama's taxation scheme at www.ador.state.al.us/gensum.pdf.
LLC Statute	Section 10-12-1 through 10-12-61 of the Code of Alabama
ALASKA	
Contact Information for Business Formation Assistance	Corporations Section Alaska Department of Community and Economic Development P.O. Box 110808 Juneau, AK 99101-0808 907-465-2530 phone 907-465-2549 fax
Web Site Address	www.commerce.state.ak.us/occ/
Incorporation Information and Fees	The fee for filing Articles of Incorporation is $250.

LLC Organization Information and Fees	The fee for filing Articles of Organization is $250 ($150 filing fee plus a biennial license fee of $100). Foreign LLCs wishing to conduct business in Alaska, must register as a foreign limited liability company. The filing fee is $350 ($150 filing fee plus a biennial license fee of $200).
Corporate Name Reservation Information and Fees	Alaska incorporators may pay a $25 name reservation fee to reserve a name. The name reservation remains effective for 120 days.
LLC Name Reservation Information	Alaska organizers may pay a $25 name reservation fee to reserve an LLC name. The name reservation remains effective for 120 days.
Where to Get Corporate & LLC Formation Forms	www.dced.state.ak.us/bsc/cforms.htm.
Periodic Corporation Reporting Requirements	Alaska corporations and qualified foreign corporations must file a biennial report in January of each alternate year with the Corporations Section. Visit the web site to obtain a form. The biennial corporation tax is $100 for domestic corporations and $200 for foreign corporations.
Periodic LLC Reporting Requirements	Alaska LLCs and qualified foreign LLCs must file a biennial report by January 2 of each alternate year with the Corporations Section. The biennial corporation tax is $100 for domestic corporations and $200 for foreign corporations.
Where to Get Corporate & LLC Tax Forms	www.tax.state.ak.us/forms.asp
Corporate Tax Summary	Alaska collects an annual Corporate income tax. A discussion is beyond the scope of this title. Contact the Alaska Department of Revenue for more information.
"S" Corporation Information	Alaska recognizes the federal S corporation provision. The subchapter S election is automatic and no state specific forms need be filed to make the subchapter S election.
LLC Tax Summary	Alaska LLCs are treated as partnerships, enjoy pass-through taxation, and are subject to the biennial license fee described above.
LLC Statute	Title 10, Chapter 10.50 of the Alaska Statutes

ARIZONA	
Contact Information for Business Formation Assistance	Corporations Division Arizona Corporation Commission 14 North 18th Avenue Phoenix, AZ 85007 (602) 542-6187
Web Site Address	www.azsos.gov
Incorporation Information and Fees	The fee for filing Articles of Incorporation is $60. A fill-in-the-blank form is available on the Arizona Corporation Commission's web site. Within 60 days after filing its Articles of Incorporation, domestic corporations must publish a "Notice for Publication" (sample at: www.cc.state.az.us/corp/filings/forms/) advising the public of the corporation's business address and statutory agent in a newspaper of general circulation in the county where the corporation conducts business. For a list of acceptable "news-papers of general circulation," see www.cc.state.az.us/corp/filings/forms/newspubs.htm. Thereafter, within 90 days of filing its Articles of Organization and publishing the notice, domestic corporations must file with the Corporation Commission an affidavit evidencing the publication of notice. There is no form for the affidavit; the newspaper filing your notice will usually draft the affidavit and may even file it on your behalf. Be sure to ask before publishing your notice.
LLC Organization Information and Fees	The fee for filing Articles of Organization is $50 for Arizona domestic LLCs and $150 for foreign LLCs registering in Arizona. Within 60 days after filing its Articles of Organization, domestic LLCs must publish a "Notice for Publication" (sample at: www.cc.state.az.us/corp/filings/forms/) advising the public of the LLC's business address and statutory agent in a newspaper of general circulation in the county where the LLC conducts business. For a list of acceptable "newspapers of general circu-lation," see www.cc.state.az.us/corp/filings/forms/newspubs.htm. Thereafter, within 90 days of filing its Articles of Organization and publishing the notice, domestic LLCs must file with the Corporation Commission an affidavit evidencing the publication of notice. There is no form for the affidavit; the newspaper filing your notice will usually draft the affidavit and may even file it on your behalf. Be sure to ask before publishing your notice.

Corporate Name Reservation Information and Fees	The Arizona Corporation Commission offers informal preliminary name availability information by telephone at (602) 542-3230. Arizona incorporators may reserve a corporate name by filing a reservation of name form with the Arizona Corporation Commission along with a $10 fee. Use the form provided on the web site to reserve a name.
LLC Name Reservation Information	The Arizona Corporation Commission offers informal preliminary name availability information by internet at www.cc.state.az.us/corp/filings/namesrch.htm, and by telephone at (602) 542-3230. Arizona organizers may reserve a LLC name by filing a reservation of name form with the Arizona Corporation Commission along with a $10 fee. The reservation is effective for 120 days. Use the form provided on the web site to reserve a name.
Where to Get Corporate & LLC Formation Forms	www.cc.state.az.us/corp/filings/forms/index.htm
Periodic Corporation Reporting Requirements	Arizona corporations are required to file an annual report with the Arizona Corporation Commission. The filing fee is $45. Financial disclosures are no longer required. The due date is dependent upon the first letter of the corporate name. Visit the web site for a schedule of due dates.
Periodic LLC Reporting Requirements	Arizona LLCs are not required to file periodic reports.
Where to Get Corporate & LLC Tax Forms	www.revenue.state.az.us/
Corporate Tax Summary	Arizona collects an annual Corporate income tax. A discussion is beyond the scope of this title. Contact the Alaska Department of Revenue for more information.
"S" Corporation Information	Arizona requires S corporations to file Form 120S annually.
LLC Tax Summary	If the limited liability company is classified as a partnership for federal income tax purposes, the limited liability company must report its income to Arizona as a partnership on Arizona Form 165. If the limited liability company is classified as a corporation for federal income tax purposes, the limited liability company must report its income to Arizona as a corporation on Arizona Form 120.
LLC Statute	Title 10, Chapter 29 of the Arizona Revised Statutes

ARKANSAS	
Contact Information for Business Formation Assistance	Corporations Division Arkansas Secretary of State State Capitol, Room 256 Little Rock, AR 72201-1094 (501) 682-3409 (888) 233-0325
Web Site Address	sos.state.ar.us
Incorporation Information and Fees	The fee for filing Articles of Incorporation is $50. Online filing is available at the Arkansas Secretary of State's web site, for a reduced fee of $45.
LLC Organization Information and Fees	The fee for filing a domestic LLCs Articles of Organization is $50 (online filing is $45). Foreign LLCs must pay a $300 filing fee along with their Application for Certificate of Registration of Limited Liability Company. Online filing is available for most forms at the Arkansas Secretary of State's web site, but you'll have to register and give a credit card number. Organizers must also file a Limited Liability Company Franchise Tax Registration form at the time of filing of Articles of Organization or registration of foreign LLC. The purpose of this form is so LLCs will receive their annual Franchise Tax Report form (see below).
Corporate Name Reservation Information and Fees	Arkansas incorporators may reserve a corporate name by filing a name reservation application with the Arkansas Secretary of State along with a $25 name reservation fee. The name reservation remains effective for 120 days.
LLC Name Reservation Information	Arkansas organizers may reserve an LLC name by filing a name reservation application with the Arkansas Secretary of State along with a $25 name reservation fee. The name reservation remains effective for 120 days.
Where to Get Corporate & LLC Formation Forms	sos.state.ar.us/corp_forms.html
Periodic Corporation Reporting Requirements	Arkansas corporations are required to file an Arizona Corporation Franchise Tax Report by June 1 of each year with the Arkansas Secretary of State.
Periodic LLC Reporting Requirements	Arkansas LLCs are required to file an annual LLC Franchise Tax Report. The Franchise Tax Report is mailed to LLCs in February of each year, and must be filed by June 1 of each year with the Arkansas Secretary of State.

Where to Get Corporate & LLC Tax Forms	sos.state.ar.us/corp_forms/.html
Corporate Tax Summary	Corporate taxes are based on total outstanding capital stock and assets in use in Arkansas. A complete discussion is beyond the scope of this title. For more information, contact the Arkansas Corporate Franchise Tax Division at (501) 682-3464.
"S" Corporation Information	Arkansas recognizes the federal S corporation provision. The subchapter S election is automatic and no state specific forms need be filed to make the subchapter S election.
LLC Tax Summary	Both foreign and domestic LLCs pay a $50 franchise tax at the time of filing their LLC Franchise Tax Report.
LLC Statute	Title 4, Chapter 32 of the Arkansas Code
CALIFORNIA	
Contact Information for Business Formation Assistance	California Secretary of State (For LLCs: Note "LLC Unit") 1500 11th Street Sacramento, CA 95814 (916) 657-5448
Web Site Address	www.ss.ca.gov
Incorporation Information and Fees	The fee for filing Articles of Incorporation is $100. While incorporators need not name initial directors in the Articles of Incorporation, if initial directors are named, all initial directors must sign and acknowledge the articles.
LLC Organization Information and Fees	The fee for filing Articles of Organization is $70.
Corporate Name Reservation Information and Fees	California incorporators may pay a $10 fee to reserve a name. The name reservation remains effective for 60 days.
LLC Name Reservation Information	California organizers may pay a $10 fee to reserve a name. The name reservation remains effective for 60 days.
Where to Get Corporate & LLC Formation Forms	www.ss.ca.gov/business/corp/corp_formsfees.htm
Periodic Corporation Reporting Requirements	California corporations and registered corporations must file a Statement of Information (Form SI-200C) within 90 days of organization along with a fee of $20. The Statement of Information must be filed biennially thereafter. The Statement of Information must be accompanied by a $5 disclosure fee.

Periodic LLC Reporting Requirements	California LLC and registered foreign LLCs must file a Statement of Information (Form LLC-12) within 90 days of organization accompanied by a $20 fee, and biennially thereafter on the Statement of Information Renewal Form (Form LLC-12R) accompanied by a $20 fee. The Statement of Information must be accompanied by a $5 disclosure fee.
Where to Get Corporate & LLC Tax Forms	www.ftb.ca.gov/forms/index.html
Corporate Tax Summary	California corporations and foreign corporations doing business in California are required to pay a minimum $800 annual franchise tax due within three months of the close of the accounting year, but see above under "Incorporation Information and Fees" for first and second year exemptions. C Corporations pay 8.84 percent and S corporations pay 1.5 percent of the corporation's income.
"S" Corporation Information	California requires the filing of Form FTP3560 (S Corporation Election or Termination/Revocation) to qualify as an S corporation. S corporations pay the $800 minimum franchise tax, OR 1.5 percent of income.
LLC Tax Summary	California LLCs and foreign LLCs doing business in California are required to pay a minimum $800 annual Limited Liability Company Tax due within three months of the close of the accounting year.
LLC Statute	Title 2.5 of the California Corporation Code
COLORADO	
Contact Information for Business Formation Assistance	Business Division Colorado Secretary of State 1560 Broadway, Suite 200 Denver, CC 80202 (303) 894-2251
Web Site Address	www.sos.state.co.us
Incorporation Information and Fees	Colorado has recently instituted aggressive online filing fees, and the online fee for filing is now among the least expensive in the country. The fee for filing Articles of Incorporation on paper is $125, and the online fee is $25.
LLC Organization Information and Fees	Colorado has recently instituted aggressive online filing fees, and the online fee for filing is now among the least expensive in the country. The fee for filing Articles of Organization is on paper is $125, and the online fee is $25.

Corporate Name Reservation Information and Fees	Colorado incorporators may check the availability of a proposed name by searching the online database at the Secretary of State's web site. If the requested name does not return an existing match, the incorporator can follow the link "Reserve This Name" to be taken to an automatic name reservation online form. The fee is only $0.99 to reserve a name for 120 days, and another $0.99 to renew for an additional 120 days.
LLC Name Reservation Information	Colorado organizers may check the availability of a proposed name by searching the online database at the Secretary of State's web site. If the requested name does not return an existing match, the organizer can follow the link "Reserve This Name" to be taken to an automatic name reservation online form. The fee is only $0.99 to reserve a name for 120 days, and another $0.99 to renew for an additional 120 days.
Where to Get Corporate & LLC Formation Forms	www.sos.state.co.us/pubs/business/forms_main.htm
Periodic Corporation Reporting Requirements	As of January 1, 2002, annual reports (the "Annual Business Report") are now due annually (formerly biennially) by the end of the second month in which the report is mailed to the corporation. The annual fee is $125 for foreign corporations to qualify and register in Colorado; foreign corporations can only file by paper. The annual fee for domestic corporations is $100 for paper filing and only $10 for online filing.
Periodic LLC Reporting Requirements	As of January 1, 2002, annual reports (the "Annual Business Report") are now due annually (formerly biennially) by the end of the second month in which the report is mailed to the corporation. The annual fee is $125 for foreign LLCs to qualify and register in Colorado; foreign LLCs can only file by paper. The annual fee for domestic LLCs is $100 for paper filing and only $10 for online filing.
Where to Get Corporate & LLC Tax Forms	www.revenue.state.co.us/TPS_Dir/wrap.asp?incl=forms_download
Corporate Tax Summary	Colorado corporations and foreign corporations doing business in Colorado must pay a corporate income tax. The tax rate is 4.63 percent.
"S" Corporation Information	Colorado recognizes the federal S corporation provision. The subchapter S election is automatic and no state specific forms need be filed to make the subchapter S election.
LLC Tax Summary	Colorado LLCs and foreign LLCs doing business in Colorado must file a Colorado Partnership or S Corporation Return of Income on

	Form 106. Colorado's treatment of LLCs is complex due to its non-resident member rules; Non-resident members of LLCs must file a special Statement of Colorado Tax Remittance for Nonresident Partner or Shareholder on Forms 107 and 108. See the instructions to Form 106 for detailed information.
LLC Statute	Title 7, Article 80 of the Colorado Revised Statutes
CONNECTICUT	
Contact Information for Business Formation Assistance	Connecticut Secretary of State 30 Trinity Street Hartford CT 06106 (860) 509-6002
Web Site Address	www.sots.state.ct.us
Incorporation Information and Fees	The fee for filing Articles of Incorporation (called a Certificate of Incorporation in Connecticut) is $275. The Certificate of Incorporation form carries a $200 filing fee, which includes a $150 minimum franchise tax and $50 to file the Certificate of Incorporation. Connecticut imposes an additional filing requirement: an Organization and First Report, which carries an additional filling fee of $75.
LLC Organization Information and Fees	The fee for filing Articles of Organization is $60. A foreign LLC must file an Application for Registration along with a $60 filing fee.
Corporate Name Reservation Information and Fees	The Connecticut Secretary of State's office provides informal information regarding corporate name availability by calling (860) 509-6002. Connecticut incorporators may reserve corporate names by filing the form entitled "Application for Reservation of Name for Domestic or Foreign Stock & Non-Stock Corp., The fee is $30, and The name reservation remains effective for 120 days.
LLC Name Reservation Information	The Connecticut Secretary of the State's office provides informal information regarding LLC name availability by calling (860) 509-6002. Connecticut organizers may reserve LLC names by filing the form entitled "Application for Reservation of Name for Domestic or Foreign Stock & Non-Stock Corp, LLC, LP, LLP & Statutory Trust." The fee is $30, and the name reservation remains effective for 120 days.
Where to Get Corporate & LLC Formation Forms	www.sots.ct.gov/CommercialRecording/crdforms.html

Periodic Corporation Reporting Requirements	Connecticut corporations and qualified foreign corporations must file annual reports by the last day of the month in which the entity originally filed in the state. The annual report fee is $75. Annual report forms are not available online.
Periodic LLC Reporting Requirements	Connecticut LLCs must file annual reports by the end of the anniversary month of the LLCs initial filing with the Division. The annual report fee is $10. Annual report forms are not available online.
Where to Get Corporate Tax Forms	www.ct.gov/drs/taxonomy/ ct_taxonomy.asp?DLN=41128&drsNav=41128
Corporate Tax Summary	Connecticut corporations and foreign corporations doing business in Connecticut pay a tax based either upon net income or upon capital stock, whichever is higher. The minimum tax is $250.
"S" Corporation Information	Connecticut recently phased out business tax on S corporations. Connecticut recognizes the federal S corporation provision. The subchapter S election is automatic and no state specific forms need be filed to make the subchapter S election.
LLC Tax Summary	If the LLC is classified as a partnership for federal income tax purposes, it must report its income to Connecticut as a partnership using the Department of Revenue's CT-1065 form. If the LLC is classified as a corporation for federal income tax purposes it must report its income to the state as a corporation using the Connecticut Department of Revenue's CT-1120 form.
LLC Statute	Volume 10, Title 34 of the General Statutes of Connecticut
DISTRICT OF COLUMBIA	
Contact Information for Business Formation Assistance	Corporations Division District of Columbia Department of Consumer Regulatory Affairs 941 North Capitol Street, N.E. Washington, DC 20002 (202) 442-4430
Web Site Address	http://dcra.dc.gov/dcra/site/
Incorporation Information and Fees	The fee for filing Articles of Incorporation is $100, plus a minimum license fee of $20, which varies with the amount of authorized stock. The $20 license fee covers up to $100,000 of authorized stock. The Department of Consumer Regulatory

	Affairs offers a helpful "Articles of Incorporation Instruction Sheet" on their web site.
LLC Organization Information and Fees	The fee for filing Articles of Organization is $100. A completed "Written Consent to Act as Registered Agent" form must be attached to the Articles of Organization. A "Combined Business Tax Registration Application," form F500 must also be filed with the LLCs articles. Foreign LLCs must file an Application for Certificate of Registration for a Foreign Limited Liability Company and submit a filing fee of $150.
Corporate Name Reservation Information and Fees	District of Columbia incorporators may pay a $25 fee to reserve a corporate name by filing an "Application for Reservation of Corporate Name." The form is available on the Department of Consumer Regulatory Affairs' web site. The name reservation remains effective for 60 days.
LLC Name Reservation Information	District of Columbia organizers may pay a $25 fee to reserve an LLC name by filing an "Application for LLC Name Reservation Information" form available on the Department of Consumer Regulatory Affairs' web site. The name reservation remains effective for 60 days.
Where to Get Corporate & LLC Formation Forms	http://mblr.dc.gov/corp/forms/index.shtm
Periodic Corporation Reporting Requirements	District of Columbia corporations and qualified foreign corporations must file an "Annual Report for Foreign and Domestic Corporations" with the Department of Consumer Regulatory Affairs. Corporate reports are due by April 15. The filing fee is $100.
Periodic LLC Reporting Requirements	District of Columbia LLCs must file a "Two-Year Report for Foreign and Domestic Limited Liability Companies." The reports are due on or before the first June 16 to fall following the LLCs registration and on or before June 16 every two years thereafter.
Where to Get Corporate & LLC Tax Forms	http://cfo.dc.gov/cfo/cwp/view,a,1324,q,590950, cfoNav,l33210l,.asp
Corporate Tax Summary	District of Columbia corporations and foreign corporations doing business in the District of Columbia are required to file a "Corporation Franchise Tax Return," Form D-20 by the 15th day of the 3rd month following the close of the taxable year. Annual corporate taxes are based on income, not on shares of stock. The tax rate is 9.975 percent of income attributable to DC operations, and the minimum tax is $100.

"S" Corporation Information	The District of Columbia recognizes the federal S corporation provision. The subchapter S election is automatic and no state specific forms need be filed to make the subchapter S election.
LLC Tax Summary	LLCs must file the District of Columbia's "Declaration of Estimated Franchise Tax Voucher" if it expects its franchise tax liability to exceed $1,000 for the taxable year. LLCs engaging in business activity in which its receipts exceed $12,000 for the taxable year must also file an "Unincorporated Business Franchise Tax Return."
LLC Statute	Title 29, Chapter 13 of the Code of Laws of the District of Columbia
DELAWARE	
Contact Information for Business Formation Assistance	Corporate Filing Section Division of Corporations Delaware Secretary of State John G. Townsend Building 401 Federal Street – Suite # 4 Dover, DE 19901 (302) 739-3073
Web Site Address	www.state.de.us/corp/default.shtml
Incorporation Information and Fees	The fee for filing Articles of Incorporation is $89. The Division of Corporations offers a range of expedited options. See their web site for more information.
LLC Organization Information and Fees	The fee for filing a Certificate of Formation is $90. The qualification filing fee for a foreign LLC is $100.
Corporate Name Reservation Information and Fees	Name availability can be checked by following the "Name Reservation" link on the left menu bar on the web site. The name reservation is done online, and the fee is $75.
LLC Name Reservation Information	Name availability can be checked by following the "Name Reservation" link on the left menu bar on the web site. The name reservation is done online, and the fee is $75.
Where to Get Corporate & LLC Formation Forms	www.state.de.us/corp/corpforms.shtml
Periodic Corporation Reporting Requirements	A domestic corporation's annual franchise tax report is due in March. Forms are mailed to resident agents in January. The filing fee is $25.

Periodic LLC Reporting Requirements	An LLC's annual franchise tax report is due in March. Forms are mailed to resident agents in December and the filing fee is $25.
Where to Get Corporate & LLC Tax Forms	www.state.de.us/revenue/services/Business_Tax/Forms.shtml
Corporate Tax Summary	All corporations incorporated in the State of Delaware are required to file an Annual Franchise Tax Report and to pay a franchise tax. Taxes and annual reports are to be received no later than March 1 each year. The minimum tax is $35 with a maximum of $165,000. Taxes are based on the number of shares of stock issued. Corporations with 3,000 authorized shares or less automatically pay the minimum of $35. Corporations with more than 3,000 authorized shares pay tax according to an annoyingly complex formula that you may find described at the Department of Revenue's web site. Delaware also imposes an income tax, but corporations not conducting business within Delaware are exempt. The Delaware state corporate income tax rate is 8.7 percent of federal taxable income attributable to Delaware activities.
"S" Corporation Information	Delaware recognizes the federal S corporation provision. The subchapter S election is automatic and no state specific forms need be filed to make the subchapter S election. S corporations conducting business in Delaware must file Form 1100S, S Corporation Reconciliation and Shareholders Information Return.
LLC Tax Summary	All Delaware LLCs are required to pay a minimum Franchise Tax of $200, due by June 1 of each year.
LLC Statute	Title 6, Chapter 18, Delaware Code
FLORIDA	
Contact Information for Business Formation Assistance	Division of Corporations Florida Department of State Corporate Filings P.O. Box 6327 Tallahassee, FL 32314
(850) 488-9000	
Web Site Address	www.sunbiz.org
Incorporation Information and Fees	The fee for filing Articles of Incorporation is $70. Incorporators must file Articles of Incorporation and a Resident Agent Designation. A certified copy fee of $8.75 is optional.

LLC Organization Information and Fees	The fee for filing Articles of Organization of $100 which must be accompanied by a completed "Designation of RA" (Resident Agent) form. The fee for filing the Designation of RA form is $25. A foreign LLC must file an Application by Foreign Limited Liability Company for Authority to Transact Business in Florida. The filing fee is $100 and the Application must be accompanied by a Designation of Registered Agent ($25 filing fee)
Corporate/LLC Name Reservation Information and Fees	Florida no longer maintains a name reservation program. However, the Secretary of State's web site allows free searches of existing corporate names.
Where to Get Corporate & LLC Formation Forms	www.dos.state.fl.us/doc/form_download.html
Periodic Corporation Reporting Requirements	Florida corporations must file an annual report by May 1 of each year. The filing fee is $150.
Periodic LLC Reporting Requirements	LLCs must complete and file Florida's Limited Liability Company Uniform Business Report (UBR) annually by May 1. The fee for filing the UBR is $50.
Where to Get Corporate & LLC Tax Forms	http://dor.myflorida.com/dor/eservices/apps/filepay/cit/
Corporate Tax Summary	Florida has no franchise tax. Corporations that conduct business, earn or receive income in Florida, including out-of-state corporations, must file a Florida corporate income tax return. Florida corporate income tax liability is computed using federal taxable income, modified by certain Florida adjustments, to determine adjusted federal income. A corporation doing business within and without Florida may apportion its total income.
"S" Corporation Information	Florida recognizes the federal S corporation provision. The subchapter S election is automatic and no state specific forms need be filed to make the subchapter S election.
LLC Tax Summary	Most LLCs will be required to file the Florida Partnership Information Return (Form F-1065). This is for informational purposes only. LLCs classified as corporations for federal tax purposes must file the Florida Corporate Income/Franchise and Emergency Excise Tax Return (Form F-1120).
LLC Statute	Title XXXVI, Chapter 608 of the Florida Statutes

GEORGIA	
Contact Information for Business Formation Assistance	Georgia Secretary of State Corporations Division Suite 315 West Tower 2 Martin Luther King, Jr. Drive Atlanta, GA 30334 (404) 656-2817 (404) 657-2248 (fax)
Web Site Address	www.sos.state.ga.us
Incorporation Information and Fees	The fee for filing Articles of Incorporation is $100. All corporations must publish a notice of intent to incorporate in the newspaper which is the official legal organ of the county where the initial registered office of the corporation is to be located, or in a newspaper of general circulation in such county and for which at least 60 percent of its subscriptions are paid. The Clerk of Superior Court can advise you as to the legal organ in your county. The notice of intent to incorporate and a $40 publication fee should be forwarded directly to the newspaper no later than the next business day after filing Articles of Incorporation with the Secretary of State.
LLC Organization Information and Fees	The fee for filing Articles of Organization is $100. Foreign LLC's must file an Application for Certificate of Authority for Foreign Limited Liability Company, accompanied by the filing fee of $200.
Corporate Name Reservation Information and Fees	Georgia incorporators may informally search existing corporate names on the Georgia Secretary of State's web site. Georgia incorporators may reserve names online for free by visiting www.sos.state.ga.us/cgi-bin/namerequest.asp. The fee is $25, and the name reservation remains effective for 90 days.
LLC Name Reservation Information	Georgia organizers may informally search existing corporate names on the Georgia Secretary of State's web site. Georgia incorporators may reserve names online for free by visiting www.sos.state.ga.us/cgi-bin/namerequest.asp. The fee is $25, and the name reservation remains effective for 90 days.
Where to Get Corporate & LLC Formation Forms	www.sos.state.ga.us/corporations/forms.htm
Periodic Corporation Reporting Requirements	Annual reports are due by April 1 of each year. Corporations must also make an original report within 90 days of incorporation. The annual registration fee is $15. Online filing is available through the Georgia Secretary of State's web site.

Periodic LLC Reporting Requirements	LLCs operating in Georgia must file an annual registration by April 1. Registration forms can be found online. Registrations can also be filed online at the Corporation Division's web site.
Where to Get Corporate & LLC Tax Forms	www.etax.dor.ga.gov/inctax/corporate_tax_index_page.shtml and www.etax.dor.ga.gov/inctax/partnership_information_and_repo.shtml
Corporate Tax Summary	Georgia corporate taxes have two components. The first is a 6 percent income tax, and the second is a graduated tax based on corporate net worth.
"S" Corporation Information	Georgia recognizes the federal S corporation provision. The subchapter S election is automatic and no state specific forms need be filed to make the subchapter S election. S corporations must file a special tax return on form 600-S.
LLC Tax Summary	LLCs engaged in business or deriving income from property located in Georgia must file the Georgia Partnership Income Tax Return (Form 700)
LLC Statute	Title 14, Chapter 11 of the Code of Georgia
HAWAII	
Contact Information for Business Formation Assistance	Department of Commerce and Consumer Affairs Business Registration Division P.O. Box 3469 Honolulu, Hawaii 96801 (808) 586-2744 (808) 586-2733 (fax)
Web Site Address	www.hawaii.gov/dcca
Incorporation Information and Fees	The fee for filing Articles of Incorporation is $50.
LLC Organization Information and Fees	The fee for filing Articles of Organization is $50. A foreign LLC must file an Application for Certificate of Authority, along with a filing fee of $50.
Corporate Name Reservation Information and Fees	Hawaii incorporators may reserve a corporate name by filing form X-1 with the Business Registration Division along with a $10 filing fee. The name reservation remains effective for 120 days.

LLC Name Reservation Information and Fees	Hawaii organizers may search an LLC name online at www.ehawaiigov.org/dcca/bizsearch/exe/bizsearch.cgi. Organizers can reserve an LLC name by filing form X-1 with the Business Registrations Division along with a $10 filing fee.
Where to Get Corporation & LLC Formation Forms	www.hawaii.gov/dcca/areas/breg/registration/
Periodic Corporation Reporting Requirements	Hawaii corporations and qualified foreign corporations must file an annual report by March 31 with the Business Registration Division. The filing fee is $25.
Periodic LLC Reporting Requirements	LLCs must file an Annual Report each year. Annual Report forms and specific filing instructions will be automatically mailed to the LLC in March.
Where to Get Corporate & LLC Tax Forms	www.state.hi.us/tax/taxforms.html
Corporate Tax Summary	Hawaii corporations and foreign corporations doing business in Hawaii are subject to a corporate income tax. The corporate tax rate is 4.4 percent of income up to $25,000, 5.4 percent of taxable income up to $100,000, 6.4 percent of income exceeding $100,000.
"S" Corporation Information	Hawaii recognizes the federal S corporation provision. The subchapter S election is automatic and no state specific forms need be filed to make the subchapter S election.
LLC Tax Summary	LLCs are subject to Hawaii's General Excise Tax. The tax rate is .4% to .5% depending on the source of the LLC's income. Hawaii's Franchise Tax is only levied on financial institutions and thus generally not applicable to LLCs.
LLC Statute	Chapter 428 of the Hawaii Revised Statutes.
IDAHO	
Contact Information for Business Formation Assistance	Office of the Secretary of State 700 W Jefferson, Room 203 PO Box 83720 Boise, ID 83720-0080 (208) 334-2300 (208) 334-2282 (fax)
Web Site Address	www.idsos.state.id.us
Incorporation Information and Fees	The fee for filing Articles of Incorporation is $100.

LLC Organization Information and Fees	The fee for filing Articles of Organization is $100. Foreign LLCs must file an Application for Registration of Foreign Limited Liability Company accompanied by a filing fee of $100. For an excellent discussion on starting a business in Idaho visit www.idoc.state.id.us/Business/starting.html.
Corporate Name Reservation Information and Fees	Idaho incorporators may reserve a corporate name by filing an "Application for Reservation of Legal Entity Name" and paying a $20 fee. The name reservation remains effective for four months.
LLC Name Reservation Information and Fees	Idaho organizers may reserve an LLC name by filing an "Application for Reservation of Legal Entity Name" and paying a $20 fee. The name reservation remains effective for four months.
Where to Get Corporate & LLC Formation Forms	www.idsos.state.id.us/corp/corpform.htm
Periodic Corporation Reporting Requirements	Idaho corporations and qualified foreign corporations must file an annual corporate report. The report is due in the anniversary month of incorporation or qualification. If timely, the report has no filing fee. The Secretary of State's office mails the form two months before its due date.
Periodic LLC Reporting Requirements	LLCs must file an annual report with the Secretary of State by the end of the month in which the LLC originally organized. The filing fee is $30.
Where to Get Corporate & LLC Tax Forms	http://tax.idaho.gov/forms.htm
Corporate Tax Summary	Idaho corporations and foreign corporations doing business in Idaho must pay a corporate income tax. The income tax rate is 7.6%.
"S" Corporation Information	Idaho recognizes the federal S corporation provision. The subchapter S election is automatic and no state specific forms need be filed to make the subchapter S election.
LLC Tax Summary	Most LLCs must file the Idaho Partnership Return of Income (Form 65). The tax rate is 7.6% with a minimum payment of $20. LLCs classified as corporations for federal tax purposes must file the Idaho Corporation Income Tax Return (Form 41)
LLC Statute	Title 53, Chapter 6 of the Idaho Statutes

ILLINOIS	
Contact Information for Business Formation Assistance	Department of Business Services Illinois Secretary of State 501 S. Second St., Suite 328 Springfield, Illinois 62756 (217) 782-6961
Web Site Address	www.sos.state.il.us
Incorporation Information and Fees	The fee for filing Articles of Incorporation is $150, plus franchise tax. The initial franchise tax is assessed at the rate of 15/100 or 1 percent ($150 per $1,000) on the paid-in capital represented in Illinois, with a minimum of $25. The Department of Business Services in Springfield will provide assistance in calculating the total fee if necessary. Call (217) 782-9522 or 9523 for assistance.
LLC Organization Information and Fees	The fee for filing Articles of Organization is $500—the highest LLC organization fee in the nation. Foreign LLCs must register by filing an Application for Admission to Transact Business along with a filing fee of $500.
Corporate Name Reservation Information and Fees	Illinois incorporators may reserve a corporate name by filing for BCA-4.10 with the Illinois Secretary of State and paying a $25 fee per reserved name. The name reservation remains effective for 90 days.
LLC Name Reservation Information and Fees	Illinois organizers may reserve a LLC name by filing form LLC-1.15 and paying a $300 fee per reserved name—the highest name reservation fee in the nation. The name reservation remains effective for 90 days. Available names can be searched at the Department of Business Services web site.
Where to Get Corporate Formation Forms	www.cyberdriveillinois.com/departments/business_services/publications_and_forms/home.html
Periodic Corporation Reporting Requirements	Domestic corporations must file a Domestic Corporation Annual Report annually, and qualified foreign corporations must file a Foreign Corporation Annual Report annually.
Periodic LLC Reporting Requirements	LLCs must file an Annual Report (Form LLC-50.1) each year prior to the anniversary date of the LLCs initial filing with the Section. The filing fee is $200.
Where to Get Corporate & LLC Tax Forms	Franchise tax is reported on the annual report form, discussed above. Income tax forms can be found at http://tax.illinois.gov/Businesses/index.htm.

Corporate Tax Summary	Illinois corporations and foreign corporations doing business in Illinois must pay an income tax and a "replacement" tax based upon the value of the corporation's gross assets in Illinois and the gross amount of business transacted in the state.
"S" Corporation Information	Illinois recognizes the federal S corporation provision. The subchapter S election is automatic and no state specific forms need be filed to make the subchapter S election.
LLC Tax Summary	Most LLCs must file an Illinois Partnership Replacement Tax Return (Form IL-1065). The Replacement Tax rate is 1.5% of the LLCs net income. LLCs classified as corporations for federal tax purposes must file an Illinois Corporation Income and Replacement Tax Return (Form IL-1120).
LLC Statute	Chapter 805, Subheading 180 of the Illinois Compiled Statutes
INDIANA	
Contact Information for Business Formation Assistance	Corporations Division Indiana Secretary of State 302 West Washington Street, Room #E018 Indianapolis, IN 46204 (317) 232-6576
Web Site Address	www.state.in.us/sos/
Incorporation Information and Fees	The fee for filing Articles of Incorporation is $90.
LLC Organization Information and Fees	The fee for filing Articles of Organization and is $90. A foreign LLC may register by filing an Application for Certificate of Authority of a Foreign Limited Liability Company and submitting a filing fee of $90.
Corporate Name Reservation Information and Fees	Indiana offers free preliminary name availability information by telephone (317) 232-6576. Indiana incorporators may reserve a corporate name by filing a name reservation application along with a $20 fee. The reservation is effective for 120 days.
LLC Name Reservation Information and Fees	Indiana offers free preliminary name availability information by telephone (317) 232-6576 or online at www.ai.org/sos/bus_service/online_corps/default.asp. Indiana organizers may reserve an LLC name by filing a name reservation application along with a $20 fee. The reservation is effective for 120 days.

Where to Get Corporate & LLC Formation Forms	www.state.in.us/sos/business/forms.html
Periodic Corporation Reporting Requirements	Indiana corporations and qualified foreign corporations must file a biennial corporate report with the Indiana Secretary of State along with a $30 fee, although a $20 online filing fee is available.
Periodic LLC Reporting Requirements	Indiana LLCs must file a biennial Indiana Business Entity Report every two years by the last day of the month in which the LLC was originally registered. The fee filing the report is $30, although a $20 online filing fee is available.
Where to Get Corporate & LLC Tax Forms	www.in.gov/dor/taxforms
Corporate Tax Summary	Indiana corporations and foreign corporations doing business in Indiana must pay two corporate income taxes: a corporate income tax based upon gross income, and an adjusted gross income tax. The gross income tax has two rates, a high rate of 1.2 percent and a low rate of .3 percent. The adjusted gross income tax rate is 3.4 percent.
"S" Corporation Information	Indiana recognizes the S corporation provision. Indiana corporations must elect to be deemed "special" corporation (equivalent to an S corporation) using form IT-20SC. Indiana special corporations are exempt from the gross income tax.
LLC Tax Summary	Most LLCs must file Indiana's Partnership Return (Form IT-65). The return is purely informational. LLCs classified as corporations for federal tax purposes must file a Corporation Income Tax Return (IT-20).
LLC Statute	Title 23, Article 18 of the Indiana State Code
IOWA	
Contact Information for Business Formation Assistance	Business Services Division Office of the Secretary of State 1st Floor, Lucas Building Des Moines, Iowa 50319 (515) 281-5204
Web Site Address	www.sos.state.ia.us
Incorporation Information and Fees	The fee for filing Articles of Incorporation is $50.
LLC Organization Information and Fees	The fee for filing Articles of Organization is $50. Foreign LLCs must file an Application for Certificate of Registration along with the fee of $100.

Corporate Name Reservation Information and Fees	Iowa incorporators may reserve a name by filing an Application to Reserve Corporate Name and paying a $10 fee. The name reservation remains effective for 120 days.
LLC Name Reservation Information and Fees	Iowa incorporators may reserve a name by filing an Application to Reserve LLC name and paying a $10 fee. The name reservation remains effective for 120 days. To search available names visit the Secretary of State's web site.
Where to Get Corporate & LLC Formation Forms	www.sos.state.ia.us/business/form.html
Periodic Corporation Reporting Requirements	Iowa corporations and qualified foreign corporations must file a biennial corporate report with the Secretary of State. Reports are due between January and April 1 of even-numbered years following the year of incorporation. The report filing fee is $45.
Periodic LLC Reporting Requirements	Iowa LLCs and qualified foreign LLCs must file a biennial corporate report with the Secretary of State. Reports are due between January and April 1 of even-numbered years following the year of incorporation. The report filing fee is $45.
Where to Get Corporate & LLC Tax Forms	www.state.ia.us/tax/forms/loadform.html
Corporate Tax Summary	Iowa corporations and foreign corporations doing business in Iowa must pay a corporate income tax. The corporate income tax rate ranges from 6 percent to 12 percent. For more information, contact the Iowa Department of Revenue at (515) 281-3114.
"S" Corporation Information	Iowa recognizes the federal S corporation provision. The subchapter S election is automatic and no state specific forms need be filed to make the subchapter S election.
Additional Information	Iowa's Department of Revenue & Finance publishes an informative guide to starting a business in Iowa at www.state.ia.us/government/drf/business/newbus.html
LLC Tax Summary	Most LLCs must file an Iowa Partnership Return (Form IA-1065), but are not required to pay state income tax. LLCs classified as corporations for federal tax purposes must file an Iowa Corporation Return (Form IA 1120)
LLC Statute	Title XII, Chapter 490A of the Iowa Code

KANSAS	
Contact Information for Business Formation Assistance	Kansas Secretary of State Corporation Division First Floor, Memorial Hall 120 S. W. 10th Ave. Topeka, KS 66612-1594 (785) 296-4564 (785) 296-4570 (fax)
Web Site Address	www.kssos.org
Incorporation Information and Fees	The fee for filing Articles of Incorporation is $90.
LLC Organization Information and Fees	The fee for organizing an LLC is $150. Foreign LLCs may file a Foreign Limited Liability Company form and submit a filing fee of $150.
Corporate Name Reservation Information and Fees	Kansas incorporators may reserve a corporate name by filing form NR with the Kansas Secretary of State and paying a $20 fee. The name reservation remains effective for 120 days.
LLC Name Reservation Information and Fees	Name reservation is not available for LLCs.
Where to Get Corporate & LLC Formation Forms	www.kssos.org/forms/forms.html
Periodic Corporation Reporting Requirements	Corporations must pay an annual Franchise Tax—now called a "Franchise Fee"—of $55; see below for information on the separate Franchise Tax. The franchise fee must be paid to the Kansas Secretary of State with the entity's annual report. Both may be submitted electronically at the Kansas Business Center. To file the annual report and pay the franchise fee by mail, you may visit this Web site to download and print forms and instructions.
Periodic LLC Reporting Requirements	LLCs must pay an annual Franchise Tax—now called a "Franchise Fee"—of $55; see below for information on the separate Franchise Tax. The franchise fee must be paid to the Kansas Secretary of State with the entity's annual report. Both may be submitted electronically at the Kansas Business Center. To file the annual report and pay the franchise fee by mail, you may visit this web site to download and print forms and instructions.
Where to Get Corporate & LLC Tax Forms	www.ksrevenue.org/forms-bustax.htm
Corporate Tax Summary	Kansas recently enacted changes to its franchise tax law. The new franchise tax and fee law requires businesses to pay a franchise tax to the Kansas Department of Revenue and a separate franchise fee to the Secretary of State (discussed above).

	Both are due the 15th day of the fourth month following the tax year end; e.g. April 15, 2005, for entities with a December 31 tax year end.
	The new franchise tax, which carries a maximum of $20,000, works as follows. Business entities that have $100,000 of net worth or more in the state must pay to the Kansas Department of Revenue a franchise tax of 0.125% of the total net worth. Business entities required to pay the tax will file a return with the Department of Revenue, which must be accompanied by the taxpayer's balance sheet.
"S" Corporation Information	Kansas recognizes the federal S corporation provision. The subchapter S election is automatic and no state specific forms need be filed to make the subchapter S election. Corporations which elect subchapter S status must file a Kansas Small Business Income Tax Return, Form K120S.
Additional Information	Kansas publishes a thorough and helpful "Kansas Corporate Handbook," available from the Secretary of State's web site.
LLC Tax Summary	Kansas recently enacted changes to its franchise tax law. The new franchise tax and fee law requires businesses to pay a franchise tax to the Kansas Department of Revenue and a separate franchise fee to the Secretary of State (discussed above). Both are due the 15th day of the fourth month following the tax year end; e.g. April 15, 2005, for entities with a December 31 tax year end.
	The new franchise tax, which carries a maximum of $20,000, works as follows. Business entities that have $100,000 of net worth or more in the state must pay to the Kansas Department of Revenue a franchise tax of 0.125% of the total net worth. Business entities required to pay the tax will file a return with the Department of Revenue, which must be accompanied by the taxpayer's balance sheet.
LLC Statute	Chapter 17, Article 76 of the Kansas Statutes

KENTUCKY	
Contact Information for	Kentucky Secretary of State Business Formation Assistance 700 Capital Avenue Suite 152, State Capitol Frankfort, KY 40601 (502) 564-3490 (502) 564-5687 (fax)
Web Site Address	www.kysos.com
Incorporation Information and Fees	The fee for filing Articles of Incorporation is $40, plus organization tax based on number of authorized shares. The organization tax is as follows: $.01 per share up to 20,000 shares, $5 per share on the next 180,000 shares, $2 per share on the remaining shares, with a minimum tax fee of $10 for 1,000 shares or less.
LLC Organization Information and Fees	The fee for filing Articles of Organization is $40. A foreign LLC must file an Application for a Certificate of Authority accompanied by a filing fee of $90.
Corporate Name Reservation Information and Fees	Kentucky incorporators may reserve a corporate name by filing an Application for Reserved Name, Form SSC-105, with the Kentucky Secretary of State along with a $15 fee. The name reservation remains effective for 120 days. Informal searches are available online, and by calling (502) 564-2848.
LLC Name Reservation Information and Fees	Kentucky organizers may reserve an LLC name for 120 days. The filing fee is $15. Informal searches are available online, and by calling (502) 564-2848.
Where to Get Corporate & LLC Formation Forms	http://sos.ky.gov/forms.htm
Periodic Corporation Reporting Requirements	Kentucky corporations and qualified foreign corporations must file an annual report, due by June 30 of each year beginning with the calendar year following the date of the corporation's formation or qualification. The filing fee is $15. The annual report form is not available online, the Secretary of State's office mails the form to registered agents between January and March of each year.
Periodic LLC Reporting Requirements	LLCs must file an annual report, due by June 30 of each year beginning with the calendar year following the date of the LLCs initial filing. The filing fee is $15. The annual report form is not available online, however the Secretary of State's office mails the form to registered agents between January and March of each year.

Where to Get Corporate & LLC Tax Forms	www.revenue.ky.gov/business/corptax.htm
Corporate Tax Summary	Kentucky corporations and foreign corporations doing business in Kentucky are subject to an income tax, payable annually on Form 720. The tax rate is progressive, beginning at 4 percent and graduating to 8.25 percent.
"S" Corporation Information	Kentucky recognizes the federal S corporation provision. The subchapter S election is automatic and no state specific forms need be filed to make the subchapter S election.
LLC Tax Summary	Most LLCs must file a Kentucky Partnership Income Return (Form 765). The return is for informational purposes only. LLCs classed as corporations for federal tax purposes must file the Kentucky Corporations Income and License Tax Return (Form 720)
LLC Statute	Chapter 275 of the Kentucky Revised Statutes
LOUISIANA	
Contact Information for Business Formation Assistance	Commercial Division Louisiana Secretary of State PO. Box 94125 Baton Rouge, LA 70804 (225) 925-4704
Web Site Address	www.sec.state.la.us
Incorporation Information and Fees	The fee for filing Articles of Incorporation is $60. Corporations must also file a Domestic Corporation Initial Report, Form 341, concurrently with the articles. If a corporation does not name directors in its Domestic Corporation Initial Report, then the corporation must disclose its directors in a Corporation Supplemental Initial Report.
LLC Organization Information and Fees	The fee for filing Articles of Organization is $60. Foreign LLCs must file an Application for Authority to Transact Business in Louisiana and submit a filing fee of $100.
Corporate Name Reservation Information and Fees	Informal inquiries regarding corporate name availability may be made by phone (225) 925-4704, by fax (225) 925-4727, or by mail to P. O. Box 94125, Baton Rouge, LA. 70804. Louisiana incorporators may reserve a corporate name by filing Form 398. Reservations are effective for 60 days. Two 30-day extensions are available upon request. The fee for reservations is $25 each.

LLC Name Reservation Information and Fees	Informal inquiries regarding LLC name availability may be made by phone (225) 925-4704, by fax (225) 925-4727, or by mail to PO Box 941125, Baton Rouge, LA 70804. Louisiana organizers may reserve an LLC name by filing Form 398. Reservations are effective for sixty days. Two thirty-day extensions are available upon request. The fee for reservations is $25.
Where to Get Corporate & LLC Formation Forms	www.sec.state.la.us/comm/corp/corp-filings.htm
Periodic Corporation Reporting Requirements	Louisiana corporations and qualified foreign corporations must file annual reports before the anniversary date of incorporation or qualification in Louisiana. The Secretary of State mails the form to the corporation at least 60 days prior to the anniversary date. The Secretary of State does not provide blank forms. The filing fee is $25.
Periodic LLC Reporting Requirements	LLCs must file annual reports before the anniversary date of the LLCs initial filing in Louisiana. The Secretary of State mails the form to the corporation at least thirty days prior to the anniversary date. The Secretary of State does not provide blank forms. The filing fee is $10.
Where to Get Corporate & LLC Tax Forms	www.rev.state.la.us/sections/taxforms
Corporate Tax Summary	Louisiana corporations and foreign corporations doing business in Louisiana are subject to corporate franchise tax and corporate income tax. The franchise tax is calculated as follows: $1.50 for each $1,000 of capital employed in Louisiana up to $300,000, and $3 for each $1,000 of capital employed in Louisiana in excess of $300,000. The income tax rate is progressive, beginning at 4 percent and graduating to 8 percent.
"S" Corporation Information	Louisiana recognizes the federal S corporation provision. No state specific forms are required to effect the subchapter S election. Louisiana taxes "S" corporations in the same manner as regular corporations, with one exception. A corporation classified by the IRS as an "S" corporation may be entitled to an exclusion of part or all of its income for Louisiana income tax purposes, depending on the percentage of shares owned by Louisiana resident individuals. In general terms, the portion of income that can be excluded is determined by the ratio of outstanding shares owned by Louisiana resident individuals to total shares outstanding.

LLC Tax Summary	Most LLCs must file a Partnership Return of Income (Form IT-565). The return is required for informational purposes only. LLCs classified as corporations for federal tax purposes must file a Corporation Income and Franchise Tax Return (Form 620).
LLC Statute	Title 12 of the Louisiana Revised Statutes
MAINE	
Contact Information for Business Formation Assistance	Bureau of Corporations Maine State Department 101 State House Station Augusta, ME 04333 (207) 287-3676 (207) 287-5874 (fax)
Web Site Address	www.state.me.us/sos/
Incorporation Information and Fees	The fee for filing Articles of Incorporation is $145, plus a minimum fee of $30 based upon authorized shares of stock.
LLC Organization Information and Fees	The fee for filing Articles of Organization (on Form No. MLLC-6) is $175. A foreign LLC must file an Application for Authority to do Business (Form MLLC-12) and submit a filing fee of $250.
Corporate Name Reservation Information and Fees	Maine incorporators may reserve a corporate name by filing form MBCA1 with the Bureau of Corporations along with a $20 fee. The name reservation remains effective for 120 days.
LLC Name Reservation Information and Fees	Maine organizers may reserve a name by filing form MLCC-1 and submitting a filing fee of $25. The reservation is effective for 120 days.
Where to Get Corporate & LLC Formation Forms	www.state.me.us/sos/cec/corp/corp.html
Periodic Corporation Reporting Requirements	Maine corporations must file an annual report on form MBCA 13. The filing fee is $60. The form is not available online. The Maine State Department mails annual reports to corporations each year.
Periodic LLC Reporting Requirements	Domestic and qualified foreign LLCs must file an Annual Report by June 1. The filing fee is $60. Annual Report forms are not available online but may be ordered by contacting the Corporate Reporting and Information Section at (207) 624-7752.
Where to Get Corporate & LLC Tax Forms	www.state.me.us/revenue/forms/homepage.html

Corporate Tax Summary	Maine corporations and foreign corporations doing business in Maine are subject to an income tax.
"S" Corporation Information	Maine recognizes the federal S corporation provision. The subchapter S election is automatic and no state specific forms need be filed to make the subchapter S election. Maine S corporations must file an information return on Form 1120S-ME.
LLC Tax Summary	Most LLCs must file Maine's Partnership Return (1065ME). The return is required for informational purposes only. LLCs classified as corporations for federal tax purposes must file a Corporation Income Tax Return (1120ME).
LLC Statute	Title 31, Chapter 13 of the Maine Revised Statutes.
MARYLAND	
Contact Information for Business Formation Assistance	Maryland Secretary of State 301 West Preston Street Baltimore, MD 21201 (410) 974-5521 (888) 874-0013 (410) 974-5190 (fax)
Web Site Address	www.sos.state.md.us
Incorporation Information and Fees	The fee for filing Articles of Incorporation is $100 unless the aggregate par value of the stock exceeds $100,000 or, if no par value stock is used, the corporation has authority to issue more than 5,000 shares. If stock exceeds these amounts, call (410) 767-1340 for the fee.
LLC Organization Information and Fees	The fee for filing Articles of Organization is $100. Foreign LLCs wishing to conduct business in Maryland must file a Limited Liability Company Registration and submit a $100 filing fee with the Division.
Corporate Name Reservation Information and Fees	Maryland incorporators may reserve a corporate name by paying a $25 fee. The name reservation remains effective for 30 days.
LLC Name Reservation Information and Fees	Organizers may reserve a name by filing a written request and a payment of $25 with the Division.
Where to Get Corporate & LLC Formation Forms	www.dat.state.md.us/sdatweb/sdatforms.html

Periodic Corporation Reporting Requirements	Maryland corporations and qualified foreign corporations must file an annual Personal Property Report (Form 1) no later than April 15. The annual report fee recently increased to $300 per year.
Periodic LLC Reporting Requirements	Maryland LLCs and qualified foreign LLCs must file an annual Personal Property Report (Form 1) no later than April 15. The annual report fee recently increased to $300.
Where to Get Corporate & LLC Tax Forms	http://business.marylandtaxes.com/taxforms/default.asp
Corporate Tax Summary	Maryland corporations and foreign corporations with Maryland income must pay a corporate income tax. The tax rate is 7 percent.
"S" Corporation Information	Maryland recognizes the federal S corporation provision. The subchapter S election is automatic and no state specific forms need be filed to make the subchapter S election.
LLC Tax Summary	LLCs must file Maryland's Pass-Through Entity Income Tax Return (Form 510). Generally the return is made for informational purposes only, however LLCs are required to pay the personal income tax on behalf of non-residents at a rate of 4.8%.
LLC Statute	Title 4A of the Corporations and Associations Section of the Maryland Code.
MASSACHUSETTS	
Contact Information for Business Formation Assistance	Corporations Division Massachusetts Secretary of State One Ashburton Place, 17th Floor Boston, MA 02108 (617) 727-9640
Web Site Address	www.state.ma.us/sec/
Incorporation Information and Fees	The fee for filing Articles of Incorporation is a minimum of $275 for up to 275,000 authorized shares and $100 for each additional 100,000 shares.
LLC Organization Information and Fees	The fee for filing a Certificate of Organization is $500. A foreign LLC wishing to do business in Massachusetts must file an Application for Registration as a Foreign Limited Liability Company with the Division along with a filing fee of $500.

Corporate Name Reservation Information and Fees	Massachusetts incorporators may reserve a corporate name by paying a $15 fee.
LLC Name Reservation Information and Fees	An organizer may reserve an LLC name for a period of thirty days. The filing fee is $15.
Where to Get Corporate & LLC Formation Forms	www.state.ma.us/sec/cor/Functionality/DownloadForm.htm
Periodic Corporation Reporting Requirements	Massachusetts corporations must file a Massachusetts Corporation Annual Report. The annual report is due on or before the 15th day of the third month after the close of the corporation's fiscal year. The filing fee is $125.
Periodic LLC Reporting Requirements	An LLC must file an annual report each year with the Division on or before the anniversary date of the filing of the LLC's original Certificate of Organization or Application for Registration with the Division. The filing fee is $500.
Where to Get Corporate & LLC Tax Forms	www.dor.state.ma.us/Forms/FormsMenu2.htm
Corporate Tax Summary	Massachusetts corporations and foreign corporations with taxable operations in Massachusetts must pay a corporate excise tax. Corporations incorporated within the Commonwealth of Massachusetts file Form 355A. Corporations chartered in foreign states file Form 355B. The excise tax is calculated as follows: $2.60 per $1,000 of taxable Massachusetts tangible property, and 9.5 percent of income attributable to Massachusetts.
"S" Corporation Information	Massachusetts recognizes the federal S corporation provision. The subchapter S election is automatic and no state specific forms need be filed to make the subchapter S election.
LLC Tax Summary	Most LLCs must file Massachusetts' Partnership Return (Form 3). The return is for informational purposes only. LLCs that are classified as corporations for federal tax purposes must file the Corporate Excise Return (Forms 355).
LLC Statute	Title XXII, Chapter 156 of the General Laws of Massachusetts.

MICHIGAN	
Contact Information for Business Formation Assistance	Bureau of Commercial Services Corporations Division P.O. Box 30702 Lansing, MI 48909-8202 (517) 241-6470 (517) 334-8048 (Mich. fax filing service)
Web Site Address	www.michigan.gov/cis
Incorporation Information and Fees	The fee for filing Articles of Incorporation is $60, up to 20,000 authorized shares of stock.
LLC Organization Information and Fees	To organize, an LLC must file Articles of Organization and submit a $50 filing fee. Foreign LLCs must file an Application for Certificate of Authority to Transact Business in Michigan accompanied by a filing fee of $50.
Corporate Name Reservation Information and Fees	Michigan incorporators may reserve a corporate name by filing an Application for Reservation of Name on Form C&S-540 with the Corporations Division accompanied by a $10 fee.
LLC Name Reservation Information and Fees	Michigan organizers may reserve an LLC name by filing an Application for Reservation of name with the Division accompanied by the $25 filing fee. The reservation is effective for six months.
Where to Get Corporate & LLC Formation Forms	www.michigan.gov/cis/0,1607,7-154-35299_35413_36736---,00.html
Periodic Corporation Reporting Requirements	Michigan corporations must file a recently simplified annual report form. The annual report form is not available online. The Michigan Bureau of Commercial Services mails the form to corporations each year. The form carries a $15 charge.
Periodic LLC Reporting Requirements	All LLCs doing business in Michigan are required to file an Annual Statement each year by February 15. LLCs organized after September 30 need not file an Annual Statement until the second February 15th after their formation
Where to Get Corporate & LLC Tax Forms	www.michigan.gov/treasury
Corporate Tax Summary	Corporations engaged in a business activity in Michigan whose adjusted gross receipts are $250,000 or more in a tax year are required to file a Single Business Tax (SBT) return.
"S" Corporation Information	Michigan recognizes the federal S corporation provision. The subchapter S election is automatic and no state specific forms

	need be filed to make the subchapter S election. However, S corporations remain subject to the SBT.
LLC Tax Summary	Michigan does not levy a business income tax. However, it does collect a Single Business Tax on any business with adjusted gross receipts that exceed $250,000 in a tax year. LLCs are generally exempt from this tax. However, LLCs classified as corporations for federal tax purposes may be required to pay.
LLC Statute	Michigan Statutes Section 450.4101 through 450.5200.
MINNESOTA	
Contact Information for Business Formation Assistance	Minnesota Secretary of State 180 State Office Building St. Paul, MN 55155-1299 (651) 296-2803 (877) 551-6767
Web Site Address	www.sos.state.mn.us
Incorporation Information and Fees	The fee for filing Articles of Incorporation is $135. Foreign corporations must file a certificate of authority and pay a fee of $200.
LLC Organization Information and Fees	An LLC may organize by filing Articles of Organization along with a fee of $135. Foreign LLCs must file a Certificate of Authority for a Foreign Limited Liability Company and pay a filing fee of $185.
Corporate Name Reservation Information and Fees	Minnesota incorporators may reserve a corporate name by filing a Request for Reservation of Name with the Minnesota Secretary of State and paying a $35 filing fee. The name reservation remains effective for one year.
LLC Name Reservation Information and Fees	Minnesota organizers may reserve an LLC name by filing a Request for Reservation of Name with the Minnesota Secretary of State and paying a $35 filing fee. The name reservation remains effective for one year.
Where to Get Corporate & LLC Formation Forms	www.sos.state.mn.us/business/forms.html
Periodic Corporation Reporting Requirements	Minnesota corporations must file a Domestic Corporation Annual Registration by December 31 of each year. There is no filing fee. Foreign corporations must file a Foreign Corporation Annual Registration by December 31 of each year. The filing fee is $115. The Secretary of State now offers online filing through its web site.

Periodic LLC Reporting Requirements	Domestic and foreign LLCs must file an Annual Registration accompanied by a filing fee of $35 each year by December 31. The Secretary of State now offers online filing through its web site.
Where to Get Corporate & LLC Tax Forms	www.taxes.state.mn.us/taxes/current_forms.shtml
Corporate Tax Summary	Minnesota corporations are subject to an annual corporate franchise tax, and must file a Corporation Franchise Tax Return (Form M4).
"S" Corporation Information	Minnesota recognizes the federal S corporation provision. The subchapter S election is automatic and no state specific forms need be filed to make the subchapter S election.
LLC Tax Summary	Most LLCs must file a Minnesota Partnership Return (Form M3). LLCs filing the Partnership Return may be subject to a minimum fee of $100 through $5,000. LLCs classified as corporations for federal tax purposes must file a Corporation Franchise Tax Return (Form M4)
LLC Statute	Chapter 322B of the Minnesota Statutes.
MISSISSIPPI	
Contact Information for Business Formation Assistance	Mississippi Secretary of State P.O. Box 136 Jackson, MS 39205 (601) 359-1350 (601) 359-1499 (fax)
Web Site Address	www.sos.state.ms.us
Incorporation Information and Fees	The fee for filing Articles of Incorporation is $50.
LLC Organization Information and Fees	Domestic LLCs must file a Certificate of Formation with Business Services and pay a filing fee of $50. A foreign LLC must file an Application for Registration of Foreign Limited Liability Company along with a filing fee of $250 with Business Services.
Corporate Name Reservation Information and Fees	Mississippi incorporators may reserve a corporation name by filing a Reservation of Name on Form F0016 with the Mississippi Secretary of State. The filing fee is $25. The name reservation remains effective for 180 days.

LLC Name Reservation Information and Fees	Mississippi organizers may reserve an LLC name by filing a Reservation of Name on Form F0016 with the Mississippi Secretary of State. The filing fee is $25 and the name reservation remains effective for 180 days.
Where to Get Corporate & LLC Formation Forms	www.sos.state.ms.us/forms/forms.asp?Unit=Corporations
Periodic Corporation Reporting Requirements	Mississippi corporations and qualified foreign corporations must file a Corporate Annual Report. The report is due April 1. The filing fee is $25.
Periodic LLC Reporting Requirements	LLCs are not required to file annual reports.
Where to Get Corporate & LLC Tax Forms	www.mstc.state.ms.us/downloadforms/main.htm
Corporate Tax Summary	Mississippi corporations and foreign corporations doing business in Mississippi must pay an income tax and a franchise tax. The minimum franchise tax is $25.
"S" Corporation Information	Mississippi does not recognize the federal S corporation provision.
LLC Tax Summary	LLCs must file a Mississippi Partnership/Limited Liability Company/Limited Liability Partnership income tax return (Form 86-105) each year by April 15. However, Mississippi LLCs do not pay tax on its income unless classified as a corporation for federal tax purposes.
LLC Statute	Title 79, Chapter 29 of the Mississippi Code
MISSOURI	
Contact Information for Business Formation Assistance	Missouri Corporations Division James C. Kirkpatrick State Information Center P.O. Box 778 Jefferson City, MO 65102-0778 (573) 751-4153
Web Site Address	www.sos.mo.gov
Incorporation Information and Fees	The minimum fee for filing Articles of Incorporation is $58 and graduates upward based upon the corporation's authorized capital, plus a fee for issuing the Certificate of Incorporation ($3), and a technology fund fee ($5).
LLC Organization Information and Fees	To organize, an LLC must file Articles of Organization and submit a filing fee of $105. Foreign LLCs must file an Application for Registration as a Foreign Limited Liability Company.

Corporate Name Reservation Information and Fees	Missouri incorporators may reserve a corporate name by filing an Application for Reservation of Name with the Missouri Corporations Division. The filing fee is $25. The name reservation remains effective for 60 days.
LLC Name Reservation Information and Fees	Missouri organizers may reserve an LLC name by filing an Application for Reservation of Name with the Division. The filing fee is $25. The name reservation remains effective for 60 days.
Where to Get Corporate & LLC Formation Forms	www.sos.mo.gov/business/corporations/forms.asp
Periodic Corporation Reporting Requirements	Missouri corporations and qualified foreign corporations must file an annual registration report. Annual reports are due by the 15th day of the fourth month of the corporation's fiscal year. The Secretary of State's office mails the form to the corporation's registered agent. The form is not available online.
Periodic LLC Reporting Requirements	Missouri LLCs are not required to file periodic reports.
Where to Get Corporate & LLC Tax Forms	www.dor.mo.gov/tax/forms/
Corporate Tax Summary	Missouri corporations and foreign corporations doing business in Missouri pay both a franchise and income tax.
"S" Corporation Information	Missouri recognizes the federal S corporation provision. The subchapter S election is automatic and no state specific forms need be filed to make the subchapter S election. Missouri S corporations must file Form MO-1120S.
LLC Tax Summary	Most LLCs must file a Partnership Return of Income (Form MO-1065). This return is informational only. LLCs classified as corporations for federal tax purposes must file a corporation income tax return (Form MO-1120)
LLC Statute	Title XXII, Chapter 347 of the Missouri Revised Statutes
MONTANA	
Contact Information for Business Formation Assistance	Montana Office of the Secretary of State Business Service Bureau Room 260, Capitol P.O. Box 202801 Helena, MT 59620-2801 (406) 444-2034 (406) 444-3976 (fax)
Web Site Address	www.sos.state.mt.us

Incorporation Information and Fees	The minimum fee for filing Articles of Incorporation is $70, which includes a filing fee of $20 and a license fee of $50 for up to 50,000 authorized shares.
LLC Organization Information and Fees	To organize, domestic LLCs must file Articles of Organization for Domestic Limited Liability Company. The filing fee for doing so is $70. Foreign LLCs wishing to conduct business in Montana must file an Application for Certificate of Authority of Foreign Limited Liability Company with a filing fee of $70.
Corporate Name Reservation Information and Fees	Montana incorporators may reserve a corporate name by filing an Application for Reservation of Name with the Business Services Bureau accompanied by a $10 filing fee. The name reservation remains effective for 120 days.
LLC Name Reservation Information and Fees	Montana organizers may reserve an LLC name by filing an Application for Reservation of Name with Business Services accompanied by a $10 filing fee. The name reservation remains effective for 120 days.
Where to Get Corporate & LLC Formation Forms	www.sos.state.mt.us/BSB/Business_Forms.asp
Periodic Corporation Reporting Requirements	Montana corporations and qualified foreign corporations must file an Annual Corporation Report accompanied by a $10 fee.
Periodic LLC Reporting Requirements	Montana LLCs must file an Annual Report accompanied by a $10 fee by April 15.
Where to Get Corporate & LLC Tax Forms	mt.gov/revenue/formsandresources/forms.asp
Corporate Tax Summary	Montana corporations and foreign corporations doing business in Montana must pay a corporation license tax, which is based upon corporate income attributable to Montana.
"S" Corporation Information	Montana recognizes the federal S corporation provision. The subchapter S election is automatic and no state specific forms need be filed to make the subchapter S election.
LLC Tax Summary	Most LLCs must file a Partnership Return of Income (Form PR-1). The Partnership Return is informational only. LLCs classified as corporations for federal tax purposes must file a Corporation License Tax Return (Form CLT-4).
LLC Statute	Title 35, Chapter 8 of the Missouri Code Annotated.

NEBRASKA	
Contact Information for Business Formation Assistance	Nebraska Corporate Division Room 1301 State Capitol P.O. Box 94608 Lincoln, NE 68509-4608 (402) 471-4079 (402) 471-3666 (fax)
Web Site Address	www.sos.state.ne.us/business/corp_serv
Incorporation Information and Fees	The minimum fee for filing Articles of Incorporation is $60, which includes up to $10,000 in authorized capital. Authorized capital is the total authorized shares multiplied by the shares' par value.
LLC Organization Information and Fees	Domestic LLCs may organize by filing Articles of Organization and submitting a filing fee of $100. A fee of $10 must also be submitted for the Certificate of Organization. A foreign LLC wishing to conduct business in Nebraska must file an Application for Certificate of Authority and submit a filing fee of $120.
Corporate Name Reservation Information and Fees	Nebraska incorporators may reserve a corporate name by filing an Application for Reservation of Corporate Name with the Nebraska Corporate Division accompanied by a filing fee of $30. The name reservation remains effective for 120 days.
LLC Name Reservation Information and Fees	Nebraska organizers may reserve an LLC name by filing an Application for Reservation of LLC name with the Division accompanied by a filing fee of $15. The name reservation remains effective for 120 days.
Where to Get Corporate & LLC Formation Forms	www.sos.state.ne.us/business/corp_serv/corp_form.html
Periodic Corporation Reporting Requirements	Nebraska corporations and qualified foreign corporations must file an annual corporation occupation tax report. The fee is based upon the paid up capital stock (for domestic corporations) and the real estate and personal property in use in Nebraska (for foreign corporations).
Periodic LLC Reporting Requirements	LLCs are not required to file annual reports.
Where to Get Corporate & LLC Tax Forms	www.revenue.state.ne.us/businc.htm
Corporate Tax Summary	Nebraska corporations and foreign corporations doing business in Nebraska are subject to an income tax.

"S" Corporation Information	Nebraska recognizes the federal S corporation provision. The subchapter S election is automatic and no state specific forms need be filed to make the subchapter S election.
LLC Tax Summary	LLCs must file a Nebraska Partnership Return of Income each year by the fifteenth day of the fourth month of the fiscal year. An LLC that's members are all Nebraska individual residents and with income solely derived from Nebraska is not required filing the Partnership Return.
LLC Statute	Section 21-2601 through 21-2653 of the Nebraska Statutes.
NEVADA	
Contact Information for Business Formation Assistance	Nevada Secretary of State, Annex Office 202 North Carson Street Carson City, NV 89701-4786 (775) 684-5708
Web Site Address	sos.state.nv.us
Incorporation Information and Fees	The fee for filing Articles of Incorporation is $75, but graduates upward based on the authorized capital. Authorized capital is the total authorized shares multiplied by the shares' par value. A Nevada corporation must name all its initial directors in its Articles of Incorporation. The Articles of Incorporation must include a declaration of the corporation's Resident Agent accepting his or her designation. Corporations must file an Initial List of Officers and Directors form by the 1st day of the 2nd month following the incorporation date. The filing fee for the Initial List is $125.
LLC Organization Information and Fees	To organize, domestic LLCs must file Articles of Organization and submit a filing fee of $75. Foreign LLCs wishing to do business in Nevada must file an Application for Registration of Foreign Limited Liability Company to the Division accompanied by the $75 filing fee. Domestic and foreign LLCs must also file an Initial List of Managers or Members and Resident Agent by the first day of the second month after initially filing with the Division (for example, if the LLC originally filed on January 18, it would be required to file the Initial List on or before March 1). The filing fee for the Initial List is $125.
Corporate Name Reservation Information and Fees	Nevada incorporators may reserve a corporate name by paying a $40 fee. The name reservation can be effected through the Secretary of State's web site and remains effective for 90 days.

LLC Name Reservation Information and Fees	Nevada organizers may reserve an LLC name by paying a $40 fee. Application can be made through the Division's web site. The name reservation remains effective for 90 days.
Where to Get Corporate & LLC Formation Forms	sos.state.nv.us/comm_rec/crforms/crforms.htm
Periodic Corporation Reporting Requirements	Nevada corporations must file an Initial List of Officers and Directors form by the 1stday of the 2nd month following the incorporation date; the filing fee is $125. Each year thereafter, Nevada corporations must file an Annual List of Officers and Directors form; the filing fee is $125, but graduates upward based on the authorized capital.
Periodic LLC Reporting Requirements	Domestic and foreign LLCs must also file an Initial List of Managers or Members and Resident Agent by the first day of the second month after initially filing with the Division (for example, if the LLC originally filed on January 18, it would be required to file the Initial List on or before March 1). The filing fee for the Initial List is $125. Thereafter, Nevada LLCs must file an Annual List of Managers or Members and Registered Agent; the filing fee is $125.
Corporate Tax Summary	Nevada has one of the least burdensome tax structures in the United States. Nevada has no corporate income tax, and no corporate franchise tax.
"S" Corporation Information	Because Nevada does not impose a corporate income tax, S corporation status is not relevant to Nevada taxation.
LLC Tax Summary	Nevada does not levy a corporate, partnership or LLC income tax.
LLC Statute	Chapter 86 of the Nevada Revised Statutes
NEW HAMPSHIRE	
Contact Information for Business Formation Assistance	State Corporation Division State House 107 North Main Street Concord, NH 03301 (603) 271-3244
Web Site Address	state.nh.us/sos/

Incorporation Information and Fees	The fee for filing Articles of Incorporation is $85. Note that Articles of Incorporation must accompany Form 11-A, entitled Addendum to Articles of Incorporation. Form 11-A requires the incorporator(s) to vouch for the corporation's registration or exemption from the state's securities laws.
LLC Organization Information and Fees	To organize, an LLC must file a Certificate of Formation (Form No. LLC1) and submit a filing fee of $35. A foreign LLC must file an Application for Registration as a foreign LLC and submit a filing fee of $200.
Corporate Name Reservation Information and Fees	The Corporation Division provides informal information on corporate name availability at (603) 271-3246. New Hampshire incorporators may reserve a corporate name by filing an Application for Reservation of Name accompanied by a $15 filing fee. The name reservation remains effective for 120 days.
LLC Name Reservation Information and Fees	LLCs may reserve a name by filing an Application for Reservation of Name and submitting a filing fee of $15. The name reservation remains effective for 120 days.
Where to Get Corporate & LLC Formation Forms	www.sos.nh.gov/corporate/Forms.html
Periodic Corporation Reporting Requirements	New Hampshire corporations and qualified foreign corporations must file an annual report form. The form is not available online. The State Corporation Division mails the form in January of each year. The form is due April 1 of each year. The filing fee is $100.
Periodic LLC Reporting Requirements	Domestic and foreign LLCs doing business in New Hampshire must file an Annual Report with the Division each year by April 1. The Division issues pre-printed forms by mail to all registered LLCs in January. The filing fee is $100.
Where to Get Corporate & LLC Tax Forms	www.state.nh.us/revenue/forms/
Corporate Tax Summary	New Hampshire corporations and foreign corporations doing business in New Hampshire must pay an income tax called a business profits tax. The tax rate is 8 percent. However, organizations with $50,000 or less of gross receipts from all their activities in New Hampshire are not required to file a return. In addition, corporations are subject to a business enterprise tax. The business enterprise tax is a 0.50 percent tax is assessed on the enterprise value tax base, which is the sum of all compensation paid or accrued, interest paid or accrued, and dividends paid by the business enterprise, after special adjustments and apportionment.

"S" Corporation Information	New Hampshire does not recognize the federal S corporation provision.
LLC Tax Summary	LLCs with more than $50,000 in annual gross receipts from business activity within New Hampshire must file a Business Profits Tax return. The Business Profits Tax rate is 8.5%. LLCs with more than $150,000 in annual gross receipts from business activity within New Hampshire must file a Business Enterprise Tax return. The Business Enterprise Tax rate is .75% of the enterprise's value.
LLC Statute	Title XXVIII, Chapter 304-C of the New Hampshire Revised Statutes
NEW JERSEY	
Contact Information for Business Formation Assistance	New Jersey Division of Revenue Business Services P.O. Box 308 Trenton, NJ 08625 (609) 292-9292 (609) 984-6851 (fax)
Web Site Address	www.state.nj.us/treasury/revenue/dcr/dcrpg1.html
Incorporation Information and Fees	The fee for filing Articles of Incorporation is $125.
LLC Organization Information and Fees	To organize, an LLC must file a Certificate of Formation and submit a filing fee of $125. Foreign LLCs must file a Certificate of Registration for a Foreign LLC along with a filing fee of $125.
Corporate Name Reservation Information and Fees	New Jersey incorporators may reserve a corporate name by filling out a Business Entity Name Availability Check & Reservation at the Business Services web site at https://www.state.nj.us/treasury/revenue/checkbusiness. The fee is $50. The name reservation remains effective for 120 days.
LLC Name Reservation Information and Fees	New Jersey incorporators may reserve a LLC name by filing an Application for Reservation of Name. The fee is $50 and the reservation remains effective for 120 days.
Where to Get Corporate & LLC Formation Forms	www.state.nj.us/treasury/revenue/dcr/geninfo/corpman.html
Periodic Corporation Reporting Requirements	New Jersey corporations and qualified foreign corporations must file an annual report accompanied by a $50 fee.
Periodic LLC Reporting Requirements	An LLC must file an annual report each year. The filing fee is $50.

Where to Get Corporate & LLC Forms	www.state.nj.us/treasury/taxation/forms.htm
Corporate Tax Summary	New Jersey corporations and foreign corporations doing business in New Jersey must pay a Corporate Business Tax (CBT). The CBT rate is 9 percent on the adjusted net income attributable to new Jersey operations.
"S" Corporation Information	New Jersey requires state specific forms to recognize the federal S corporation provision, specifically, New Jersey S Corporation Election Form CBT- 2553. Further information on New Jersey S corporations is available at www.state.nj.us/treasury/taxation/ot5.htm.
LLC Tax Summary	Most LLCs must file a Partnership Return of Income (Form NJ-1065). The return is for informational purposes only. LLCs classified as corporations for federal tax purposes must file a Corporation Business Tax Return (CBT-100).
LLC Statute	Section 42:2B-1 through 42:2B-70 of the New Jersey Permanent Statutes.
NEW MEXICO	
Contact Information for Business Formation Assistance	Corporations Division 1120 Paseo De Peralta P.O. Box 1269 Santa Fe, New Mexico 87504 (505) 827-4508 (800) 947-4722
Web Site Address	www.nmprc.state.nm.us
Incorporation Information and Fees	The minimum filing fee for filing Articles of Incorporation is $100, and the maximum filing fee is $1,000, the filing fee increases by $1 for each 1,000 authorized shares of stock.
LLC Organization Information and Fees	Organizers wishing to register with the Bureau must file Articles of Organization and submit a filing fee of $50. Foreign LLCs wishing to do business in New Mexico must file an Application for Registration along with a filing fee of $100.
Corporate Name Reservation Information and Fees	New Mexico incorporators may reserve a corporate name by filing a Reservation of Corporate Name form with the Corporations Division. The form is not available online, but is available by calling (505) 827-4504 or 4509. The filing fee is $25. The name reservation remains effective for 120 days.

LLC Name Reservation Information and Fees	Request for name reservation may be made in writing to the Public Registration commission. The filing fee is $20.
Where to Get Corporate & LLC Formation Forms	www.nmprc.state.nm.us/cf.htm
Periodic Corporation Reporting Requirements	New Mexico corporations and qualified foreign corporations must file a First Report within 30 days from the date of incorporation or qualification in New Mexico. The filing fee is $25. Thereafter, New Mexico corporations and qualified foreign corporations must file a biennial report on or before the 15th day of the third month following the end of the corporation's fiscal year.
Periodic LLC Reporting Requirements	LLCs are not required to file annual reports.
Where to Get Corporate & LLC Tax Forms	www.state.nm.us/tax/trd_form.htm
Corporate Tax Summary	New Mexico corporations and foreign corporations doing business in New Mexico are subject to a corporate franchise tax and a corporate income tax. The corporate franchise tax is $50 per year. The income tax rate is progressive and ranges from 4.8 percent of net income to 7.6 percent of net income.
"S" Corporation Information	New Mexico recognizes the federal S corporation provision. The subchapter S election is automatic and no state specific forms need be filed to make the subchapter S election. S corporations remain subject to the corporate franchise tax.
LLC Tax Summary	New Mexico LLCs must file a New Mexico Income and Information Return for Pass Through Entities (Form PTE). LLCs that file a federal corporate income tax return are required to pay the New Mexico franchise tax ($50 per year).
LLC Statute	Section 53-19-1 through 53-19-74 of the New Mexico Statutes Annotated
NEW YORK	
Contact Information for Business Formation Assistance	New York Department of State Division of Corporations 41 State Street Albany, NY 12231-0001 (518) 474-2492 (518) 474-1418
Web Site Address	www.dos.state.ny.us/corp/corpwww.html

Incorporation Information and Fees	The fee for filing a Certificate of Incorporation is $125, plus the applicable tax on shares pursuant to Section 180 of New York's tax law. Contact the Division of Corporations for more information.
LLC Organization Information and Fees	To register with the Division a domestic LLC must file Articles of Organization and a filing fee of $200. Foreign LLCs wishing to conduct business in New York must file an Application for Authority and submit a filing fee of $250.
Corporate Name Reservation Information and Fees	New York incorporators may reserve a corporate name by filing an Application for Reservation of Name Form with the Division of Corporations accompanied by a filing fee of $20. The name reservation remains effective for 60 days.
LLC Name Reservation Information and Fees	New York organizers may reserve an LLC name by filing an Application for Reservation of Name Form with the Division of Corporations accompanied by a filing fee of $20. The name reservation remains effective for 60 days.
Where to Get Corporate & LLC Formation Forms	www.dos.state.ny.us/corp/filing.html
Periodic Corporation Reporting Requirements	New York corporations and qualified foreign corporations must fine a Biennial Statement accompanied by a $9 filing fee. The statement is due in the calendar month in which the corporation filed its original Certificate of Incorporation.
Periodic LLC Reporting Requirements	LLCs must file a Biennial Statement with the Division every two years. Shortly before the due date, the Division will mail a Statement form to the LLC. The filing fee is $9.
Where to Get Corporate & LLC Tax Forms	www.tax.state.ny.us/forms/default.htm
Corporate Tax Summary	New York corporations and foreign corporations doing business in New York must pay an annual Maintenance Fee Tax, a corporate franchise tax, and an income tax. Foreign corporations are also subject to a New York State license fee, and domestic corporations are also subject to an organization tax. New York taxation is onerous and complex, and is beyond the scope of this volume. Contact the New York Department of Taxation and Finance for more information.
"S" Corporation Information	New York requires corporations to file Form CT-6 to elect S Corporation status.
LLC Tax Summary	LLCs are usually considered partnerships for New York tax purposes and must pay the Department of Revenue's annual filing fee ($325 - $10,000 depending on the number of LLC

	members). An LLC that is treated as a partnership for federal income tax purposes will be treated as a partnership for NY personal income and corporate franchise tax purposes.
LLC Statute	Chapter 34 of the Consolidated Laws of New York
NORTH CAROLINA	
Contact Information for Business Formation Assistance	Corporations Division North Carolina Secretary of State P.O. Box 29622 Raleigh, NC 27626-0622 (919) 807-2225 (888) 246 7636 (call back line)
Web Site Address	www.secstate.state.nc.us
Incorporation Information and Fees	The fee for filing Articles of Incorporation is $125.
LLC Organization Information and Fees	Domestic LLCs may register with the Division by filing Articles of Organization and submitting a filing fee of $125. A foreign LLC wishing to conduct business in North Carolina must file an Application for Certificate of Authority and submit a filing fee of $125.
Corporate Name Reservation Information and Fees	North Carolina incorporators may reserve a corporate name by filing an Application to Reserve a Corporate Name accompanied by a filing fee of $10. The name reservation remains effective for 120 days.
LLC Name Reservation Information and Fees	North Carolina organizers may reserve an LLC name by filing an Application to Reserve an LLC name accompanied by a filing fee of $10. The name reservation remains effective for 120 days.
Where to Get Corporate & LLC Formation Forms	www.secretary.state.nc.us/corporations/indxfees.asp
Periodic Corporation Reporting Requirements	North Carolina corporations and qualified foreign corporations must file an annual report with the Secretary of State.
Periodic LLC Reporting Requirements	Domestic and foreign LLCs must file an annual report by the fifteenth day of the fourth month after the close of the fiscal year. The filing fee is $200.
Where to Get Corporate Tax Forms	www.dor.state.nc.us/downloads/corporate.html
Corporate Tax Summary	North Carolina corporations and foreign corporations doing business in North Carolina must pay a franchise tax and an income tax. The franchise tax rate is $1.50 of each $1,000 of the "capital stock, surplus, and undivided profits base"—essentially

	a tax on corporate property. The minimum franchise tax is $35. The income tax rate is 6.9 percent.
"S" Corporation Information	North Carolina recognizes the federal S corporation provision. The subchapter S election is automatic and no state specific forms need be filed to make the subchapter S election.
LLC Tax Summary	LLCs are not subject to North Carolina's corporate income or franchises taxes.
LLC Statute	Chapter 57C of the North Carolina General Statutes
NORTH DAKOTA	
Contact Information for Business Formation Assistance	North Dakota Secretary of State 600 East Boulevard Bismark, ND 58505-0500 (701) 328-4284 (800) 352-0867, ext. 8-3365 (701) 328-2992 (fax)
Web Site Address	www.state.nd.us/sec
Incorporation Information and Fees	The minimum fee for filing Articles of Incorporation is $90. This includes a $30 filing fee, $10 consent of agent fee, and a $50 minimum license fee. The license fee is based upon the number of authorized shares. Incorporators must include with their filing a Registered Agent Consent to Serve form.
LLC Organization Information and Fees	Domestic LLCs may organize by filing Articles of Organization and submitting a filing fee of $135. A foreign LLC wishing to conduct business in North Dakota must file a Certification of Authority Application and submit a filing fee of $135.
Corporate Name Reservation Information and Fees	North Dakota incorporators may reserve a corporate name by filing a Reserve Name Application on Form SFN13015 with the North Dakota Secretary of State accompanied by a filing fee of $10. The name reservation remains effective for twelve months.
LLC Name Reservation Information and Fees	North Dakota organizers may reserve an LLC name by filing a Reserve Name Application on Form SFN13015 with the North Dakota Secretary of State accompanied by a filing fee of $10. The name reservation remains effective for twelve months.
Where to Get Corporate & LLC Formation Forms	www.state.nd.us/sec/Business/forms/ businessinforegformsmnu.htm

Periodic Corporation Reporting Requirements	North Dakota corporations and qualified foreign corporations must file an annual report each year following the year in which they were incorporated or qualified. Annual report forms are not available on the Secretary of State's web site. The report is due on August 1. The filing fee is $25.
Periodic LLC Reporting Requirements	LLCs that engage in business or provide professional services must file an annual report by November 15. LLCs engaged in farming or ranching must file by April 15. The filing fee for both is $50.
Where to Get LLC & Corporate Tax Forms	www.state.nd.us/taxdpt/genforms/
Corporate Tax Summary	North Dakota corporations and foreign corporations doing business in North Dakota must pay an annual corporate income tax, and a license fee based upon the corporation's authorized shares.
"S" Corporation Information	North Dakota recognizes the federal S corporation provision The subchapter S election is automatic and no state specific forms need be filed to make the subchapter S election.
LLC Tax Summary	LLCs typically must file a North Dakota Return of Income (Form 1065) and will benefit from pass-through taxation. LLCs classified as corporations for federal tax purposes will be required to file a Corporation Income Tax Return (Form 40).
LLC Statute	North Dakota Century Code, Chapter 10-32
OHIO	
Contact Information for Business Formation Assistance	Ohio Secretary of State Business Services Division P.O. Box 670 Columbus, Ohio 43216 (614) 466.3910 (877) 767-3453 (614) 466.3899 (fax)
Web Site Address	www.state.oh.us/sos/
Incorporation Information and Fees	The fee for filing Articles of Incorporation is $85 for corporations authorizing up to 850 shares. For corporations authorizing more than 850 shares, the following fee table applies: For 851 to 1,000 authorized shares, the filing fee is 10 cents per share. From 1,001 to 10,000 authorized shares, the filing fee is 5 cents

	per share. From 10,001 to 50,000 authorized shares, the filing fee is 2 cents per share. From 50,001 to 100,000 authorized shares, the filing fee is 1 cent per share. From 100,001 to 500,000 authorized shares, the filing fee is 1/2 cent per share. For all authorized shares in excess of 500,000 shares, the filing fee is 1/4 cent per share.
LLC Organization Information and Fees	Domestic and foreign LLCs may register with Business Services by filing an Organization/Registration of Limited Liability Company. The filing fee is $125.
Corporate Name Reservation Information and Fees	Ohio offers informal name availability information by telephone by phone at (614) 466-3910 or (877) 767-3453, and by email at busserv@sos.state.oh.us. Ohio incorporators may reserve a corporate name by sending a written request (no form is available) to the Secretary of State accompanied by a $5 fee. The name reservation remains effective for 60 days.
LLC Name Reservation Information and Fees	Ohio offers informal name availability information by telephone by phone at (614) 466-3910 or (877) 767-3453, and by email at busserv@sos.state.oh.us. Ohio organizers may reserve a LLC name by filing Form 534 with Business Services. The name reservation remains effective for 180 days.
Where to Get Corporate & LLC Formation Forms	www.sos.state.oh.us/SOSApps/SOS/FormRefbs.aspx
Periodic Corporation Reporting Requirements	Ohio corporations and qualified foreign corporations must file an annual report. The annual report form is not available on the Secretary of State's web site. Contact the Secretary of State's office to obtain an annual report form.
Periodic LLC Reporting Requirements	LLCs are not required to file annual reports.
Where to Get Corporate & LLC Tax Forms	http://dw.ohio.gov/tax/dynamicforms/
Corporate Tax Summary	Ohio corporations and foreign corporations doing business in Ohio must pay an annual corporate franchise tax. The franchise tax is based upon the corporation's income attributable to Ohio operations and the net worth of the corporation. The minimum tax is $50.
"S" Corporation Information	Ohio recognizes the federal S corporation provision. Ohio corporations and qualified foreign corporations must file a Notice of S Corporation Status on Form FT-1120-S.
LLC Tax Summary	LLCs are not subject to the Ohio Corporate Franchise Tax Report.
LLC Statute	Title XVII, Chapter 1705 of the Ohio Revised Code

OKLAHOMA	
Contact Information for Business Formation Assistance	Oklahoma Secretary of State Business Filing Department 2300 N. Lincoln Blvd., Room 101 Oklahoma City OK 73105-4897 (405) 522-4560 (405) 521-3771 (fax)
Web Site Address	www.sos.state.ok.us
Incorporation Information and Fees	The minimum fee for filing Articles of Incorporation is $50. Oklahoma bases its filing fee on the corporation's authorized capital. Authorized capital is the total authorized shares multiplied by the shares' par value. The filing fee is $1 per $1,000 of authorized capital.
LLC Organization Information and Fees	To organize, LLCs must file Articles of Organization along with a filing fee of $100. Foreign LLCs must file an Application for Registration of Foreign Limited Liability Company and submit a filing fee of $300.
Corporate Name Reservation Information and Fees	Oklahoma incorporators may reserve a corporate name by either submitting an Application for Reservation of Name form to the Oklahoma Secretary of State or by telephone. The filing fee is $10. The name reservation remains effective for 60 days.
LLC Name Reservation Information and Fees	Oklahoma organizers may reserve an LLC name by either submitting an Application for Reservation of Name form to the Oklahoma Secretary of State or by telephone. The filing fee is $10. The name reservation remains effective for 60 days.
Where to Get Corporate & LLC Formation Forms	www.sos.state.ok.us/forms/FORMS.HTM
Periodic Corporation Reporting Requirements	Foreign corporations must file an annual certificate on or before the anniversary date of its qualification in Oklahoma. The Secretary of State mails the forms to the corporation's last known address.
Periodic LLC Reporting Requirements	LLCs must file an annual report each year by July 1. The Department will automatically mail forms to registered LLCs in May. The filing fee is $25.
Where to Get Corporate & LLC Tax Forms	www.oktax.state.ok.us/btforms.html
Corporate Tax Summary	Oklahoma levies an annual franchise tax on all corporations that do business in the state. Corporations are taxed $1.25 for each $1,000 of capital invested or used in Oklahoma. Foreign

	corporations are additionally assessed $100 per year, payable to the Oklahoma Tax Commission, for the Secretary of State acting as their registered agent. The franchise tax return, unless an election is made to file in conjunction with the filing of the Oklahoma income tax, is due July 1. Corporations are also subject to an income tax. The tax rate is 6 percent.
"S" Corporation Information	Oklahoma recognizes the S corporation provision. The subchapter S election is automatic and no state specific forms need be filed to make the subchapter S election.
LLC Tax Summary	LLCs are not required to file a return for the Oklahoma Franchise Tax.
LLC Statute	Section 18-2001 through 18-2060 of the Oklahoma Statutes
OREGON	
Contact Information for Business Formation Assistance	Oregon Office of the Secretary of State Corporation Division Public Service Building Suite 151 255 Capitol Street NE Salem OR 97310 phone (503) 986-2200
Web Site Address	www.sos.state.or.us
Incorporation Information and Fees	The fee for filing Articles of Incorporation is $50.
LLC Organization Information and Fees	To organize, domestic LLCs must file Articles of Organization and submit a filing fee of $20. Foreign LLCs must submit an Application for Authority to transact business along with a filing fee of $20.
Corporate Name Reservation Information and Fees	Oregon corporations may pay a $10 fee to reserve a name for 120 days.
LLC Name Reservation Information and Fees	Oregon organizers may pay a $10 fee to reserve a name for 120 days.
Where to Get Corporate & LLC Formation Forms	www.sos.state.or.us/corporation/forms
Periodic Corporation Reporting Requirements	Oregon corporations and qualified foreign corporations must file an annual report by a corporation's anniversary date. The Corporation Division mails annual report forms to corporations approximately 45 days prior to the due date. Corporations must pay a renewal fee. Oregon corporations pay $30 and Foreign corporations pay $220.

Periodic LLC Reporting Requirements	Annual Reports along with a filing fee of $20 are due by an LLC's anniversary date. An Annual Report form is mailed to the LLC by the Division approximately 45 days prior to the due date. The Annual Report is only filed the first year after organizing. LLCs must only file a renewal coupon with the Division in subsequent years. The Division mails the renewal coupon form approximately 45 days prior to the due date. The filing fee is $20.
Where to Get Corporate & LLC Tax Forms	www.oregon.gov/DOR/forms.shtml
Corporate Tax Summary	Oregon corporations and foreign corporations doing business in Oregon must pay an annual corporate income tax. The income tax rate is 6.6 percent.
"S" Corporation Information	Oregon recognizes the S corporation provision. The subchapter S election is automatic and no state specific forms need be filed to make the subchapter S election.
LLC Tax Summary	Most LLCs will be required to file a Partnership Return (Form 65). The return is generally for informational purposes only and no tax will be due. LLCs classified as corporations for federal tax purposes must file an Oregon Corporation Excise Tax Return (Form 20).
LLC Statute	Chapter 63 of the Oregon Revised Statutes
PENNSYLVANIA	
Contact Information for Business Formation Assistance	Department of State Corporation Bureau Commonwealth Avenue & North Street 206 North Office Building Harrisburg, PA 17120 (717) 787-1057
Web Site Address	www.dos.state.pa.us
Incorporation Information and Fees	The fee for filing Articles of Incorporation is $125. Foreign qualification is $250. Incorporators must also file a "docketing statement" along with the articles; the form is available at the Secretary of State's web site.
LLC Organization Information and Fees	To organize, an LLC must file a Certificate of Organization and submit a filing fee of $125. Organizers must also file a "docketing statement" along with the certificate; the form is available

	at the Secretary of State's web site. A foreign LLC must file an Application for Registration and submit a filing fee of $250.
Corporate Name Reservation Information and Fees	Pennsylvania incorporators may reserve a corporate name by submitting a written or faxed request to the Corporation Bureau. The fee is $52. The name reservation remains effective for 120 days.
LLC Name Reservation Information and Fees	Pennsylvania organizers may reserve an LLC name by submitting a written or faxed request to the Corporation Bureau. The fee is $52. The name reservation remains effective for 120 days.
Where to Get Corporate & LLC Formation Forms	www.dos.state.pa.us/corps/site/default.asp
Periodic Corporation Reporting Requirements	Pennsylvania corporations and qualified foreign corporations are not required to file annual reports. However, they are required to notify the Corporation Bureau upon a change in the name or address of the registered agent by filing a Statement of Change of Registered Agent.
Periodic LLC Reporting Requirements	Pennsylvania and foreign LLCs doing business in the state are not required to file annual reports, however, they are required to notify the Bureau upon a change in the name or address of the registered agent by filing a Statement of Change of Registered Agent.
Where to Get Corporate & LLC Tax Forms	www.revenue.state.pa.us/revenue/cwp/view.asp?a=190&q=209828
Corporate Tax Summary	Pennsylvania corporations and foreign corporations doing business in Pennsylvania must pay a corporate net income tax and a corporate loans tax. The corporate income tax rate changes from year to year, but is generally burdensome. The corporate loans tax is imposed at the rate of 4 mills (4/10 of a cent) on each dollar of the nominal value of all scrip, bonds, certificates, and evidences of indebtedness. In addition, Pennsylvania corporations must pay a capital stock tax. The capital stock tax for domestic firms is imposed on the corporation's capital stock value, as derived by the application of a formula. Foreign corporations must remit foreign franchise tax. The foreign franchise tax is a tax on the privilege of doing business in Pennsylvania, rather than on property, and is imposed on the capital stock value attributable to Pennsylvania.
"S" Corporation Information	Pennsylvania requires that corporations file form REV-1640 to elect S corporation status. Pennsylvania S corporations must file an annual information return of form PA-20S.

LLC Tax Summary	Most LLCs must file the Pennsylvania S Corp/Partnership Information Return (Form PA-20S/PA-65), which is for informational purposes only. LLCs may also have to file form RCT-101 for Pennsylvania's Capital Stock/Franchise Tax.
LLC Statute	Title 15, Chapter 89 of the Pennsylvania Consolidated Statutes
RHODE ISLAND	
Contact Information for Business Formation Assistance	Corporation Division Rhode island Secretary of State Office of the Secretary of State 100 North Main Street, First Floor Providence, RI 02903 (401) 222-2357 (401) 222-1356 (fax)
Web Site Address	www.sec.state.ri.us
Incorporation Information and Fees	The fee for filing Articles of Incorporation is $150 for up to 8,000 authorized shares. The fee graduates upward for additional authorized shares.
LLC Organization Information and Fees	The fee for filing Articles of Organization is $150. A foreign LLC must file an Application for Registration and submit a filing fee of $150.
Corporate Name Reservation Information and Fees	Rhode Island incorporators may reserve a corporate name by filing an Application for Reservation of Entity Name with the Corporation Division accompanied by a $50 filing fee. The name reservation remains effective for 120 days.
LLC Name Reservation Information and Fees	Rhode Island organizers may reserve an LLC name by filing an Application for Reservation of Entity Name with the Corporations Division accompanied by a $50 filing fee. The name reservation remains effective for 120 days.
Where to Get Corporation & LLC Formation Forms	www2.corps.state.ri.us/corporations/forms
Periodic Corporation Reporting Requirements	Rhode Island corporations and qualified foreign corporations must file an annual report. Annual reports are not available on the Secretary of State's web site, but can be requested by calling (401) 222-3040. The filing fee is $50.
Periodic LLC Reporting Requirements	Annual Reports must be filed with the Division between September 1 and November 1. Annual Report forms are not

	available on the Division's web site, but can be requested by calling (401) 222-3040. The filing fee is $50.
Where to Get Corporate & LLC Tax Forms	www.tax.state.ri.us/form/form.htm
Corporate Tax Summary	Rhode Island corporations and qualified foreign corporations must pay an income tax. The tax rate is 9 percent of net income attributable to Rhode Island. In addition, Rhode Island corporations and qualified foreign corporations must pay a franchise tax of $2.50 for each $10,000 of authorized capital. Authorized capital is the total authorized shares multiplied by the shares' par value. No par stock is valued at $100 per share. The minimum franchise tax is $250.
"S" Corporation Information	Rhode Island recognizes the federal S corporation provision. The subchapter S election is automatic and no state specific forms need be filed to make the subchapter S election.
LLC Tax Summary	Most LLCs must only pay the Rhode Island Franchise Tax of $250. LLCs classified as a corporation for federal tax purposes must file Rhode Island's corporate income tax return.
LLC Statute	Chapter 7-16 of the General Laws of Rhode Island
SOUTH CAROLINA	
Contact Information for Business Formation Assistance	South Carolina Secretary of State Edgar Brown Building P.O. Box 11350 Columbia, SC 29211 (803) 734-2158
Web Site Address	www.scsos.com
Incorporation Information and Fees	The fee for filing Articles of Incorporation is $135.
LLC Organization Information and Fees	The fee for filing Articles of Organization is $110. A foreign LLC must file an Application for a Certificate of Authority by a Foreign Limited Liability Company to Transact Business in South Carolina. The filing fee for foreign LLCs is also $110.
Corporate Name Reservation Information and Fees	South Carolina incorporators may reserve a corporate name by filing an Application to Reserve Corporate accompanied by a $10 filing fee. The name reservation remains effective for 120 days.
LLC Name Reservation Information and Fees	South Carolina organizers may reserve an LLC name by filing an Application to Reserve LLC name with the South Carolina

	Secretary of State accompanied by a $25 filing fee. The name reservation remains effective for 120 days.
Where to Get Corporate & LLC Formation Forms	www.scsos.com/forms.htm
Periodic Corporation Reporting Requirements	Annual reports are not filed with the Secretary of State's office; they are included in a corporation's tax filings and filed with the South Carolina Department of Revenue.
Periodic LLC Reporting Requirements	LLCs conducting business in South Carolina must file an Annual Report and a filing fee of $10 each year. The Annual Report must be filed between January 1 and April 1 the year after the LLC first organizes or registers in South Carolina. Thereafter, an LLC must file its Annual Report by the fifteenth day of the fourth month after the close of the LLCs taxable year
Where to Get Corporate & LLC Tax Forms	www.sctax.org
Corporate Tax Summary	South Carolina corporations and foreign corporations doing business in South Carolina must pay an annual license tax of .001 times their capital stock and paid-in-surplus plus $15. The license tax is payable by the original due date for filing the income tax return and is paid along with the return or the request for an extension for filing the income tax return. The initial license tax is $25 and is paid at the time of incorporation or at the time of qualification by a foreign corporation. In addition, South Carolina corporations and foreign corporations doing business in South Carolina must pay an income tax equal to 5 percent of a corporation's net income attributable to South Carolina.
"S" Corporation Information	South Carolina recognizes the federal S corporation provision. The subchapter S election is automatic and no state specific forms need be filed to make the subchapter S election.
LLC Tax Summary	Typically, domestic and foreign LLCs conducting business in South Carolina must file a Partnership return (Form SC-1605). LLCs classified as corporations for federal tax purposes must file a Corporate Income Tax return (Form SC-1120).
LLC Statute	Section 33-44 of the South Carolina Code of Laws

SOUTH DAKOTA	
Contact Information for Business Formation Assistance	South Dakota Secretary of State Capitol Building 500 East Capitol Avenue Suite 204 Pierre, SD 57501-5070 (605) 773-4845
Web Site Address	www.state.sd.us/sos/sos.htm
Incorporation Information and Fees	The minimum fee for filing Articles of Incorporation is $90 for corporations with an authorized capital of up to $25,000. Authorized capital is the total authorized shares multiplied by the shares' par value. See the sample Articles of Incorporation on the Secretary of State's web site for a fee schedule.
LLC Organization Information and Fees	To organize, an LLC must file Articles of Organization. To register, Foreign LLCs must file a Certificate of Authority Application. Articles of Organization and the Certificate of Authority Application must be accompanied by the First Annual Report. The fee schedule for the First Annual Report is • $90 for LLCs with member contributions less than $50,000 • $150 for LLCs with member contributions from $50,000 - $100,000. • $150 for LLCs with member contributions in excess of $100,000 plus $50 for each additional $1,000 of member contributions. • the maximum filing fee is $16,000.
Corporate Name Reservation Information and Fees	South Dakota incorporators may reserve a corporate name by filing an Application for Reservation of Name with the South Dakota Secretary of State accompanied by a $15 filing fee. The name reservation remains effective for 120 days.
LLC Name Reservation Information and Fees	South Dakota organizers may reserve an LLC name by filing an Application for Reservation of Name with the South Dakota Secretary of State accompanied by a $15 filing fee. The name reservation remains effective for 120 days.
Where to Get Corporate & LLC Formation Forms	www.state.sd.us/sos/Corporations/forms.htm
Periodic Corporation Reporting Requirements	South Dakota corporations must file a domestic annual report. The filing fee is $25. Qualified foreign corporations must file a foreign annual report. The filing fee is $25.

Periodic LLC Reporting Requirements	LLCs must file an Annual Report before the first day of the second month following the anniversary month of the LLCs initial filing.
Where to Get Corporate & LLC Tax Forms	www.state.sd.us/drr2/forms/btaxforms.htm
Corporate Tax Summary	South Dakota does not have a corporate or personal income tax. South Dakota corporations and qualified foreign corporations may be subject to a sales and use tax.
"S" Corporation Information	South Dakota recognizes the federal S corporation provision. The subchapter S election is automatic and no state specific forms need be filed to make the subchapter S election.
LLC Tax Summary	South Dakota does not have a corporate or personal income tax. LLCs conducting business in South Dakota may be subject to a sales and use tax.
LLC Statute	Title 47, Chapter 34A of the South Dakota Code
TENNESSEE	
Contact Information for Business Formation Assistance	Tennessee Department of State Division of Business Services 312 Eighth Avenue North 6th Floor, William R. Snodgrass Tower Nashville, TN 37243 (615) 741-2286
Web Site Address	www.state.tn.us/sos/soshmpg.htm
Incorporation Information and Fees	The fee for filing Articles of Incorporation is $100.
LLC Organization Information and Fees	Tennessee LLCs may organize by filing Articles of Organization. Foreign LLCs may register by filing an Application for Certificate of Authority to Transact Business. The fees for organizing/registering are $50 per member in existence at the date of filing. The minimum filing fee is $300 and the maximum is $3,000. LLCs must also obtain a Certificate of Formation by paying a filing fee of $20.
Corporate Name Reservation Information and Fees	Tennessee offers informal name availability information by telephone at (615) 741-2286. Tennessee incorporators may reserve a corporate name by filing an Application for Reservation of Name with the Division of Business Services accompanied by a $20 fee. The name reservation remains effective for four months.

LLC Name Reservation Information and Fees	Tennessee offers informal name availability information by telephone at (615) 741-2286. Tennessee organizers may reserve a LLC name by filing an Application for Reservation of Name with the Division of Business Services accompanied by a $20 fee. The name reservation remains effective for four months.
Where to Get Corporate & LLC Formation Forms	www.state.tn.us/sos/forms.htm
Periodic Corporation Reporting Requirements	Tennessee corporations and qualified foreign corporations must file an annual report on or before the first day of the fourth month following the close of the corporation's fiscal year. The Division of Business Services automatically prepares and mails an annual report form to each active corporation during the ending month of the corporation's fiscal year. The annual report filing fee is $20.
Periodic LLC Reporting Requirements	LLCs conducting business in Tennessee must file an Annual Report on the first day of the fourth month following the close of the fiscal year. The filing fees are identical to those for organizing or registering an LLC.
Where to Get Corporate & LLC Tax Forms	www.state.tn.us/revenue/forms/taxspec.htm
Corporate Tax Summary	Tennessee corporations and foreign corporations doing business in Tennessee must pay an excise tax equal to 6 percent of net earnings. In addition, corporations must pay a franchise tax equal to 25 cents per $100 of corporate net worth.
"S" Corporation Information	Tennessee does not recognize the federal S corporation provision.
LLC Tax Summary	Tennessee LLCs must file a Franchise, Excise Tax Return (FAE 170). The franchise tax is $.25 per $100 of the LLC's net worth at the close of the tax year (minimum tax is $100). The excise tax is 6% on earnings from business conducted in Tennessee.
LLC Statute	Title 48, Chapters 201-248 of the Tennessee Code
Additional Information	The Division of Business Services publishes a Filing Guide for Limited Liability Companies which can be found at www.state.tn.us/sos/forms/fg-llc.pdf.

TEXAS	
Contact Information for Business Formation Assistance	Secretary of State Corporations Section Texas Secretary of State P.O. Box 13697 Austin, TX 78711 (512) 463-5555
Web Site Address	www.sos.state.tx.us
Incorporation Information and Fees	The fee for filing Articles of Incorporation is $300. Foreign corporations may qualify with the Corporations Section by filing an Application for a Certificate of Authority by a Corporation along with a filing fee of $750.
LLC Organization Information and Fees	The fee for filing Articles of Organization is $300. Foreign LLCs may register with the Corporations Section by filing an Application for a Certificate of Authority by a Limited Liability Company along with a filing fee of $750.
Corporate Name Reservation Information and Fees	Texas incorporators may reserve a corporate name by filing an Application for Reservation of Entity Name with the Corporations Section accompanied by a filing fee of $40. The name reservation remains effective for 120 days.
LLC Name Reservation Information and Fees	Texas organizers may reserve an LLC name by filing an Application for Reservation of Entity Name with the Corporations Section accompanied by a filing fee of $25. The name reservation remains effective for 120 days.
Where to Get Corporate & LLC Formation Forms	www.sos.state.tx.us/corp/business.shtml
Periodic Corporation Reporting Requirements	Texas corporations and qualifying foreign corporations must file an initial Franchise Tax Report and Public Information Report within one year and 89 days after the corporation's original filing date. Thereafter, corporations must file annual reports each May 15. The Secretary of State mails the annual report forms to corporations each year.
Periodic LLC Reporting Requirements	LLCs are not required to file an annual report with the Secretary of State.
Where to Get Corporate & LLC Tax Forms	www.window.state.tx.us/taxinfo/taxforms/05-forms.html
Corporate Tax Summary	Texas corporations and foreign corporations doing business in Texas must pay an annual corporate franchise tax. Corporations pay the greater of the tax on net taxable capital or net taxable earned surplus.

"S" Corporation Information	Texas does not recognize S corporation status.
LLC Tax Summary	LLCs doing business in Texas must file and pay Texas' franchise tax (Form 05-143). The tax rate is .25% on the LLC's net taxable capital
LLC Statute	Title 32, Article 1528n of the Texas Civil Statutes
UTAH	
Contact Information for Business Formation Assistance	Division of Corporations Utah Department of Commerce 160 East 300 South Salt Lake City, UT 84114-6705 (801) 530-4849 (877) 526-3994 (801) 530-6111 (fax)
Web Site Address	www.commerce.state.ut.us
Incorporation Information and Fees	The fee for filing Articles of Incorporation is $52.
LLC Organization Information and Fees	To organize, LLCs must file Articles of Organization accompanied by a $50 filing fee. Foreign LLCs may register with the Division of Corporations by filing an Application for Authority to Transact Business along with a filing fee of $52.
Corporate Name Reservation Information and Fees	Utah incorporators may reserve a corporate name by filing an Application for Reservation of Business Name with the Division of Corporations accompanied by a filing fee of $20. The name reservation remains effective for 120 days.
LLC Name Reservation Information and Fees	Utah organizers may reserve an LLC name by filing an Application for Reservation of Business Name with the Division of Corporations accompanied by a filing fee of $20. The name reservation remains effective for 120 days.
Where to Get Corporate & LLC Formation Forms	http://corporations.utah.gov/llpllclp.html http://corporations.utah.gov/corpdba.html
Periodic Corporation Reporting Requirements	Utah corporations must file an annual Application for Renewal Form accompanied by a $10 fee.
Periodic LLC Reporting Requirements	LLCs conducting business in Utah must file an Annual Report/Renewal Form by the anniversary date of the original filing with the Division.

Where to Get Corporate & LLC Tax Forms	www.tax.utah.gov/forms/current.html
Corporate Tax Summary	Utah corporations and foreign corporations doing business in Utah must pay a corporation franchise tax equal to 5 percent of income attributable to Utah operations. The minimum tax is $100.
"S" Corporation Information	Utah recognizes the federal S corporation provision. The subchapter S election is automatic and no state-specific forms need be filed to make the subchapter S election. However, Utah requires that a copy of the IRS approval letter be filed with the Utah Tax Commission. S corporations are treated as "Utah Small Business Corporations."
LLC Tax Summary	Most LLCs must file Utah's Partnership Limited Liability Company Return of Income (Form TC-65). If an LLC is classified as a corporation for federal tax purposes the LLC is subject to the Utah corporate income and franchise taxes.
LLC Statute	Title 48, Chapter 2C of the Utah Code
VERMONT	
Contact Information for Business Formation Assistance	Corporations Division Vermont Secretary of State Heritage I Building 81 River Street Montpelier, VT 05609-1104 (802) 828-2386 (802) 828-2853 (fax)
Web Site Address	www.sec.state.vt.us
Incorporation Information and Fees	The fee for filing Articles of Incorporation is $75.
LLC Organization Information and Fees	The fee for filing Articles of Organization of $75. Foreign LLCs may also register by filing Vermont's Articles of Organization form and submitting a filing fee of $100. Foreign LLCs must also submit a Good Standing Certificate from their state of organization.
Corporate & LLC Name Reservation Information and Fees	Vermont incorporators and LLC organizers may reserve a name by filing an Application to Reserve a Name, available at www.sec.state.vt.us/tutor/dobiz/forms/reservat.htm. The filing fee is $20. The name reservation remains effective for 120 days. Vermont offers informal name searches via the Secretary of State's web site at www.sec.state.vt.us/seek/database.htm.

Where to Get Corporate & LLC Formation Forms	www.sec.state.vt.us/tutor/dobiz/dobizdoc.htm
Periodic Corporation Reporting Requirements	Vermont corporations and qualified foreign corporations must file an annual/biennial report form. You may generate a form online. The fee for domestic corporations is $25. The fee for foreign corporations is $150. For more information, contact the Vermont Secretary of State.
Periodic LLC Reporting Requirements	LLCs doing business in Vermont must file an annual report within the first 2-? months following the end of a fiscal year. The filing fee is $15.
Where to Get Corporate & LLC Tax Forms	www.state.vt.us/tax/formsall.shtml
Corporate Tax Summary	Vermont corporations and foreign corporations doing business in Vermont must pay a corporate income tax. The corporate tax rate ranges from 7 percent to 9.75 percent. The minimum tax is $250.
"S" Corporation Information	Vermont recognizes the federal S corporation provision. The subchapter S election is automatic and no state specific forms need be filed to make the subchapter S election.
LLC Tax Summary	LLCs must file a Vermont Business Income Tax Return. Pass through taxation is granted to LLCs, but they must pay a minimum tax of $250.
LLC Statute	Title II, Chapter 21 of the Vermont Statutes
VIRGINIA	
Contact Information for Business Formation Assistance	Office of the Clerk Virginia State Corporation Commission 1300 East Main Street Richmond, VA 23219 (804) 371-9967 (800) 552-7945
Web Site Address	www.state.va.us/scc/index.html
Incorporation Information and Fees	The minimum fee for filing Articles of Incorporation is $75. This includes a $25 filing fee, and a $50 minimum charter fee. The minimum charter fee of $50 applies to corporations with 25,000 authorized shares or less. The charter fee increases by $50 for each additional 25,000 authorized shares or fraction thereof. The maximum filing fee is $2,500.

LLC Organization Information and Fees	To organize, an LLC must file Articles of Organization and submit a filing fee of $100. Foreign LLCs may register by filing an Application for Registration as a Foreign Limited Liability Company accompanied by a filing fee of $100.
Corporate Name Reservation Information and Fees	Virginia incorporators may reserve a corporate name by filing an Application for Reservation or for Renewal of Reservation of Corporate Name on form SCC631/830 accompanied by a filing fee of $10. The name reservation remains effective for 120 days.
LLC Name Reservation Information and Fees	Virginia organizers may reserve an LLC name by filing an Application for Reservation or for Renewal of Reservation of LLC name on form LLC-1013 accompanied by a filing fee of $10. The name reservation remains effective for 120 days.
Where to Get Corporate & LLC Formation Forms	www.state.va.us/scc/division/clk/fee_bus.htm
Periodic Corporation Reporting Requirements	Virginia corporations and qualified foreign corporations must file an annual report. The Virginia State Corporation Commission mails an Annual Assessment Packet to eligible corporations. Corporations must file their annual report by the last day of the calendar month of the anniversary date of their incorporation. The annual report must accompany an annual registration fee. The annual registration fee is based upon the corporation's authorized shares and ranges from $50 to $850. A table appears at www.state.va.us/scc/division/clk/fee_annual.htm.
Periodic LLC Reporting Requirements	The Commission collects an annual registration fee of $50 from each LLC doing business in Virginia. The fee is due each year by September 1.
Where to Get Corporate & LLC Tax Forms	www.tax.virginia.gov/site.cfm?alias=busforms
Corporate Tax Summary	Virginia corporations and foreign corporations doing business in Virginia must pay a corporate income tax.
"S" Corporation Information	Virginia recognizes the federal S corporation provision. The subchapter S election is automatic and no state specific forms need be filed to make the subchapter S election.
LLC Tax Summary	LLCs are not required to file an annual return with the Virginia Department of Taxation.
LLC Statute	Title 13.1, Chapter 12 of the Code of Virginia

WASHINGTON	
Contact Information for Business Formation Assistance	Corporations Division Washington Secretary of State 801 Capitol Way S. P.O. Box 40234 Olympia, WA 98504-0234 (360) 753-7115
Web Site Address	www.secstate.wa.gov
Incorporation Information and Fees	The fee for filing Articles of Incorporation is $175.
LLC Organization Information and Fees	To organize, an LLC must file an Application to Form a Limited Liability Company and submit a filing fee of $175. A foreign LLC may register by filing an Application for Foreign Limited Liability Company Registration accompanied by a filing fee of $175. Newly filed LLCs must also file an Initial Report within 120 days of the LLCs initial filing.
Corporate Name Reservation Information and Fees	Washington incorporators may reserve a corporate name by paying a $30 name reservation fee. The form is not available online. Contact the Washington Secretary of State for more information.
LLC Name Reservation Information and Fees	Washington organizers may reserve an LLC name by paying a $30 name reservation fee. The form is not available online. Contact the Division for more information.
Where to Get Corporate & LLC Formation Forms	www.secstate.wa.gov/corps/forms.htm
Periodic Corporation Reporting Requirements	Washington corporations may file their annual reports online at www.secstate.wa.gov/corps/renew.aspx.
Periodic LLC Reporting Requirements	Washington LLCs may file their annual reports online at www.secstate.wa.gov/corps/renew.aspx.
Where to Get Corporate & LLC Tax Forms	http://dor.wa.gov/content/forms
Corporate Tax Summary	Washington corporations and foreign corporations doing business in Washington must pay a Business and Occupation income tax that is based upon gross income from activities conducted in the state.
"S" Corporation Information	Washington recognizes the federal S corporation provision. The subchapter S election is automatic and no state specific forms need be filed to make the subchapter S election.

LLC Tax Summary	LLCs must pay the Business and Occupation Tax each year. The tax is levied on gross income, proceeds of sales or the value of the LLC's products. The rate is .47% on retailing, .484% on manufacturing and 1.5% on services.
LLC Statute	Chapter 25.15 of the Revised Code of Washington
WEST VIRGINIA	
Contact Information for Business Formation Assistance	Corporations Division West Virginia Secretary of State Building 1, Suite 157-K 1900 Kanawha Boulevard East Charleston, West Virginia, WV 25305-0770 (304) 558-8000
Web Site Address	www.wvsos.com
Incorporation Information and Fees	The fee for filing Articles of Incorporation is based upon the month of filing. You must visit the Secretary of State's web site to determine the filing fee.
LLC Organization Information and Fees	To organize, an LLC must file Articles of Organization and submit a filing fee of $100. Foreign LLCs must register by filing an Application for Certificate of Authority for a Limited Liability Company along with a filing fee of $150.
Corporate Name Reservation Information and Fees	West Virginia incorporators may reserve a corporate name by filing an Application for Reservation of Name on Form NR-1 accompanied by a $15 filing fee. The name reservation remains effective for 120 days.
LLC Name Reservation Information and Fees	West Virginia organizers may reserve an LLC name by filing an Application for Reservation of Name on Form NR-1 accompanied by a $15 filing fee. The name reservation remains effective for 120 days.
Where to Get Corporate & LLC Formation Forms	www.wvsos.com/business/services/formindex.htm
Periodic Corporation Reporting Requirements	West Virginia corporations and foreign corporations with operations in West Virginia must file an annual report. The Corporations Division mails the annual report to registered corporations. The report is due July 1 of each year. The report must be accompanied by a $10 attorney-in-fact fee and the annual corporate license tax.
Periodic LLC Reporting Requirements	LLCs doing business in West Virginia must file an annual report by April 1 each year. The filing fee is $10.

Where to Get Corporate & LLC Tax Forms	www.state.wv.us/taxrev/forms.html
Corporate Tax Summary	West Virginia corporations and foreign corporations doing business in West Virginia must pay a business franchise tax. The tax is based upon the corporation's capital structure. Corporations must also pay a corporation net income tax. The income tax rate is 9 percent. Contact the West Virginia State Tax Department for more information.
"S" Corporation Information	West Virginia recognizes the federal S corporation provision. The subchapter S election is automatic and no state specific forms need be filed to make the subchapter S election.
LLC Tax Summary	LLCs doing business in West Virginia must file a Business Franchise Tax Return each year. The tax rate is $.75 per $100 of taxable income, with a minimum annual tax of $50.
LLC Statute	Chapter 31B of the West Virginia Code

WISCONSIN

Contact Information for Business Formation Assistance	Dept. of Financial Institutions P.O. Box 7846 Madison, WI 53707-7846 (608) 261-7577
Web Site Address	www.wdfi.org
Incorporation Information and Fees	The fee for filing Articles of Incorporation is $100.
LLC Organization Information and Fees	Wisconsin offers two means of filing Articles of Organization: traditional paper filing, and "QuickStart LLC." QuickStart LLC is a web-based application which allows the organizer of a Wisconsin limited liability company to draft, sign and deliver their Articles of Organization on-line. The fee for QuickStart is $130. The fee for traditional paper filing of Articles of Organization is $170.
Corporate Name Reservation Information and Fees	Wisconsin offers informal name availability information by telephone. Wisconsin incorporators may reserve a corporate name by filing a Corporate Name Reservation Information and Fees Application on Form 1 accompanied by a filing fee of $15. Name reservation is also available for a fee of $30. The name reservation remains effective for 120 days.
LLC Name Reservation Information and Fees	Wisconsin offers informal name availability information by telephone. Wisconsin organizers may reserve an LLC name by filing a LLC Name Reservation Information and Fees Application on

	Form 1 accompanied by a filing fee of $15. Name reservation is also available over the telephone for a fee of $30. The name reservation remains effective for 120 days.
Where to Get Corporate & LLC Formation Forms	www.wdfi.org/corporations/forms
Periodic Corporation Reporting Requirements	Wisconsin corporations and qualified foreign corporations must file an annual report. The form is not available online. The filing fee is $25 for domestic corporations and a minimum of $50 for foreign corporations.
Periodic LLC Reporting Requirements	Domestic LLCs do not have to file an annual report with the Corporations Section, however registered foreign LLCs do. The filing fee for doing so is $50 and the report is due by the end of the first quarter of each calendar year.
Where to Get Corporate & LLC Tax Forms	www.dor.state.wi.us/html/formpub.html
Corporate Tax Summary	Wisconsin has both a franchise tax and in income tax. However, only one tax is imposed against a corporation in a taxable year for the privilege of exercising its Wisconsin franchise or for doing business in Wisconsin. Franchise tax applies to Wisconsin corporations foreign corporations doing business in Wisconsin. The tax rate is 7.9 percent. Income tax applies only to foreign corporations which are not subject to the franchise tax and which own property in Wisconsin or whose business in Wisconsin is exclusively in foreign or interstate commerce. The tax rate is 7.9 percent.
"S" Corporation Information	Wisconsin recognizes the federal S corporation provision. The subchapter S election is automatic and no state specific forms need be filed to make the subchapter S election.
LLC Tax Summary	Most LLCs must file a Partnership Return of Income (Form 3). The return is informational only. LLCs classified as a corporation must file a Corporation Franchise or Income Tax Return (form 4).
LLC Statute	Chapter 183 of the Wisconsin Statutes.
WYOMING	
Contact Information for Business Formation Assistance	Wyoming Office of the Secretary of State Capitol Building Cheyenne, WY 82002 (307) 777-7378 (307) 777-6217

Web Site Address	soswy.state.wy.us
Incorporation Information and Fees	The fee for filing Articles of Incorporation is $100.
LLC Organization Information and Fees	To organize, an LLC must file Articles of Organization and pay a filing fee of $100. Foreign LLCs must file an Application for Certificate of Authority for Foreign Limited Liability Company and submit a filing fee of $100.
Corporate Name Reservation Information and Fees	Wyoming incorporators may reserve a corporate name by filing an Application for Reservation of Corporate Name accompanied by a $50 filing fee.
LLC Name Reservation Information and Fees	Wyoming organizers may reserve an LLC name by filing an Application for Reservation of LLC name accompanied by a $50 filing fee.
Where to Get Corporate & LLC Formation Forms	soswy.state.wy.us/corporat/corporat.htm
Periodic Corporation Reporting Requirements	Annual corporation reports are due on or before the 1st day of the anniversary month of the corporation's initial filing. The report may be drafted and printed online at the Secretary of State's web site.
Periodic LLC Reporting Requirements	Annual Reports may be filed online at soswy.state.wy.us/Annual_Rpt_Main.asp.
Where to Get Corporate & LLC Tax Forms	soswy.state.wy.us/Annual_Rpt_Main.asp
Corporate Tax Summary	Wyoming has no corporate income tax. Wyoming corporations and foreign corporations doing business in Wyoming pay an Annual Report License tax based upon all assets located and employed in Wyoming. The Annual Report License Tax is the greater of $50 or two-tenths of one mil (.02 cents) of the company's Wyoming assets.
"S" Corporation Information	Wyoming recognizes the federal S corporation provision. The subchapter S election is automatic and no state specific forms need be filed to make the subchapter S election.
LLC Tax Summary	Wyoming has no income tax applicable to LLCs. Wyoming LLCs doing business in Wyoming pay an Annual Report License Tax based upon all assets located and employed in Wyoming. The Annual Report License Tax is the greater of $50 or two-tenths of one mil (.02 cents) of the company's Wyoming assets.
LLC Statute	Section 17-15-101 through 17-15-144 of the Wyoming Statutes

Glossary

Acquisition: The purchase of one corporation by another, through either the purchase of its shares, or the purchase of its assets.

Administrative Dissolution: The involuntary dissolution of a corporation by the Secretary of State, or other equivalent department, due to the failure of a corporation to meet statutory requirements such as periodic filing and tax reporting requirements.

Advisory Board: A body that advises the board of directors and management of a corporation but does not have authority to vote on corporate matters.

Agent: Anyone who is authorized to act on behalf of another. A corporation can only act through its agents; therefore, it is important to define what action an agent is authorized to perform.

Agent for Service of Process: The person or entity that is authorized to receive legal papers on behalf of a corporation.

Alter Ego Liability: Doctrine that attaches liability to corporate shareholders in cases of commingling of assets and failure to observe corporate formalities.

Amendment of Articles of Incorporation: The procedure by which one or more changes is made to a corporation's articles of incorporation.

Annual Meeting of Directors: A meeting held each year to elect officers of a corporation, and to address other corporate matters. Usually follows immediately after an Annual Meeting of Shareholders.

Annual Meeting of Shareholders: A meeting held each year to elect directors of a corporation, and to address other corporate matters.

Apparent Authority: The doctrine that a Principal is responsible for the acts of his Agent where the principal by his words or conduct suggests to a third person that the agent may act on the principal's behalf, and where the third person believes in the authority of the agent.

Apportionment: The allocation of income earned from activities in a particular state or assets present in a particular state to determine the tax due in that state.

Articles of Incorporation: The document which gives birth to a corporation by filing in the state of incorporation. Articles cover foundational matters such as the name of the corporation, the shares it is authorized to issue, its corporate purpose, and its agent for service of process.

Articles of Organization: The document which gives birth to an LLC by filing in the state of organization. Articles of organization cover foundational matters such as the name of the LLC, its business purpose, and its agent for service of process. Articles of organization are to LLCs what articles of incorporation are to corporations.

Authorized Capital: The total number of a corporation's authorized shares multiplied by the share's par value. For example, 1,000,000 authorized shares of stock with a one cent par value equals an authorized capital of $10,000.

Authorized Shares: The number of shares of a corporation's stock that the corporation has the authority to issue. The authorized shares of a class of stock is stated in a corporation's articles of incorporation.

Blue Sky Laws: The securities laws of individual states, collectively. These laws seek to protect people from investing in sham companies offering nothing more than "blue sky."

Board of directors: The directors of a corporation, collectively. The directors of a corporation are its governing board. Elected by shareholders, they vote on major corporate matters such as the issuing of shares of stock, election of officers, and approval of mergers and acquisitions.

Business Judgment Rule: The rule that shields directors from liability for mismanagement of the corporations that they serve.

Bond: An interest-bearing instrument issued by a corporation or other entity that serves as evidence of a debt or obligation.

Bylaws: The internal operating rules of a corporation, usually set out in a five- to twenty—page document. Bylaws govern such matters as holding meetings, voting, quorums, elections, and the powers of directors and officers.

C Corporation: Any corporation that has not elected S Corporation status.

Capital Contribution: The total amount of cash, other property, services rendered, promissory note, and/or other obligation contributed to a company for such owners' interest in a company.

Certificate of Authority: A document issued by the secretary or state or equivalent department that authorizes a foreign corporation to operate in a state other than its state of incorporation.

Certificate of Good Standing: A document issued by the secretary or state or equivalent department that certifies that a corporation in validly existing and in compliance with all periodic and taxation requirements.

Close Corporation: A corporation owned by a small number of individuals. Corporations must elect to be close corporations by inserting a statement in their articles of incorporation. State laws typically permit close corporations to be operated more informally than non-close corporations

Common Stock: A corporation's primary class of stock. Common stock holders typically have voting rights.

Conversion; Conversion Rights: Rights allowing the holder of shares of stock or other financial instrument to convert to other shares of stock.

Convertible Instrument: Financial instruments such as bonds or notes that can be converted into shares of stock. Shares of stock may also be convertible into shares of another class.

Corporate Secretary: A corporate officer, elected by the directors, usually charged with record-keeping responsibilities.

Cumulative Dividends: Dividends that accumulate if they are not paid according to the terms of the cumulative preferred shares under which they are granted. Unlike a dividend on common stock that the company can pay out to shareholders under its discretion, dividends on cumulative preferred shares are an obligation regardless of the earnings of the company. The unpaid accumulated preferred stock dividends must be paid before any common stock dividends are paid.

Cumulative Voting: A system of voting shares of stock used in some states. Cumulative voting gives minority shareholders additional voting power by allowing them to "cumulate" their votes for a single director.

Deadlock: The circumstance that arises when either the board of directors or shareholders are evenly split on a vote and cannot take action. Deadlock can lead to judicial resolution of the underlying dispute.

Debt Financing: A method of financing where the company receives a loan and gives its promise to repay the loan. See also: Equity Financing.

Dilution: The effect of reducing an existing shareholder's interest in a corporation when new shares are issued.

Director: The directors of a corporation are its governing board. Elected by shareholders, they vote on major corporate matters such as the issuing of shares of stock, election of officers, and approval of mergers and acquisitions.

Dissolution: The process of shutting down a corporation, settling its affairs, and ending its life.

Distribution: A transfer of profits or property by a corporation to its shareholders.

Dividend: A share of profits issued to the holders of shares in a corporation. Dividends can be paid in shares of stock or other property such as shares in a subsidiary or parent company.

Dividend Priority: Special rights enjoyed by holders of a secondary class of stock that entitle holders to receive dividends before other shareholders.

Doing Business As (DBA): A company whose operating name differs from its legal name is said to be "doing business as" the operating name. Some states require DBA or "fictitious business name" filings to be made for the protection of consumers conducting business with the entity.

Domestic Corporation: In general, a corporation whose articles of incorporation are filed in the state in which it operates and maintains its principal office.

Equity Interest: Another term for an ownership interest in a company.

Equity Financing: A method of financing where a company issues shares of its stock and receives money. See also: Debt Financing.

Express Authority. Authority possessed by an individual to act on behalf of a corporation that arises naturally from his or her title or position, or by resolution of a corporation.

Fictitious Business Name: A company whose operating name differs from its legal name is said to be doing business under a fictitious business name. Some states require DBA (doing business as) or fictitious business name filings to be made for the protection of consumers conducting business with the entity.

Fiduciary: one who holds or administers property for another and is held to a high standard of trust and responsibility with respect to that property.

Fiduciary Relationship: A special relationship in which one party, the fiduciary, owes heightened duties of good faith and responsibility to the other party with respect to the property and rights of the other party.

Foreign LLC: In general, an LLC that operates in one state but whose articles of organization are filed in another state; the state in which it operates refers out-of-state LLCs as "foreign." The term also refers to LLCs chartered in foreign nations.

Franchise Tax: A tax levied in consideration for the privilege of either incorporating or qualifying to do business in a state. A franchise tax may be based upon income, assets, outstanding shares, or a combination.

Fully Reporting Company: A public company that is subject to the Securities and Exchange Commission's periodic reporting requirements.

Go Public: The process of becoming a public, fully reporting company either by filing a registrations statement with the SEC, or by merging with a public company.

Good Standing: A state a corporation enjoys when it is in full compliance with the law.

Illiquidity Discount: A discount in the value of an interest in a business because of legal restrictions on the resale of such interest.

Initial Director(s): The first director or directors of a corporation, named in the original articles of incorporation filed with the secretary of state.

Incorporator: The person or entity that organizes a corporation and files its Articles of Incorporation. The incorporator can take corporate actions before directors and officers are appointed.

Indemnification: A legally enforceable promise to reimburse a party for expenses, claims, fees, and/or judgments incurred by that party.

Involuntary Dissolution: The forced dissolution of a corporation by a court or administrative action.

Judicial Dissolution: The forced dissolution of a corporation by a court at the request of a state attorney general, shareholder, or creditor.

Liability Shield: The protection from liabilities, debts, and lawsuits enjoyed by the owners of a well-operated LLC or corporation that maintains its good standing. The owners of such an LLC or corporation are said to be "shielded from liability."

Liquidation Preference: Certain classes of stock (usually preferred stock) may have a liquidation preference, which entitles the holders to be paid first in the event of the liquidation of a corporation's assets.

Limited Liability Company (LLC): A new and flexible business organization that offers the advantages of liability protection with the simplicity of a partnership.

Limited Partnership: A business organization that allows limited partners to enjoy limited personal liability while general partners have unlimited personal liability.

Manager(s): The person or persons who are granted the authority to manage and operate an LLC.

Manager-Managed LLC: An LLC that is managed by managers appointed by the members (owners) of LLC.

Member(s): The owner or owners of an LLC.

Membership Ledger: A ledger indicating the owners of an LLC, and their proportion of ownership. A corporation's ledger is called a "share ledger."

Member Managed LLC: An LLC that is managed by its members (owners), and not by appointed managers.

Merger: The combination of one or more corporations, LLCs or other business entities into a single business entity.

No Par Shares: Shares for which there is no designated par value.

Nonprofit Corporation: A business organization that serves some public purpose, and therefore enjoys special treatment under the law. Nonprofits corporations, contrary to their name, can make a profit, but cannot be designed primarily for profit-making. Distributions upon liquidation typically must be made to another nonprofit.

Novation: The substitution of a new contract for an old one or the substitution of one party in a contract with another party.

Officer: The managers of a corporation such as the President, CFO, and Secretary. The officers are appointed by the board of directors.

Operating Agreement: The agreement that governs the internal structure and operation of an LLC and governs the relationship between its members and managers.

Outside Director: A independent member of the board of directors that is not a shareholder or regular employee of a corporation.

Par Value: The issued price of a security that bears no relation to the market price.

Parent Corporation: A corporation that either owns outright or controls a subsidiary.

Partnership: A business organization formed when two or more persons or entities come together to operate a business for profit. Partnerships do not enjoy limited liability, except in the case of limited partnerships.

Partnership Agreement: The agreement that governs the internal structure and operation of a partnership and governs the relationship between its partners.

Pass-Through Taxation: Partnerships and LLCs enjoy "pass through taxation." This means the entities are not taxed on their income, but the income and profits that the entities pay out to owners and employees is taxable. The income is said to "pass through" the entity.

Percentage Ownership: One's ownership in an LLC, partnership or corporation, expressed as a percentage of the total ownership.

Pierce the veil: Doctrine that attaches liability to corporate shareholders in cases of commingling of assets and failure to observe corporate formalities.

Preemptive Rights : Rights enjoyed by existing shareholders to purchase additional shares of stock in the same proportion to their existing holdings.

Preferred Stock: A separate and/or secondary class of stock issued by some corporations. Preferred stock typically has limited or no voting rights, but its holders are paid dividends or receive repayment priority in the event the corporation is liquidated.

Professional Corporation: A corporation whose members are all licensed professionals, such as doctors, lawyers, accountants and architects.

Professional LLC: An LLC organized to offer services that normally require a license, such as the practice of medicine or law.

Promoter: A person who organizes a business venture or is a major participant in organizing the venture.

Proxy: An authorization by one shareholder giving another person the right to vote the shareholder's shares. Proxy also refers to the document granting such authority.

Qualification: The process by which a foreign corporation registers in a state of operation other than its state of incorporation.

Quorum: The minimum percentage of either shareholders or directors that must be present at a meeting in order for a vote to be legally effective.

Record Date: The date, set by a company, used to determine when an individual must own shares or units in a company in order to receive certain benefits from a company, such as dividend rights and voting rights. The record date is important for shareholders in publicly traded companies because shares are constantly changing hands.

Redemption: A repurchase of shares from shareholders by a corporation.

Redemption Rights: Right of repurchase enjoyed by a corporation that exist for certain shares of stock.

Registered Agent: The person or entity that is authorized to receive legal papers on behalf of a corporation.

Registered Office: The official address of a corporation. Typically this address is the same as that of the registered agent.

Registered Shares: Share of stock that are registered with the US Securities and Exchange Commission following the filing of a registrations statement.

Representative Management: The form of management used by modern business entities where the owners elect managers, directors, and officers to operate and manage the business entity.

Resident Agent: The person or entity that is authorized to receive legal papers on behalf of a corporation.

S Corporation: A "subchapter S" corporation is a corporation that elects by filing with the IRS to be treated as a partnership for taxation purposes.

Secretary (Corporate Secretary): A corporate officer, elected by the directors, usually charged with record-keeping responsibilities.

Secretary of State: A state official charged with responsibility for the filing of legal documents, including corporation papers. In some states, and the District of Columbia, this responsibility falls upon another department, such as Hawaii's Department of Commerce and Consumer Affairs, or Arizona's Corporation Commission.

Securities: The broad term that refers to shares of stock, bonds, and some debt instruments.

Share Ledger/Share Transfer Ledger: A ledger indicating the owners of a corporation, and their proportion of ownership, as well as transfers of such ownership. An LLC's ledger is called a "membership ledger."

Shareholder: An owner of a corporation and one who holds shares of stock in a corporation.

Shareholder's Agreement: An agreement between the shareholders of a corporation that can cover various matters such as a commitment to vote particular persons as directors and allowing other shareholders to have a right of first refusal to purchase the shares of departing shareholders.

Shareholder's Equity: The total net worth of a company, the amount by which assets exceed liabilities. It's also referred to as "book value."

Shelf Corporation: A fully formed corporation without operations, assets, or liabilities that remains in inventory, or on a "shelf," waiting for a buyer. The advantages: a shelf corporation can be operating within hours, and uses its original formation date.

Simple Majority: With respect to shareholder and director voting, more than 50%.

Sole Proprietorship: Simply, a business owned and managed by one person. Sole proprietorships do not enjoy liability protection.

Special Allocation: A device whereby an LLC or Corporation's profits are divided in a proportion not equal to the ownership percentages of the entity.

Special Meeting of Directors: A meeting of directors, but not an annual meeting, called for a specific purpose.

Special Meeting of Shareholders: A meeting of shareholders, but not an annual meeting, called for a specific purpose.

Staggered Board: A board of directors a portion of whose members are elected each year instead of all members being elected annually.

Statute of Limitations: A law which sets the maximum period in which one must bring a lawsuit. Lawsuits cannot be brought after the expiration of the period. Periods vary by state.

Stockholder: An owner of a corporation and one who holds shares of stock in a corporation.

Subscriber: A person who contracts to purchase the shares of a corporation.

Subscription Agreement: A contract to purchase the shares of a corporation.

Subsidiary: A corporation that is owned outright or controlled by a parent corporation.

Supermajority: With respect to shareholder and director voting, any required percentage higher than 50 percent.

Trademark: Any symbol, word, or combination of either used to represent or identify a product or service.

Undercapitalization: The condition that exists when a company does not have enough cash to carry on its business and pay its creditors.

Voluntary Dissolution: The intentional dissolution of a corporation by its own management.

Voting Right: The right enjoyed by shareholders to vote their shares.

Warrant: An instrument which grants its holder the option or right to purchase shares of stock at a future date at a specific price. Warrants are tradeable.

Winding Up: The process of paying creditors and distributing assets that occurs before the dissolution of a corporation.

Written Consent: A document executed by either the shareholders or directors of a corporation in lieu of a formal meeting.

About the Author

Michael Spadaccini is a business law author and semi-retired attorney. He practiced business law for small businesses and startups in San Francisco and Silicon Valley since 1993, and more recently in Austin, Texas. He is the author of numerous business law books for Entrepreneur Press. From 1991 to 1992, he was the Editor in Chief of The Connecticut Probate Law Journal-an academic publication operated at his Alma Mater, Quinnipiac University School of Law. He has been sought for comment on business law and intellectual property issues in publications such at *USA Today*, *The San Francisco Examiner*, and *Women's Wear Daily*.

Index

263